To Dad
With love at
Christmas 2022
Julie & Alistair
xx

BRITISH RAILWAY HISTORY IN COLOUR

Volume 5A:
GLOUCESTER to SWINDON and BRANCHES
Part 1: GLOUCESTER to STROUD

Standish Junction was a spectacular location in steam days, as this view from the Black Bridge, which carries a farm access road, shows. On 17th July 1965, with less than six months of steam action to go, Saltley-based Class '9F' No. 92150 was photographed heading towards Swindon with a very mixed freight, which included a couple of cement hoppers at the front and an ex-GWR 'Crocodile' wagon a little further back loaded with three aircraft propellers. Despite the engine's Birmingham base, this may well be a freight from Gloucester New Yard, with the propellers having come from the ex-Gloster Aircraft factory at Brockworth, which by this date had become part of Hawker Siddeley Aviation. Bill Potter/KRM

Previous Page: With its 85B shedplate on the smokebox door, 'Small Prairie' No. 5545 poses whilst stood over one of the inspection pits outside Horton Road shed on 10th May 1964. The single white lamp over the left-hand buffer suggests the engine had recently been employed on local pick-up freight duties. John Strange/NPC

BRITISH RAILWAY HISTORY IN COLOUR

Volume 5A:
GLOUCESTER to SWINDON and BRANCHES

Part 1:
GLOUCESTER to STROUD

NEIL PARKHOUSE

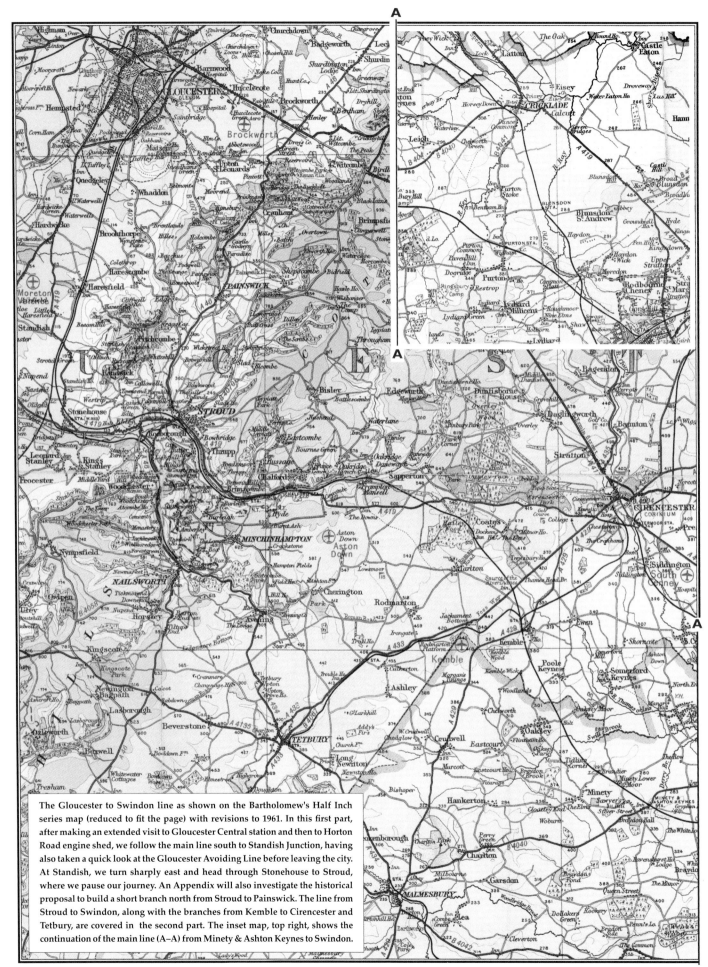

The Gloucester to Swindon line as shown on the Bartholomew's Half Inch series map (reduced to fit the page) with revisions to 1961. In this first part, after making an extended visit to Gloucester Central station and then to Horton Road engine shed, we follow the main line south to Standish Junction, having also taken a quick look at the Gloucester Avoiding Line before leaving the city. At Standish, we turn sharply east and head through Stonehouse to Stroud, where we pause our journey. An Appendix will also investigate the historical proposal to build a short branch north from Stroud to Painswick. The line from Stroud to Swindon, along with the branches from Kemble to Cirencester and Tetbury, are covered in the second part. The inset map, top right, shows the continuation of the main line (A–A) from Minety & Ashton Keynes to Swindon.

CONTENTS
VOLUME 5A: GLOUCESTER to SWINDON and BRANCHES
Part 1: GLOUCESTER to STROUD

Published by LIGHTMOOR PRESS
© Lightmoor Press & Neil Parkhouse 2021
Designed by Neil Parkhouse

British Library Cataloguing-in-Publication Data. A catalogue record for
this book is available from the British Library

ISBN: 9781911038 91 7

LIGHTMOOR PRESS
Unit 144B, Harbour Road Trading Estate,
Lydney, Gloucestershire GL15 4EJ
website: www.lightmoor.co.uk
email: info@lightmoor.co.uk

Lightmoor Press is an imprint of
Black Dwarf Lightmoor Publications Ltd

Printed in Poland
www.lfbookservices.co.uk

With the soubriquet 'Chalford Queen' chalked on its smokebox door, '14XX Class
0-4-2T No. 1455 stands in the bay Platform No. 6 at Gloucester Central on Chalford
auto duties in 1963. Note the glimpse of an old grounded coach body by the water
tank on the extreme right. DON MANN

Heavy industry – coal, iron and steel – had been the backbone of British industry and also freight traffic on the railway for a century and a half and Gloucester was one of the railway hubs that saw a proportion of this traffic passing through. Central station in particular was host to the iron ore trains and we shall see much of this traffic in this first section. Heavy loaded trains made their west from the iron ore fields of Northamptonshire to the steel furnaces of South Wales, with the empties then heading back in what must have seemed at the time as an almost continuous loop. Passing through on the Down (to South Wales) and Up main lines running through the centre of the station, invariably stops had to be made to wait for a clear road ahead and almost always so that water could be taken, whilst sometimes a crew change took place too. And whilst '9Fs' tended to predominate, as the following pictures will show there was still plenty of locomotive variety to be seen on these trains. Here, Class '9F' No. 92236 of Severn Tunnel Junction shed heads into Gloucester Central along the Up Main Line with a train of iron ore empties returning from South Wales to Northamptonshire in 1965. Don Mann

INTRODUCTION

To return to the analogy with which I began the previous volumes, 4A and 4B, the battle plan failed once again even before paging started. Volume 5 was supposed to takes us on a journey from Gloucester Central station to Swindon, with an extended stop at Kemble to traverse the branches from there, firstly east to Cirencester and then west to Tetbury. Having been through the relevant folders on the computer, chosen the likely pictures that would be used and then done a rough page count, it was clear we would be heading north of 500 pages once again, so the decision was quickly taken to split this volume in two as well. However, having been able to do this so early in the process – as compared to Volume 4 which was nearing completion before I decided that it had to be split – I was also then able to further decided on issuing the two books that will make up this fifth volume separately, as they were completed. It's also a little easier on the pocket that way!

So, I ask myself, should I be apologising for this? Well probably not. For those who like their railway books concise and their journeys along a line swift, getting from A to B as quickly as possible, then as I have pointed out before this series was never intended for you. For those of us, however, who miss that era when a day alongside the railway was filled with anticipation as to what might appear next and for whom the sheer variety was a wonder in itself, then these are most definitely the books for you. From the first few pages of this volume, where we return to the west end of Gloucester Central station which was pretty well covered in Volume 1, we loiter much longer than most books would. But who wouldn't want to be back there on the end of the Down platform in the early 1960s, snapping away with our cameras and furiously jotting down numbers in notebooks or spotters ABCs, as a succession of freights passed through on the centre lines bound to or from South Wales and with no idea until the next train appeared as to what would be on the front of it – a 'Hall'?, a '9F'?, an 8F?, a 'Dub-Dee'? The selection of pictures presented here are thus designed to give a flavour of this variety, of the surprises any potential visit could throw up.

By giving myself a susbstantially increased number of pages to fill, I was also thus able to comprehensively cover the substantial parts of the railway at Gloucester that I had not depicted so far. The city was undoubtedly one of the great railway centres of the steam age and recognised as such by many photographers back in the day. One of its many attractions, which I have alluded to before, was that despite the amount of railway infrastructure that once existed here, it was actually quite compact, much of it crammed into a fairly small area on the northern edge of the city centre, with both main stations only about ten minutes' walk from The Cross, where Gloucester's four compass point 'Gate' streets meet. Visible then from both stations were various goods yards and sidings, as well as the huge sheds and other buildings that formed Horton Road motive power depot. Therefore, I have been able to present extensive photographic coverage of Central station, Horton Road shed and much of the surrounding infrastructure too. Along the way, I have also then been able to give a very clear picture of the amount of traffic arriving at and passing through the station, and of Horton Road shed through the last few years of its existence, including the cut down version of the mid-1970s during the early years of the Rail Blue diesel era.

Once an everyday scene. An unidentified '9F' 2-10-0 stands 'Light Engine' on the Up Main Line whilst taking water in summer 1965. DON MANN

As mentioned in previous volumes, I have tried to accelerate the schedule but a new one every two years is about as good as I am able to manage because of commitments to other authors and their manuscripts. However, when Volume 5B also appears early next year, we will at least have the end of my series in sight, with only the Cheltenham and the Cotswolds Lines, and the Bristol Lines volumes still to come to complete the county – although both of those may also grow beyond the confines of a single book! No doubt for Gloucestershire railway devotees it will be a disappointment once I have finished but for those enjoying the series and seeing the railway scene of the circa 1955-75 period in colour, other volumes are planned. Indeed, one has already come out, namely Andrew Britton's *Warwickshire Western Region Lines Part 1 Fenny Compton to Snow Hill*, which has gone into the series as Volume 8 to follow on from the Gloucestershire books. Volume 9 will follow the WR line from Honeybourne back to Birmingham but terminating at Moor Street and should be out next year. I am also planning a future volume covering the Severn Valley Railway and its connecting lines – all pre-preservation – whilst Freddie Huxtable, author of *The Taunton to Barnstaple Line* trilogy, is collaborating with Amyas Crump on some West Country colour volumes to add to the 'British Railway History in Colour' series. So still lots to look forward too!

As also noted in previous volumes, I am conscious of the range of interests of those who buy these books. The general enthusiast and ex-spotter loves the feel of being back at lineside wondering what is coming next, whilst modellers want the detail, the bits they can't quite see, as well as the locomotive/traffic variety. As a modeller myself – I've

mentioned my N gauge layout of Grange Court Junction before, it's making good progress! – I am still hoping to find a good photograph of the open waiting area to the main station building, fronting onto the Down platform of Grange Court station. Much more importantly, however, as I've stated before, these books stand as a tribute to the many photographers whose work features within, whose ranks sadly reduce with the march of time. Colour photography for the masses was still in its infancy when most of these pictures were taken, hence the range of colour tones amongst the different films, something which computer software can only partially solve. All generally manage to still look 'real' however. Slides bought via internet auction sites rarely come with any clue as to the photographer's identity but if I do have a name I always give full credit.

As I have also mentioned before, I saw little of the railway system which is illustrated within these volumes. Passing glimpses of the railway at Toddington, Tewkesbury and Over Junction in the early 1960s, occasional cycle trips with schoolmates to stand on the bridge over the line at Hinton station on the Ashchurch to Evesham line – which closed when I was seven – plus a visit to collect some sacks from the goods shed there with dad in the Netherton Farm lorry are the only memories I have. There was also a brief late night visit to Eastgate a few weeks before it closed in 1975, plus I drove over the crossing past Barton Street Junction signal box a few times. Otherwise I saw nothing of the lines within the county prior to that. The Gloucester to Hereford line, the Ledbury Branch, the lines in the Forest of Dean (with the exception of Parkend Marsh Wharf) the Severn Railway Bridge, the railway across the Cotswolds to Kingham, branch lines to Cirencester, Tetbury, Fairford, Stroud Midland, Nailsworth, Dursley, Sharpness and Thornbury were all unknown to me. However, living in Worcestershire, whilst only just over the boundary from Gloucestershire, meant that visits were limited to rare sojourns to Cheltenham for the shops or equally rare trips in the Netherton Farm lorry to Healings Mill at Tewkesbury or to Gloucester Cattle Market.

The production of this series has therefore been quite a journey of discovery for me. The disappointment of never having seen most of what is featured is tempered by the surge of excitement experienced every time new images are discovered, particularly if they show something of which I do not already have a picture. I am by nature slightly obsessive about completeness and every volume that goes to print with gaps in it somewhere is an annoyance that I have had to learn to live with. New pictures do turn up of course, many that would have made it in to the original volumes and I have in fact included two follow-up supplements at the rear of this volume taking us back to Over Junction, the Llanthony Docks Branch and the Eastgate Loop.

So do I wish I'd been born perhaps ten years earlier, so that I might have been able to experience some of what I have written about and illustrated? Well no frankly! Modern life brings with it many comforts and whilst these volumes are, as previously stated, wonderful excercises in nostalgia, brought to life by the magic of colour, if I was seventy-six instead of sixty-six I probably wouldn't be doing this! And whilst I am a firm supporter and great admirer of the railway preservation scene, I would in no way advocate that we should return to that age. Indeed, the generation that my son and daughter, now twenty-two and twenty respectively – are a part of face enough challenges in securing the planet's future without worrying about what life was like fifty or a hundred years ago. Yes we remember those days with great fondness and miss the sights, sounds and smells of the steam railway. But sitting here at my computer which stores tens of thousands of high quality images, pushing non-existent buttons on my touch screen phone, eating dishes from all around the world – well would I swap all that modern life offers for a permanent return to the 1950s? Well absolutely not! However, a time machine – well that's a slightly different matter but until somebody invents one, then I offer you my version of time travel within these pages.

The driver of '9F' No. 92243 of Newport Ebbw Junction shed attends to his trusty steed with rag and oil can whilst waiting for the road on the Up Main Line on 29th July 1965. A companion view to this can be found on page 38. DON MANN

Neil Parkhouse, Lydney 2021

ACKNOWLEDGEMENTS

I must start the acknowledgements by paying tribute to Don Mann, who contacted me after seeing the first volumes and offered me the chance to scan his fine collection of local slides, mostly of Gloucester and the Stroud area. A few were used in Volume 4A but the bulk of them feature within the pages of the two parts that make up this volume and it is thanks to his extensive photographing of the railway around Gloucester in particular that I have been able to present such a comprehensive colour survey of Central station and Horton Road shed, as well as other more obscure parts of the local system. I have also used a number of them as the basis for a follow-up revisiting Over Junction and the Llanthony Docks Branch. It really does continue to amaze that the various parts of the railway in and around Gloucester were so well photographed in colour – I'm not sure that many other places were so well covered.

There is one codicil to this, however. Collectors of original colour slides will be aware how fragile they are and how susceptible to problems caused by dirt, damp and poor storage. Many of Don's slides have started to deteriorate quite badly and it is fortunate that I have been able to scan them all now, before they get any worse. The images have thus been preserved for posterity. Most of them have reacted well to being cleaned, repaired and colour balanced in Photoshop but a few still show signs of their condition. Some of them have been used within these pages because of what they show, which I trust readers will understand. With this series I always worked on the basis that if it is the only colour image that you have that shows a particular feature, then the quality becomes of secondary importance – I believe that there are enough pictures of the finest quality to balance this out in any case.

KRM curator David Postle has once again generously allowed me access to Bill Potter's colour pictures which, as in previous volumes, serve as a fitting tribute to a talented, unassuming character who photographed extensively the railways of Gloucestershire from the late 1950s and without whose work this series would never even have got off the ground. Such was his interest that Bill carried on taking pictures even after the demise of steam, when many others either gave up or switched to photographing preserved steam instead. Thus he took some now invaluable images of the early diesel era around the county. This volume benefits enormously from Bill Potter's and Don Mann's slides, and without them this picture of the railway scene at Gloucester in the late 1950s/early 1960s would have been so much the poorer.

On a similar note, great tribute should also be paid here to the late John Strange, whom I never met but I did chat to him once on the phone many years ago at my shop in Lydney. After his death, much of his archive was fortuitously rescued – I say rescued because John owned two properties and much of it disappeared, believed skipped – by Alan Sainty of Kidderminster, an assiduous collector of slides of various classes of steam locomotives. Alan sold me anything Gloucestershire from the collection that did not interest him and John's name is once again to the fore in this volume, as he took many photographs on the line and of the Gloucester-Chalford autos in particular. Sadly, Alan is none too well, having been diagnosed with Parkinsons Disease, so I would like to here pass on my best wishes to him and my thanks for the huge part he played in making this series what it has become.

Another special 'mention in dispatches' follows now for Roy Denison, about whose pictures I have waxed lyrical previously, after he kindly made his colour archive available to me in time for Volume 3 and the updated version of Volume 1. A number of Roy's superb slides again feature in this book and the soon to follow Volume 5B but sadly I must report that Roy passed away in 2020, a few months after being diagnosed with cancer. Condolences from all at Lightmoor to his widow Mya but especially from Heather and myself, who have on several occasions enjoyed her wonderful hospitality on our visits to their home in Streatley.

Tony Bowles has again been most helpful in supplying scans from slides held in the collection of the Restoration & Archiving Trust, an independent registered charity based on the Gloucestershire Warwickshire Railway at Toddington station. The Trust holds the photographic archives of Blake Patterson, Paul Riley, Mike Squire and Tony himself, and contains many useful and valuable images. Likewise, Gerry Nicholls has again kindly supplied scans from the late Mark Warburton's archive held under the auspices of the Stephenson Locomotive Society and I am grateful also to Mark's widow Margaret for permission to publish them. In addition to these, Gerry also supplied pictures taken by the late John Grainger.

Someone else well deserving of a mention is Pete Berry, who has taken a great interest in the volumes covering Gloucester in particular and who has again made some rare colour views that he took himself available to me. He has also not only dug out the truth behind Clan Line and Princess Elizabeth calling at Gloucester on their way back from Shildon in 1975 but has also provided the 'inside track' on how the SR 'West Country' 4-6-2 Salisbury came to make its final journey to the scrapyard all tarted up – on one side only! Such tales add greatly to the interest of these volumes and I am pleased that they have provided a platform for enthusiasts like Pete and also Chris Baldwin, below.

A number of photographers and others have been most generous and helpful in allowing me access to their collections over the time that I have been compiling this series and merit a further thank you here: Ben Ashworth (some of the best is still to come!), Chris Baldwin (who is always assiduous in answering queries and holds much knowledge of 1970s train workings for the area), Howard Beard (for the use of some images from his Stroud area postcard collection), David Bick, Sean Bolan (my favourite railway artist and a friend of many years' standing with whom I am now properly back in touch), Howard Burchell, John Carter, Tony Dyer (for the loan of his ticket collection), Dr Simon Fosbury (holder of the Maurice E.J. Deane archive), Michael Hale, Alan Jarvis, John Jennison (of the Rail Online archive), Rodney Lissenden, Colin Park, Gerald Peacock, David Pollard (whose monumental work, *Digging Bath Stone, A Quarry and Transport History,* was published by Lightmoor Press earlier in 2021), John Ryan, John Searle (for the pictures of Quedgeley Dow-Mac depot), Tim Stephens, David Stowell and Paul Strong.

I should mention that the Colour-Rail collection has not been plundered for this volume, apart from a couple of scans previously supplied, a decision I took as I already had a positive embarrassment of riches from which to choose.

Finally, I have collected many of the images within these pages myself, spending a small fortune on internet and other auction sites on the way. However, such slides usually come with no provenance, lost somewhere following the taker's demise, so as with previous volumes, these are credited simply 'NPC' for Neil Parkhouse Collection. Where I have received pictures from the collections of people whose names I know, they are given credit first.

As in the previous volumes, the pages that follow are further illustrated with tickets, working and ordinary time table excerpts, and other items collected over a number of years. Much of it is ephemera and tickets that I have collected but some of the latter also come from the collections of Tony Dyer and Roy Denison, so my thanks to them once more. Such items are important in building up a picture of the railway of the period. It should be noted that even small Edmonson tickets can appear large and dominating at actual size, so they have all been reduced by 25 per cent, a fact which is not immediately apparent in any case. The time table extracts and other ephemera have also all been reduced in size, generally mostly by around 40 per cent. It might be apposite also to mention here that I use railway spelling throughout these volumes, hence time table and signal box as two words, with capitals as well for the latter if in conjunction with the box name; it was GWR practice to put Signal Box on the nameplate (except in very rare instances), whereas the Midland/LM&SR did not.

Some unusual and historic maps and plans have appeared in previous volumes and I have taken the chance to present a few more within the pages of this book. As well as those from the two resignalling schemes which have reshaped the railway in and around Gloucester, I have taken the opportunity to use most of a rare ink on cloth plan for an additional Up Goods Loop bypassing the station, produced by the GWR in 1935. The original, which is in my collection, is around 8ft by 2ft 6ins in size, so was not easy to scan but I persevered because it contained much useful detail and using it here gave me the opportunity to reproduce it in colour. In the event the scheme was not proceeded with but the two extracts show a layout which changed little subsequently, so fits well with the pictures. In addition, I have long held an original plan produced by George W. Keeling in 1873 for a proposed branch railway to Painswick. Also in colour, whilst clearly well outside of the timelines of the book, I felt an appendix illustrating what might have been was not unreasonable and might just stimulate someone into producing a model. Finally, and most importantly, I also considered that the extensive coverage of Gloucester within this volume fully merited a plan showing the two stations, their associated yards, Horton Road shed and Tramway Junction. Expertly drawn up by my Lightmoor Press co-director Ian Pope and based on the 1955 25 inch OS, it is again in colour allowing the distinction between the Western and Midland lines, illustrates all of the salient features and shows just how much has been lost.

As well as crediting those who have contributed images for the book, I also need to credit several others who have helped in regards to the accuracy of the finished text and captions. First and foremost amongst these is Mike Christensen, who has kept me on the 'right track' in regards to signalling matters in particular but whose proofing of the book has also

led to numerous other corrections and amplifications. I freely admit that I really should have taken more advice from him with regards to previous volumes. Nick Freezer has again offered me the benefit of his considerable experience in regards to diesel multiple units and GWR coaches expert John Lewis continues to respond patiently and with huge authority on anything relating to carriages and occasionally wagons too. In the same vein, Peter Tatlow is always prepared to answer queries on railway cranes, so that captions can be written with authority. Finally, as previously, beyond the boundaries of the railway, Malcolm Bobbitt, a noted motoring historian, has once again been most helpful on vehicle identification.

As the internet continues to grow in size and the amount of research material available on line expands with it, so it becomes easier to do much of your research without moving from your desk. The usual codicils apply with regards to double checking, where possible, any information gleaned but as much of what you find comes from original sources, it can be trusted. The main sites consulted are listed in the bibliography but SixBellsJunction, for rail tours, is always worthy of a special mention. And whilst you cannot beat getting out on the ground when researching long closed routes, Google Earth and Google Street View are powerful research tools at times when deskbound. And as always, whilst I am hugely grateful to everyone who has provided assistance, I must emphasise that any factual errors which almost inevitably remain are entirely my responsibility. I am always happy to receive correspondence from any reader with straightforward corrections or with better or more accurate information on the pictures within these pages. And I am always pleased to hear from anyone whose memories have been stimulated by the photographs.

Finally, as regular readers will be aware, I have dedicated all of the previous volumes to my family, my late father Dennis, my mum Mary, my lovely and hugely supportive wife Heather and our two now pretty much grown up children, Theo and Freya. Having thus run out of immediate family to whom to dedicate the book, perhaps now is the time to do so instead to the many photographers who have made the series possible but in particular to four who have made this (and the following Volume 5B) as strong as they are. So step forward please and take a bow – Roy Denison, Don Mann, Bill Potter and John Strange.

SOURCES & BIBLIOGRAPHY

Books Consulted

British Railways First Generation DMUs, Hugh Longworth, Oxford Publishing Co., 2011
Great Western Auto Trailers Part Two: Post Grouping and Absorbed Vehicles, John Lewis, Wild Swan, 1995
Great Western Railway Halts Vol. 1, Kevin Robertson, Irwell Press, 1990
GWR Goods Wagons, A.G. Atkins, W. Beard & R. Tourret, Tourret Publishing, 1998 ed.
History of the Great Western Railway, Vol. 1, Part 1, E.T. MacDermot, MA, Great Western Railway Co., 1927
Industrial Locomotives of Central Southern England, Roger Hateley, Industrial Railway Society, 1981
Peto's Register of GWR Locomotives Vol. 2, Manor 4-6-0s, Irwell Press 1996
Peto's Register of GWR Locomotives Vol. 3, 14XX and 58XX 0-4-2Ts, Irwell Press 1996
Railway Cranes Vol. 3, Peter Tatlow, Crécy Publishing 2018
Railway Motor Buses and Bus Services in the British Isles 1902-1933, Vol. Two, John Cummings, Oxford Publishing Co., 1980
Railway Passenger Stations in England, Scotland & Wales, M.E. Quick, Railway & Canal Historical Society, 2003
The Locomotives of the Great Western Railway, Parts 5, 6 & 8, The Railway Correspondence & Travel Society, 1958, 1959 & 1968
Track Layout Diagrams of the GWR & BR (WR), Sec. 20: Swindon and South Gloucestershire, R.A. Cooke, 1988
Track Layout Diagrams of the GWR & BR (WR), Sec. 35: Gloucester and Cheltenham, R.A. Cooke, 1978
Various Public and Working Time Tables (WTT), Appendices and other official railway publications mostly in my own collection

Magazines & Journals Consulted

'Gloucester New Yard or 'T' Sidings', Chris Turner, *Great Western Railway Journal No. 44*, 2002
'Gloucester Old Yard', Chris Turner, *Great Western Railway Journal No. 45*, 2003
'Gloucester Docks', Chris Turner, *Great Western Railway Journal No. 47*, 2003
'Gloucester Horton Road Shed', John Copsey & Chris Turner, *Great Western Railway Journal No. 44*, 2002
'The Broad Gauge at Gloucester 1844-1872', Neil Parkhouse, *Railway Archive No. 27*, 2010
The Railway Observer, journal of the Railway Correspondence & Travel Society – various issues Vols. 30-37 (1960-67)

Websites Consulted

maps.nls.uk (*National Library of Scotland map database; covers whole of UK*)
shedbashuk.blogspot.co.uk (*loco's on shed at various dates circa 1930s to closure*)
www.brdatabase.info (*locomotives database*)
www.davidheyscollection.com (*for train reporting numbers and much else*)
www.oldmaps.co.uk (*huge database of OS maps from 19th century to 1990s*)
www.sixbellsjunction.co.uk (*huge and very useful railtour website*)
www.westernlocomotiveresearchsociety.com (*histories of all the 'Westerns'*)
www.class47.co.uk (*histories of all the Class '47' fleet*)
www.stroudtown.gov.uk (*for the stroud station heritage statement*)

CREDIT ABBREVIATIONS
KRM: Kidderminster Railway Museum
NPC: Neil Parkhouse Collection

The CHELTENHAM & GREAT WESTERN UNION RAILWAY

As recounted in Volume 3 of this series, *Gloucester Midland Lines Part 1: North*, the rails of the Birmingham & Gloucester Railway (B&GR) were the first to reach the city with the opeing of the section west from Cheltenham on 4th November 1840. The B&GR's original intention, as outlined in its prospectus issued in November 1835, was to raise its line on a gradual climb as it approached Gloucester, so that it could cross the 3ft 6ins gauge Gloucester & Cheltenham Tramroad by means of a bridge and terminate at a high level station close to the city centre. A short incline would then take a connecting line down to the docks.

However, although this plan received Parliamentary approval, two other factors combined to prevent it being implemented. The Cheltenham & Great Western Union Railway (C&GWUR) had been formed by an Act of June 1836 to build a line from Swindon to Cheltenham, via Stroud and Gloucester. However, its plans had been widely publicised well before this. The section between Cheltenham and Gloucester was to be built and operated jointly with the B&GR, and Parliament stipulated that, should their forthcoming application prove successful, their route should be adopted instead. Further, the finances of the B&GR at the time were such that a highly expensive series of arches climbing across the city to a costly raised station was completely beyond their reach. As it was, the Act compelled the

company to choose their own station site, which was to be bought by the C&GWUR and leased back to the B&GR at a peppercorn but the latter then had to build a joint station at their own expense. Hence a site was chosen on the outskirts of the city centre, on lower ground, which the two companies (the B&GR were absorbed by the Midland Railway in August 1846 and the C&GWUR by the GWR in May 1844) shared for nearly six and a half years from May 1845 to September 1851.

The GWR opened their main line from Paddington to Maidenhead on 4th June 1838, with the section between Faringdon Road (near Wantage) through Swindon to Wootton Bassett opening on 17th December 1840. The C&GWUR had gained their Act following something of a fight – with the London & Birmingham Railway, twice, who promoted a much shorter but far steeper route from Tring to Cheltenham via Thame, Witney and Northleach; with the Thames & Severn Canal Company, whose traffic was threatened and who had to be bought off to the tune of £7,500; and with Squire Robert 'Bum' Gordon of Kemble House, a bombastic and forceful character, who not only obtained a similar sum but who caused Brunel no end of problems with his demands for the railway not to intrude on his park landscape. Thus Kemble Tunnel was driven through the shallow terrain so as to hide the line, whilst the beautiful station at Kemble

I have slotted this view in here for the simple reason that I do not know exactly where it is. The slide mount is captioned simply 'Nr Stroud. Castle on Special', whilst the date stamp on it is too faint to read. Nor have I been able to identify train No. Z25. The cottage close to the line on the left should provide a good clue and there is a red brick factory or mill building just visible in the right background but careful trips along the route on Google Earth and large scale OS maps have not thrown up an answer. If anyone therefore can provide a location and also maybe identify the train I would be grateful. JOHN STRANGE/NPC

was not built until 1882, when it also first appeared in the public time tables and long after Gordon's death in 1864; up until then, simple unadvertised wooden platforms serving as the interchange with the Cirencester Branch had been all that the Squire had permitted. As a consequence, another station a mile further north beyond the boundaries of Gordon's land had to be provided to service the locality. Named Tetbury Road, it closed to passengers when the new station opened in 1882, although it remained open for goods traffic until 1st July 1963, having been renamed Coates from 1st May 1908.

Progress on building the line was, however, slow, due to a downturn in the economy in the mid 1830s, with the directors reporting in November 1837 that little, if any, progress had been made. There was also the question of where to begin construction, with both ends of the intended route having a strong case; at Swindon a direct link with the GWR main line would be made, whilst the C&GWUR had made a commitment with the B&GR to build the section between Cheltenham and Gloucester at the northern end.

In the event, it was decided that construction would begin northwards from Swindon, so as to provide a direct link between London and Cirencester, from where horse-drawn coaches could serve Stroud, Gloucester and Cheltenham. A lease was arranged with the GWR for them to work the line between Swindon, Kemble and Cirencester once completed and an application was made to Parliament for an extension of time to build the rest. However, whilst this looks an eminently sensible decision, it forced the B&GR directors to reconsider their arrangement with the C&GWUR.

Accordingly, they opposed the Bill and succeeded in having clauses inserted granting them the right to take over the Cheltenham to Gloucester section, to buy the land if the C&GWUR had not done so by 21st March 1839 and to build the railway if the latter had not done so by 24th June 1840. However, the C&GWUR could repurchase this section for half the cost of its construction if they had managed to get their line to Gloucester completed throughout by 21st June 1845, after which ownership of this section of railway would revert to them as under the original Act. The Bill for the two year extension in time also allowed for the bore of the proposed tunnel at Sapperton to be shortened and straightened, and the provision for separate B&GR and C&GWUR stations in Gloucester.

The B&GR did indeed exercise their powers to take over the Cheltenham to Gloucester line and to pay off the costs that the C&GWUR had expended on it to date, and it was handed over on 18th June 1840. Divested of this responsibility, the latter were thus able to concentrate on building the line from Swindon to Kemble and on from there to Cirencester. By November 1840, work on the line was reported to be nearing completion, with an anticipated opening in January 1841. However, there then arose an issue with the embankment near Swindon, which had been built with clay obtained from side cuttings in the wet winter of 1839-40. Several slips occurred which delayed opening by several months, as much of it had to be remade with rubble and sand. In one place, so wet was the interior that the embankment had subsided by 8 feet in 24 hours.

Board of Trade Inspecting Officer Sir Frederick Smith found it to be 'tolerably firm' when he inspected the line, recommending that a careful watch should be kept on the embankment, but with the rest of the line in good order he sanctioned the opening, which duly took place on 31st May 1841. The C&GWUR directors arranged to lease the line to the GWR for working, under terms previously agreed in 1837. The route was double track from Swindon to Kemble, with intermediate stations at Minety & Ashton Keynes and at Purton, but then single for the rest of the way to Cirencester on what would become the branch. However, for a few short years, the station in the Cotswold market town of Cirencester, albeit an important centre in Roman times, was effectively the terminus of a main line from London. As mentioned a little earlier, Kemble at this date had only basic wooden platforms.

At this stage in time, though, there was little prospect of the C&GWUR being able to raise the finances for completing the line from Kemble on to Gloucester and thus a further Act was obtained in 1842. This authorised the sale of the whole undertaking, to the GWR, the B&GR or the Bristol & Gloucester Railway (Br&GR); the latter was in the process of constructing their line, which it was intended would use C&GWUR rails to reach Gloucester. In order to be able to do this, in 1842 they decided to build their line to the broad gauge instead of standard gauge as originally planned. After some wrangling, agreement was finally reached with the GWR in 1843, the transfer of capital taking place in July, whilst the amalgamation between the two was sanctioned in an Act of 1844. Subsequently, in 1846, both the B&GR and the Br&GR were absorbed by the Midland Railway.

As it turned out, the Br&GR opened its line to Gloucester on 8th July 1844, before the erstwhile C&GWUR route was opened by the GWR. The hold up was largely caused by the directors and successive chairmen losing interest in anything other than selling their undertaking to the GWR, whilst further slips had occurred in the embankment near Swindon in January 1842. Although quickly and efficiently solved by Brunel, this no doubt further hastened their desire to divest themselves of the railway. The new Act of 1842 which authorised its sale, also provided for the raising of a further £750,00 in capital to complete it and an extension of three more years in which to do so, and also gave powers to the Br&GR to build the line between Standish and Gloucester.

Following the purchase by the GWR of the whole of the C&GWUR undertaking in July 1843, little time was then lost in completing the rest of the line, which, if done and opened by 21st June 1845, permitted the GWR to buy back the moiety of the Cheltenham to Gloucester section from the B&GR. Agreement had also been reached with the Br&GR for the GWR to build and have ready for them the line from Kemble to Gloucester by April 1844, the GWR no doubt being concerned that this section was built to the broad gauge. In the summer of 1843, four contracts were let for building the rest of the line from Kemble to Gloucester, with work commencing in the August. The 7$^{1}/_{2}$ mile section north from Standish was the first to be completed, the line from there to Gloucester being opened on 8th July 1844 as part of the Br&GR.

The other three contracts comprised the line from Stonehouse to Sapperton Tunnel, the tunnel itself and then the short section from the south end of the tunnel to Kemble. By July 1844, the route between Stonehouse and Sapperton was two thirds completed and ballasted, whilst the trackbed from the tunnel to Kemble was finished, ballasted and ready for tracklaying. The tunnel itself was nearly three-quarters done. By February 1845, the tunnel and all principal works were finished, and tracklaying was underway

The new railway was inspected by General Pasley of the BoT in early May 1845. From the 2,227 yards long Sapperton Tunnel, the line curved down the steep Sapperton Bank, hugging the valley contours and closely following the course of the Thames & Severn Canal through Chalford and Brimscombe on its way down to Stroud. Nine timber viaducts were crossed on the way, which had fairly short lives, with rebuilding of all of them in more durable materials commencing from 1859. From Stroud, the line was mostly on the level to Stonehouse and then on to Standish, where the junction with the Br&GR line was made. New stations with 'handsome stone buildings', were provided at Brimscombe, Stroud and Stonehouse, and Kemble was served by a station named Tetbury Road until 1882, whilst at Gloucester a temporary platform was added to the north side of the existing B&GR/Br&GR station. The inspector's report being favourable, the line from Kemble to Standish opened for traffic on 12th May 1845, which thus at last allowed trains to travel between Swindon and Gloucester.

Apart from the conversion of the line from broad to standard gauge in May 1872 and the aforementioned rebuilding of the

A most unusual working is seen here approaching Cashes Green Halt on Sunday 18th March 1962 – for which the photographer this time did record the details on the slide mount, although not the identity of the 'Castle' Class engine at its head! Train No. F21 was actually the Paddington to Fishguard boat train which, during the winter of 1962, was diverted at Swindon to run via Stroud and Gloucester. This is likely to have been in connection with the electrification of the Severn Tunnel pumping station, with the old steam engines being removed and replaced by electrical pumps. This took place in November 1961 but then early in 1962 work commenced on electrification of the ventilating system, which also presumably required access to the tunnel itself on weekends. John noted that this was the last winter working of the diverted train, so this was a fortunate picture indeed. We shall see much more of Cashes Green and its lineside allotments later on. JOHN STRANGE/NPC

original timber viaducts, little changed on the route in the first fifty or so years of its existence. The first new station to be added was at Chalford, which opened on 2nd August 1897. However, perhaps the biggest change occurred in the early years of the 20th century, when the GWR were trialling steam railmotor cars in the hope of providing a bus or tram style service in areas where competition from these sources was starting to bite. Although no tram service ever operated in the Stroud Valley, the line was ideal as the number of villages spread along its floor and sides provided a large number of potential passengers mostly living within walking distance of the railway. Accordingly, between October 1903 and May 1905, six new halts were opened between Chalford and Stonehouse for a new railmotor service – at Ebley Crossing, Downfield Crossing, Bowbridge Crossing, Ham Mill, Brimscombe Bridge and St. Mary's, with a seventh, at Cashes Green, added in 1931. Although the steam railmotor cars were a short-lived innovation on this route at least, a victim partly of their own success, the 'Chalford Auto' or 'Chalford Donkey' service was to survive until the end of October 1964, during which time it became synonymous with the line and latterly one of the most photographed train services in the country.

I have mentioned before that Gloucestershire was fortunate in having so many highly scenic stretches of railway and within the pages of this and the companion Volume 5B we shall traverse yet more, in particular the climb up the valley from Stroud to Sapperton Tunnel – the Golden Valley as it is often called. As well as being very photogenic, it was also steep and winding, which in steam days meant that heavy freights especially needed banking uphill. A small engine shed, a sub-shed of Horton Road, was provided at Brimscombe to house the banking engine, which could be attached there or sometimes at Stroud and, as we shall see, a fair variety of classes appeared on these duties. Further sub-sheds could be found at the termini of the Cirencester and Tetbury branches, whilst a shed was provided at Chalford in 1903 for the rail motor service but was closed in 1935.

Today, the main line to Swindon still curves away from the Bristol & Gloucester line at Standish Junction but the halts have all gone along with two of the stations, Brimscombe and Chalford. Stonehouse, Stroud and Kemble remain open but, of these, Stonehouse is but a shadow of its former self. Despite a fierce campaign by the local council and heritage campaigners, the original Brunellian station buildings were demolished in the 1990s in a

then typical act of British Railways corporate vandalism, which was accompanied by a threat to close the station completely if they were not given permission to do so, although they magnanimously said they would keep it open if the local parish council paid thousands for improvement works deemed necessary! For a time the platforms were reduced to just 60 yards in length (enough to accommodate two coaches) but recently the station has been upgraded somewhat and the platforms lengthened to around 150 yards. There is a part-time ticket office but bus shelters still suffice for passenger comfort.

Happily, Stroud and Kemble still retain their buildings, the former also having its Brunellian goods shed, complete with 'GWR Express Goods Services' lettering still extant on its rail facing side. A long period of disuse, during which it was fortunately saved from demolition by Grade II* listing, has ended with the building now in use as part of Stroud Valleys Artspace. The original station building remains but was much extended by the GWR. Kemble station buildings are listed Grade II, which also includes the limestone road over bridge at the south end of the station, the Cirencester Branch platform (which recently stopped Network Rail from part demolishing it) and the water tank at the north end of the Down platform. The branch platform is home to a short siding used mostly for stabling track machines.

On leaving the station, the line heads through Kemble Tunnel, beneath Squire Gordon's land. In one of these incredibly short-sighted decisions that blighted the railway network following the Beeching Report, in 1968 the line between Kemble and Swindon was singled as a money saving exercise, which created an unnecessary pinch-point. However, in 2014, at great expense and no doubt vastly negating any savings that had been made, the line was redoubled once more. It remains a busy trunk route, being the direct rail connection to London for the county of Gloucestershire.

Finally, for those with a particular interest in the railway traversing the Stroud Valley between Kemble and Stonehouse, Lightmoor Press will shortly be starting production work on the first part of a major two volume history of the line currently being written and compiled by Mike Fenton. This will cover everything, from inception and construction to opening as a broad gauge line, the start of the railmotor service, traffic and services, the Sapperton bankers, stations and infrastructure, railwaymen who worked on the line and signal boxes and signalling. Volume 1 is planned to come out in 2022.

'Halls' meet at Gloucester on a bright spring day, on 23rd March 1964. No. 6987 *Shervington Hall* crosses over London Road Bridge as it breasts the gently rise into the station from the west and heads along the Up Main line with a long rake of empty iron ore wagons bound for the ore fields of Northamptonshire. Meanwhile, No. 6913 *Levens Hall* waits to head to South Wales with another unseen freight of some description. Based at Cardiff East Dock, No. 6987 was one of Hawksworth's 'Modified Hall' Class, new into service under the nascent British Railways regime on 10th March 1948. Despite Hawksworth's mostly successful improvements to Collett's original design, their late introduction on the scene meant they led relatively short lives and this engine was withdrawn from East Dock shed on 21st September 1964, after just sixteen and a half years of service. No. 6913 meanwhile was a Collett 'Hall', new on 7th February 1941 and also on its final posting when seen here, at Horton Road shed where it arrived from Reading in March 1963. Withdrawal took place on 25th June 1964, three months after this picture was taken, so a working life of a slightly more respectable twenty-three years, four and a half months. DON MANN

SECTION 1

GLOUCESTER CENTRAL STATION

From a technical point of view there is much to criticise about this photograph, with the lamppost in the foreground neatly projecting out of the chimney of the unidentified 'Grange' Class 4-6-0 heading west past Gloucester West Signal Box and across London Road Bridge circa 1963 – but what an atmospheric shot! This is how many Gloucester folk would remember the railway, glimpses of steam engines crossing the span as they walked or drove beneath on their daily business. The advertisement for Purolator engine filters looks newly painted; first patented in 1923, they are still under manufacture today, under the ownership of Mann+Hummel of Germany. On the right is the Horse & Groom pub at No. 12 London Road, selling Allsopp's Ales (part of the Ind Coope group) and in steam days used for enginemen's lodgings. Closed circa 1979, the building is now is no more, the site being a car park for nearby offices. Beyond the bridge on the right is the entrance to Station Approach (also now no more) and the white building opposite, which does still remain, was the District General Manager's office. NPC

Despite the often fraught nature of daily operations, the Great Western and Midland railways operated alongside each other at the station in Gloucester for nearly six and a half years from May 1845. The GWR platform was situated on the north side of the station, their rails crossing those of the Midland on the level just outside the platforms. This situation finally came to an end on 19th September 1851, when a new station was brought into use in conjunction with the opening of the South Wales Railway to Chepstow. It comprised two short platforms with a wooden covered roof or train shed spanning them.

However, the GWR quickly decided the layout was too restricted and in 1855 rebuilt the station completely. The train shed and the northernmost platform were swept away, and the surviving platform, backing on to the Midland station, was lengthened by 280 yards. In common with other major stations across the broad gauge network at this period, there was a single long platform, which was situated on the south or Down side of the line. This single platform was divided into Up and Down faces by means of a scissors crossover midway along its length. Gloucester's association with exceptionally long platforms thus stemmed from very early days and this arrangement

is in part replicated by the station as it exists today, following the extensive rebuild it underwent in the mid-1970s, when Eastgate was closed and all services were then concentrated on Central, which was renamed just Gloucester.

However, we have got ahead of ourselves. The Up or north side platform was added in 1885, by which time the station must have become something of an operational nightmare. Ironically, in a similar vein, having closed this platform to passengers in 1968, it too has since been re-opened again to provide more operational flexibility. The main platform on the Down side was lengthened to 1,977ft during a major rebuilding of the station in 1975, enjoying the status of being the longest platform in Britain for a number of years. However, it was superceded by Colchester at 2,034ft, although this was controversial as the platform there is actually physically split, so many thought it a cheat! In any case, the argument became superfluous following the opening of the Channel Tunnel terminal at Cheriton, which has eight island platforms each 2,595ft in length.

In steam days, the four tracks through the station comprised the Down (towards South Wales) and Up Platform Lines, and the Down and Up Mains, the lines running straight through the

The old order meets the new as lime-stained No. 92155 greets an unidentified 'Hymek' diesel-hydraulic arriving 'Light Engine' from the west past Gloucester West Signal Box on 6th July 1964. The big 2-10-0s had almost criminally short working lives, Saltley-based No. 92155 being typical. New into service from Crewe Works on 30th November 1957, withdrawal off Liverpool Speke Junction shed occurred in mid-November 1966, just short of its ninth birthday. The 101 members of the 'Hymek' Class faired little better, however, as BR shied away from the diesel-hydraulic designs introduced by the Western Region. Built between 1961 and 1964, all had gone by the end of 1975. DON MANN

RIGHT: Another 'photter' had joined Don Mann here at the east end of the Down platform on 1st September 1964, as the Horton Road footplate crew of ex-GWR 'Mogul' No. 7318 watch a freight arrive from South Wales whilst they await departure with a train for Hereford, exactly two months before the service was withdrawn. The spire of St. Gregory's RC church dominates the background. DON MANN

centre. A trailing crossover linked these two lines towards the eastern end of the platforms, with another trailing crossover sited immediately to the west of London Road Bridge. The Down and Up platforms were split in two, so they could each accommodate two trains at once, by means of scissors crossovers midway along their length. There were also Down and Up bay platforms, for local services heading west and east. The platforms were thus numbered 1 and 2 on the Down Main side, and 3 for the west end bay, whilst the Up Main platform was 4 and 5, with the Stroud bay being 6. There was also an un-numbered parcels platform opposite the bay No. 3. The map on pages 74-75 shows all this more clearly.

The ex-GWR goods yard was situated on the Up side at the east end of the station and accommodated a long narrow shed, some 300ft in length by 30ft wide, which was served by one internal line running right through. Between the shed and the east end of the Up platform were the GWR carriage sidings but use seems to have been made of those on the ex-LM&SR side as well in BR days, which were to the south of Central on the site of the old Midland terminus, closed in 1896.

Plans to resite Gloucester station on
(continued on page 20)

ABOVE: On a line busy with freight to and from South Wales, these juxtapositions of motive power were common and no doubt one of the main things that drew photographers here. On 20th September 1965, '9F' No. 92218 and 'Black Five' No. 44917 meet, the latter with a train of coke hoppers bound possibly for the John Summers steelworks at Shotton, the locomotive being based at Mold Junction at this time. If so, it is a working that would have been expected to head up the 'North & West' route via Newport, Hereford and Shrewsbury. The Banbury-based '9F' has a chalked nameplate on its smoke deflector, 'The Black Prince', a name of course since bestowed by the late David Shepherd on his preserved '9F' No. 92203.

LEFT: 'Halls' to the fore again as No. 4929 Goytrey Hall, a long term resident of Horton Road shed, arrives with a train of low sided wagons, whilst No. 4951 Pendeford Hall waits for the road. This engine was withdrawn on 25th June 1964, so the view probably dates from late 1963 or early '64. No. 4929 was taken out of service on 19th March 1965. BOTH DON MANN

An unusual view showing a heavy iron ore train being banked out of the station towards South Wales by Class '4F' No. 44123 on 16th September 1964. This was a common occurrence with these workings, to assist them in starting away again after stopping for water and over the 'hump' taking the line across London Road, but one that seems to have been rarely photographed. The 0-6-0 is not coupled to the train and it is not signalled to pass the Down Starter, so is in fact about to cease pushing. With only the last ten or so wagons to clear the hump, the train will have gained enough momentum on the gentle downslope to continue on its way unassisted. In a similar vein, it was not unknown for a banker to be sent out to assist heavy Up freights into the station from the west. New from Crewe Works as LM&SR No. 4123 in July 1925, the 0-6-0 was based at Gloucester Barnwood from September 1950 until the shed closed on 4th May 1964, when it then transferred over to Horton Road, its home when photographed here. It was withdrawn in early June 1965. DON MANN

Filthy No. 6965 *Thirlestaine Hall* proceeds slowly along the Up Main with a train of steel bar loaded on bogie bolsters on 31st July 1964. The 'Modified Hall' was based at Newport Ebbw Junction at this date but transferred to Bristol Barrow Road in the November, from where it was withdrawn on 26th October 1965. Gloucestershire readers may be aware that the name is local, Thirlestaine Hall being a grand house built in 1885-87 and fronting on to Thirlestaine Road in Cheltenham. Note the parcels train departing from the bay in the left background. DON MANN

Class '8F' No. 48332 of Burton-on-Trent shed has just been given the 'right away' from Gloucester on 9th July 1965, as Newport Ebbw Junction's 2-10-0 No. 92230 arrives with a train of loaded coke hoppers. This was another '9F' with a frighteningly short working life of less than seven and a half years. New from Crewe Works on 1st August 1958, it was withdrawn off Horton Road shed, to where it had transferred ten weeks earlier, on 31st December 1965, the last day of Western Region steam. We get a good view here of the unusual signal gantry straddling the exit from the bay platform. The Starting and Calling On arms on the right pertained to the Down Platform Line, whilst those on the left were for the bay platform. The ground disc in the foreground was for the parcels bay. DON MANN

GLOUCESTER CENTRAL

ABOVE: Ex-LM&SR Class '8F' 2-8-0 No. 48266, also of Burton-on-Trent shed, waits for the road on the Down Main with a train of coal empties for South Wales on 11th May 1965. New from North British Locomotive at Glasgow in May 1942, a six week allocation to Agecroft in 1966 was to be followed by the engine spending its final six months in traffic at Lostock Hall, withdrawal occurring in June 1967. DON MANN

LEFT: Photographed in the same spot on a similar duty the previous year, these trains stopped here to take water, hence the fireman of No. 6840 *Hazeley Grange* is up on the tender in charge of the hose. Taken on 23rd September 1964, the 'Grange' was on its final allocation, to Llanelly shed, having been based in South Wales following transfer from Bristol St. Philip's Marsh in November 1950 to Pontypool Road. A move to Neath Court Sart in June 1963 preceded the transfer to Llanelly twelve months later. The engine was withdrawn in February 1965. NPC

the Avoiding Line have never been seriously pursued, so it remains something of an operational anomaly for such a large and important station with all north-south trains having to reverse. However, the four tracks through the station remain, as the long platform is still split in two and each can be accessed from the Down Main or the Up Main by a crossover, whilst freight to and from South Wales can also use the centre roads. The route can be doubly busy when the Severn Tunnel is closed for maintenance. The bay platform at the west end of the station remains but has seen little use in recent years since local stopping services from South Wales were extended to

Cheltenham, where a new turnback siding was installed. Funding was approved in 2018 for a new station building and improvements to the underpass, although the funds were not available until April 2020. Gloucester City Council began design work in February 2019 but the Coronavirus crisis has delayed the start of work and it will probably be 2022 now at the earliest before Gloucester gets its new station.

Some sidings remain in the old goods yard but no freight is either generated from or delivered here. A small logistics warehouse roughly on the site of the goods shed sits immediately adjacent to a bank of three sidings but makes no use of them.

More South Wales-bound freight, behind Saltley-based BR 'Standard' Class '4' 2-6-0 No. 76048 held waiting
for a clear road on 16th September 1964. New from Doncaster Works in March 1955, the engine moved on to
Croes Newydd in early September 1966, from where it was withdrawn at the end of January 1967. DON MANN

On a rainy Thursday 4th June 1964, work-stained Class 'WD/8' No. 90311 is undergoing a crew change. Based at Canklow shed near Rotherham, the Horton Road shedmaster
would look to find them a suitable working to take them back home to South Yorkshire, although perhaps with a night in lodgings in Gloucester first. New from North
British Locomotive as WD No. 7449 in March 1944, the engine became WD No. 77449 in Janaury 1945 and then BR No. 90311 in October 1949, when based at Mexborough.
Transferred to Canklow in January 1963, the 2-8-0 had just two months left in service when seen here at the head of a train of steel carrying bogie bolsters. DON MANN

No. 92150 poses in warm spring sunshine on 11th May 1965, at the head of another train of iron ore bound for the steelworks of South Wales. At this date there were three major plants operating making steel in the principality, at Port Talbot, Ebbw Vale and Llanwern, the latter having then only recently gone into production, in 1962. All three were voracious consumers of Oxfordshire and Northamptonshire ironstone, hence the steady procession of ore trains through Gloucester which is well shown in this series of pictures. The industry they served is also now largely confined to history. Ironstone is no longer mined in the UK, whilst steel making at Ebbw Vale ceased in 1978 (part of the works remained open until 2002 for tinplating and galvanising) and at Llanwern in 2001; again a part of the site remains in operation for hot rolling and pickling. Port Talbot is thus the only one of the plants still making steel, albeit using imported coal and ore, whilst clinging on to life by its fingertips. New from Crewe Works on 31st October 1957 and sent first to Wakefield shed, No. 92150 had transferred to Saltley in early February 1959, where it was be based for the next seven and a half years, apart from a month at Tyseley in the early summer of 1964. In October 1966, the 2-10-0 transferred north back to Wakefield where it spent its last six months in service, leading up to withdrawal in April 1967. DON MANN

A pairing of 'Manors' on 29th July 1964, as No. 7813 *Freshford Manor* heads No. 7808 *Cookham Manor* (most unusually coupled with a Collett 4,000 gallon tender) into the Up platform. Double-heading was not a common sight at Gloucester so the reason for this pairing is unknown. No. 7808 had three spells based at Horton Road – 1954-59, 1960-61 and from late 1964 until withdrawal at the end of WR steam but was based at Reading when seen here, as also was No. 7813. This engine too had transferred to Horton Road by the end of the year but then went to Didcot at the end of February 1965 for its final two months in service. Note the supposedly long gone GWR lettering fighting its way through the grime on the tender of *Freshford Manor*. Don Mann

We had a glimpse of the front end of No. 92218 on page 17 as it waited for the signal to proceed to South Wales on 20th September 1965, so here we have the corresponding view looking back towards the station. The '9F' was clearly having priming issues, a problem common with these engines on iron ore trains emanating from the limey, hard water areas where the stone was mined. The fireman is again up on the tender whilst filling it with water; it is these little glimpses of everyday tasks in the steam era, as much as the locomotives and trains themselves, which serve to bring these pictures to life. Don Mann

Class '42XX' 2-8-0 tank No. 5220 trundles slowly along the Up Main with a mixed freight which includes some Berry Wiggins tank wagons at the front of the consist. These will be returning from the company's depot at Whimsey, near Cinderford, at the top end of the Forest of Dean Branch, and were bound for Sharnal Street on the Isle of Grain (around two weeks per year they went to Manchester, presumably whilst Sharnal Street was down for maintenance). With Bullo Yard not used for branch exchange traffic latterly, they were now tripped to Llanthony Sidings or Over Sidings (or occasionally to Gloucester New Yard). No. 5220 had collected them in this instance probably from Over Sidings, along perhaps with other wagons as well for carrying forward. The slide is undated but the locomotive, which was new from Swindon Works in May 1924, was withdrawn off Cardiff East Dock shed on 28th December 1963, from where it had been based since transferring from Cardiff Canton in late August 1962, and a date within this period would seem likely. Note the black painted, rubber tyred unit on the Up platform; I have been unable to find out anything about it but am presuming that it is a battery operated tractor for towing parcels trolleys – any further information welcome. NPC

LEFT: With the writing on the wall for steam traction, the early 1960s saw locomotives becoming ever more neglected, as a consequence of which we have waited until now before seeing one here at Gloucester with its British Railways Western Region livery not covered in a layer of grime. On 10th June 1964, No. 5990 *Dorford Hall* pauses on the Up Main line with a train of iron ore empties heading back east to Oxfordshire. New into service on 6th December 1939, the engine spent the last five years of its career, from March 1960 to January 1965, based at Banbury shed, so was working back home. DON MANN

RIGHT: In contrast to the summer sunshine of the picture above, wisps of steam leaking from '8F' No. 48623 are the only evidence of warmth on the morning of a very frosty Monday 4th January 1965. The 2-8-0 was a war-time build by the Southern Railway at their Ashford Works in December 1943, and was based at Birkenhead Mollington Street shed when photographed here. It moved on to Sutton Oak three months after the picture was taken, from where it was withdrawn in early October 1966. The scissors crossover which divided the Down platform in two, allowing it to be used by two trains at once, is well shown. DON MANN

LEFT: A pair of unidentified '45XX' 'Prairie' tanks – plus at least one other engine just glimpsed behind the second one – trundle along the Down Main line, past a long rake of steel mineral wagons loaded with coal. The picture, which is undated but is circa 1964, provides us with a glimpse beneath the Platform 1 canopy, showing the stylish cast iron columns and spandrels which were swept away in the 1975 rebuilding of the station. Note too the disc signals, one set projecting from the canopy and another hung beneath it. Operated from Gloucester East Signal Box, they controlled movements through the scissors crossover, the outer set reading for the Down Main and the inner set for the Down Platform Line. The smaller Calling On disc is 'off', indicating that the locomotives are signalled to proceed part way along the Down Main but do not have a clear route all the way through the station. DON MANN

The routes through the station were controlled by a myriad of ground, disc and repeater signals, as this view of No. 5979 *Cruckton Hall* shows. Taken on 11th October 1963, the 'Hall' is seen making its way tender first along the Up Main propelling a parcels van. The disc signal just above its roof, along with the banner repeater mounted on the footbridge above the locomotive's chimney, indicate that the crew have the road right the way through the station. As on the Down side, there was another set of disc signals (hidden behind the tender) hung beneath the canopy controlling the Up Platform Line. Of interest here also are the two ground discs in the foreground, which controlled reverse movements through the Down side scissors crossover. New into service on 8th September 1938, *Cruckton Hall* was based at Horton Road when seen here, having transferred up from Reading in March 1963, and is probably engaged on station pilot duties. A further transfer to Worcester in early September 1964 preceded the engine's withdrawal two months later. Note the enamelled platform number signs on the wall on the left; Platform No. 4 was to the left (west) of the scissors crossover visible behind the van and No. 5 beyond it, whilst the Stroud bay was No. 6. DON MANN

Watched by the driver of 2-10-0 No. 92227, a pair of trainspotters check their ABCs to see if they have it noted down already. Taken on 16th August 1965, such days would soon be a thing of the past, as WR steam had just four and a half months left. Nowadays, a pair of youngsters like this would similarly have their heads down but checking mobile phones whilst being completely oblivious of any passing train! The wagons are loaded with spoil, so this is an engineers' train, as also indicated by the 'Z' headcode (carried by excursion, military or special trains), but its origin and destination are unknown. The locomotive was based at Banbury at this date. New from Crewe Works on 3rd July 1958, it was withdrawn off Speke Junction shed at the start of November 1967. DON MANN

OPPOSITE PAGE TOP: Excess steam from No. 6821 *Leaton Grange* has served to obscure its train as it heads through on the Down Main on 9th March 1964. The engine also appears to be suffering a leakage which has coated the lower half of its boiler barrel and the nameplate with a rust coloured deposit. New into service on 13th January 1937, this was a St. Philip's Marsh engine when seen here, which transferred to Barrow Road in June 1964 and was then withdrawn from Llanelly shed on 6th November that year. DON MANN

OPPOSITE PAGE BOTTOM: Horton Road's Class '94XX' 0-6-0PT No. 8471 is seen on 7th August 1964 whilst on station pilot duties. The pannier tank has coupled up to the four empty coaches of a recently arrived service from Hereford, which will be taken to the carriage sidings for cleaning and preparation for their next turn. No. 8471 was built for BR by the Yorkshire Engine Company, going to Merthyr Tydfil when new on 31st May 1951. Stints at the three Cardiff sheds followed subsequently, before it arrived at Horton Road for an eighteen month stay in July 1963. Transferred to Bristol Barrow Road in January 1965, it was withdrawn on 16th June. There is a good view of the Down Platform Line discs, the larger ones representing normal signal arms and the smaller discs Calling On arms. There is a glimpse too of the corresponding set for the Up side, beneath the canopy. DON MANN

ABOVE: A Hereford train at Platform No. 4, having just arrived on 4th June 1964 behind 2-6-2T No. 5545, whilst a freight heads away along the Down Main to the left, having just been given the 'right away'. New in October 1928, the 'Prairie' tank spent only the last seven months of its working life at Gloucester, from May to late November 1964 but, as we shall see, managed to get itself in front of the camera quite frequently! DON MANN

BELOW: Class and shedmate No. 4564 on the Up Main with a load of ballast from Whitecliff Quarry in the Forest of Dean on 31st August 1964. On the left, the local permanent way gang are carrying out some maintenance on the scissors crossover. New in October 1924, this was one of the original straight tank '45XXs', No. 5545 above being a later build with the larger capacity slope tanks. Posted to Horton Road in September 1963, No. 4564's forty year career had just three weeks left to run when seen here. DON MANN

LEFT: A small selection of J.T. Bassingdale's slides were presented in Volume 3 of this series, *Gloucester Midland Lines North*, and this view of ex-GWR '28XX' Class 2-8-0 No. 3824 at the head of a train of South Wales coal is the first of several more. They are undated but believed to have been taken in the period 1955-57. New into service on 10th September 1940, No. 3824 went to Ebbw Junction shed in early October 1954, staying there until transferred to Pontypool Road in June 1956. The picture was clearly taken on the same occasion as that of No. 5017, below, so it was still Ebbw Junction based when seen here. The engine transferred back there in November 1959 after its sojourn at Pontypool Road, where it remained until withdrawal in June 1964.

J.T. BASSINGDALE/LAURENCE BROWNHILL COLLECTION

RIGHT: 'Castle' Class No. 5017 *The Gloucestershire Regiment 28th-61st* poses on the Up Main line. New into service on 11th July 1932 as *St. Donat's Castle*, No. 5017 was reallocated to Horton Road from Worcester shed in October 1951 and was renamed on 26th April 1954, presumably in recognition of the regiment's outstanding action in the Battle of the Imjin River in April 1951 during the Korean War. The locomotive is coupled to one of the slab-sided Hawksworth 4,000 gallon tenders; it is listed as being paired with tender No. 4040 from 1st May 1954 to 28th September 1955, after which it was coupled to Collett tenders again, so that gives us a likely summer 1955 date for the picture. The engine is surprisingly grubby for what must have a local celebrity but entered Swindon Works for a heavy general overhaul on 29th August, which adds further credence to the date suggested. It was withdrawn off Horton Road in September 1962 after two months in storage there.

J.T. BASSINGDALE/LAURENCE BROWNHILL COLLECTION

LEFT: Again taken on the same day and looking very smart in its lined black British Railways livery, with the early 'Cycling Lion' emblem on the tender, 'Standard' Class '5' No. 73065 was less than a year old when seen here, having emerged from Crewe Works in October 1954. It was also some distance from home, being based at Sheffield Millhouses shed. The 4-6-0 is carrying a 'Light Engine' lamp code but its presence at Eastgate station would be more easily explained than here, facing the wrong way on the Down Main at Central! After moving to Canklow at the start of 1962, by the end of the year it had transferred down to the Southern Region and was withdrawn off Nine Elms shed in early July 1967.

J.T. BASSINGDALE/LAURENCE BROWNHILL COLLECTION

A fine study of gleaming 'Castle' Class No. 5075 *Wellington* waiting to depart east from Central station. Entering service on 3rd August 1938, the 4-6-0 was originally named *Devizes Castle* but was patriotically renamed in August 1940 after the Vickers Wellington bomber, which was then the mainstay of Bomber Command's fleet. Indeed, the type was the only bomber design built throughout the war and in greater numbers than any other. Note the 'Castle Class' designation on the plate below the name, which was appended to non-castle names, as also with No. 5017 on the previous page. This engine is also coupled to a Hawksworth tender but it was paired with four in a row between October 1953 and December 1960, so this does not help us with dating. However, it was in Swindon Works for a Heavy General Overhaul from 25th April to 16th June 1955, which would certainly explain its sparkling condition here if taken on the same day as the previous three pictures, circa August 1955. The locomotive was at that time based at Chester West, where it had been since June 1949. It subsequently transferred to Wolverhampton Stafford Road in May 1956 and was withdrawn off Bristol St. Philip's Marsh in September 1962. J.T. BASSINGDALE/LAURENCE BROWNHILL COLLECTION

Our ultimate destination through the two parts that constitute this volume is Swindon, which we shall travel to via the Stroud Valley. This is the first of what will be a multitude of sightings of the Stroud Valley auto train which, after leaving Gloucester, ran first to Stonehouse and then called at the various stations and halts all the way up to Chalford. No. 1474 and its single auto coach have arrived at Platform No. 1 but will cross over to the bay Platform No. 6 on the Up side for its next departure. Incidentally, the train is not stopped at the bracket signal jutting from the canopy by the driving end of the trailer, which did not apply to the Down Platform Line. This is a most unusual signal, protecting the crossover between the Down Main and the Up Main and equipped with a permanent route indicator – a white letter 'M' in a black circle – to remind approaching footplate crews that it applied to the Main Line. The tower of Gloucester Cathedral can be seen in the right background. DON MANN

ABOVE: No. 7817 *Garsington Manor* loads parcels on a wet and miserable day, 16th April 1964, prior to departing to Hereford. The 4-6-0 was on its final posting, to Reading shed and two months away from withdrawal, on 15th June. DON MANN

RIGHT: No. 92007 of Severn Tunnel Junction shed heads along the Up Main on 18th August 1965. The 2-10-0 moved to Horton Road seven weeks later and was withdrawn on 31st December. DON MANN

LEFT: 'Black Five' No. 45190 is an unusual sight in the No. 3 bay platform in July 1964. The 4-6-0 was based at Shrewsbury at this time, so was about to head back with a working to Hereford – yet more evidence of the variety of motive power which appeared on that line. DON MANN

ABOVE: A portion of a linen plan, dated 29th October 1935 and entitled 'GWR Gloucester, Proposed Up Relief Line and Abolition of Middle Signal Box'. Although pre-dating the photographs in this book, it is useful for illustrating the accommodation and offices within the station buildings and also for showing a proposed major track alteration. It would have required significant rebuilding of the Down side of the station, which would have become an island platform with all new buildings, whilst encroaching onto the site of the old Infirmary and Public Assistance Institution (Gloucester Workhouse), which would have required partial demolition of some of the buildings. Unsurprisingly, in the event it was never proceeded with. The Down side buildings comprised, from left to right: Gent's Lavatory (to left of footbridge steps); Booking Hall, Booking Office and Bookstall; Parcels Clerk, Parcel Office; Cloak Room; Telegraph Office;

LEFT: A second view of the bracket signal with the permanent route indicator, which here gazes down on 'BR-built 'Modified Hall' No. 7927 *Willington Hall* on 23rd September 1965. The engine, which was based at Newport Ebbw Junction, had lost its smokebox numberplate. DON MANN

BELOW: 'Mogul' No. 7318 rests having arrived with a train from Hereford in the autumn of 1964. New in December 1921, the 2-6-0 had transferred to Horton Road from Pontypool Road in the June and was withdrawn in early November after this service ceased. TIM STEPHENS

Refreshment Room; District Insp' Office; Store; General Waiting Room; WCs; Ladies Room; Lavatory; Telegraph Office; Ticket Collector's Room; Office; blank; Store. On the Up side, which are harder to read because of the proposed alterations, they are from left to right: Parcels & Cloak Room; blank; Porters Room; Guards Room; Booking Hall; Booking Office; Refreshment Room; 1st Class Ladies Waiting Room; General Waiting Room; Station Master's Office; 3rd Class Ladies Room; Gentleman's Lavatory (to right of footbridge steps); Staff Lavatory. What is noticeable is that the cramped nature of the site had meant that more of the accommodation was sited on the Up side and thus Station Approach (here marked 'Closed') formed an important entrance to that side of the station. The building partially shown top left on the north side of Station Approach was the DGM's Office, whilst the block of three rooms at the west end of the Up platform were the Oil and Lamp Rooms and a Stores. The new island platform would have had (in red, left to right) a smaller Refreshment Room; Waiting Room; Gents Lavatory; realigned footbridge steps and Offices. NPC

A change of emphasis here as we commemorate the dawn of the diesel era with a couple of views of 'Western' Class diesel-hydraulics in the attractive maroon livery which most of them carried throughout the 1960s and which married well with maroon coaching stock. No. D1070 *Western Gauntlet* is seen here at Central circa 1964 with the 3.20pm Cardiff to Leeds express, train reporting No. 1N61. Built at Crewe Works and entering into service on 28th October 1963 at Cardiff Canton, the locomotive was transferred to Swansea Landore shed in March 1964 and then moved to Plymouth Laira in April 1966. A return to Landore in February 1969 saw it working from South Wales for another two years, with the engine then moving back to Plymouth Laira in May 1971. It was withdrawn in December 1976 due to collision damage sustained at the 'B' end, having covered 1,312,000 miles in service, an indication of how intensively diesel locomotives could be worked in comparison to steam engines. DON MANN

Sadly, on this occasion on Wednesday 10th June 1964, Don did not record the identity of the maroon 'Western' clattering in past Gloucester East Signal Box at the head of a mixed loose-coupled freight. Reporting No. 7T62, this was the 6.40am Oxford, Hinksey Yard to Rogerstone working, which was due through Central at 10.54am. On the left by way of contrast stands No. 5990 *Dorford Hall* in Western Region lined green passenger livery. The 'Hall' was based at Banbury shed, so was quite possibly at the head of a train of iron ore empties and had stopped here to take water. Note the engineman visible between the two locomotives, walking the '4 foot' to the boarded crossing and presumably heading to the signal box to find out when they would be due off. New in December 1939, No. 5990 was withdrawn off Banbury shed in January 1965. DON MANN

'Hall' variety 1 – No. 6956 *Mottram Hall* stands on the Down Main Line in May 1964. The engine is carrying an ordinary passenger train lamp code, so may be waiting here to take over a service bound for Cheltenham St. James. The DMU behind, a Swindon-built unit of Class '120' of which Trailer Buffet Second Lavatory car No. 59255 is identifiable, was probably on the Swansea-Cardiff-Birmingham express service introduced in 1957. NPC

'Hall' variety 2 – No. 6942 *Eshton Hall* at the east end of the Down Platform Line on 16th July 1964. The lamp code is for a pick-up goods, which seems unlikely. However, there was often a rather lackadaisical approach to the placing of lamps in later years, particularly if the work involved was local, and the locomotive was probably on station pilot duties. NPC

RIGHT: An unusual sight on the Down Main Line, sadly at an unrecorded date. At the front of this convoy is 'Large Prairie' tank No. 4109. This '5101' Class 2-6-2T was new in September 1935 and was withdrawn off Horton Road shed in April 1964, having been based there since being transferred from Worcester in September 1961. This is clearly not a line of engines going for scrap, however, with coal piled high in No. 4109's bunker and also visible in the tenders of the two 'Hall' Class 4-6-0s behind, the nearest of which, under heavy magnification, can be identified as No. 6951 *Impney Hall*. The year is probably 1963, with No. 6951 having moved to Banbury, also from Worcester, in the March. So are these engines coming off shed or heading back and why all coupled together, or was that just to save separate 'Light Engine' moves? DON MANN

LEFT: The largest tank engines built by the GWR were the '72XX' Class 2-8-2Ts, which were actually enlarged rebuilds of '52XX' and '42XX' 2-8-0s, forty of the former being converted and then later fourteen of the latter. The rebuilds were lengthened at the rear by extending the frames by 4ft 1in., which allowed for a set of trailing wheels and a much larger capacity bunker, almost akin to a tender engine, greatly increasing their range and thus sphere of operation. The effect was quite porportional and they were impressive looking machines, and one was even tried as Lickey banker but there was found to be insufficient platform clearance at Bromsgrove. No. 7207 was rebuilt from No. 5282 in October 1934 and was based at Banbury when seen here on 15th November 1963, where it no doubt found use on the iron ore trains to South Wales. It was withdrawn a year later, in November 1964. DON MANN

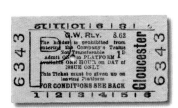

RIGHT: A rather quiet scene looking east from beneath the end of the Up platform canopy on Monday 16th August 1965. On the right, '9F' No. 92227 is seen again, this being a complementary view to that on page 27, with the 2-10-0 waiting for the road whilst heading an engineers' spoil train. In the left distance, a diesel shunter can be seen at work in the goods yard. DON MANN

A spot of routine maintenance for No. 92243 whilst held on the Up Main at the head of a train of cattle wagons on 29th July 1965. The engine had transferred from Cardiff East Dock to Newport Ebbw Junction just days before the picture was taken, hence the space on the smokebox door where the shedplate should be. The train was probably bound for Banbury to collect livestock from the market there rather than here at Gloucester, the new (1955) market being some distance from the railway. Don Mann

No. 4564 again, standing on the Up Main and taking water from the crane positioned there on a damp and misty day circa 1963. The engine may have arrived earlier with a local pick-up freight, as suggested by the lamp code, and returned for water having completed shunting the wagons in the yard. No. 1472 waits for departure from the bay platform with an auto working to Chalford. NPC

ABOVE AND BELOW: '28XX' 2-8-0 No. 2895 stops for water on 29th August 1963, whilst towing classmate No. 3802 to Swindon for repair. The latter was based at Severn Tunnel Junction at this date but moved to Taunton in April 1964 and then on to Bristol Barrow Road, from where it was withdrawn in early August 1965. No. 2895 was shedded at Cardiff East Dock, having moved there from Severn Tunnel in March 1963; it was withdrawn from Newport Ebbw Junction at the end of April 1965. The two engines were built at Swindon within a month of each other in late 1938. BOTH DON MANN

On 23rd July 1965, No. 92013 takes water whilst standing on the Up Platform Line with a train of bogie bolster wagons loaded with pipes, whilst the Starting signal in the foreground is 'off' for something coming through on the Up Main. New from Crewe Works on 31st May 1954, the locomotive went first to March shed, in Cambridgeshire, transferring then to Annesley in Nottinghamshire in February 1957, where it stayed until early May 1965, apart from a brief three week allocation to Woodford Halse in October 1959. The move from Annesley was to Banbury, where it was based when photographed here but the destination of the load of pipes is unknown. No. 92013's final allocation was to Saltley in early September, from where it was withdrawn three weeks later. DON MANN

LEFT: We now move to the Chalford Bay or Platform No. 6, to begin a series of views of the Chalford auto service. Grubby looking 0-4-2T No. 1444 is lit by a low morning sun sometime in 1964 as it waits for its next departure. New on 15th April 1935 as No. 4844, the class were renumbered into the '14XX' series in 1946, as the '48XX' numbers were required by the GWR for Class '28XX' 2-8-0s converted to oil burning. Having never been allocated there before, No. 1444 moved to Horton Road for its final posting in December 1963 and when the Chalford service finished officially on 2nd November, it was withdrawn immediately. DON MANN

RIGHT: No. 1458 gently simmers whilst sitting quietly and having its tanks filled with water on 7th August 1964. New into stock on 17th August 1935, long standing allocations for this engine included Banbury through the 1940s and Stourbridge in the 1950s. A brief stint at Hereford in 1963, which included nearly four months in store, preceded its last transfer, to Gloucester Horton Road in July 1964, where it too then succumbed to the great cull of local and branch passenger services on 2nd November. DON MANN

LEFT: Whilst the little Collett 0-4-2 tanks are synonymous with this service, it was not by any means their sole preserve, as we shall see. Auto-fitted Class '64XX' pannier tank No. 6412 transferred up to Horton Road from Yeovil in the summer of 1964, just a few weeks before the service ended, officially on Monday 2nd November although the last trains ran on Saturday 31st October, and was then immediately withdrawn itself. It was a week away from its thirtieth birthday, having gone into service on 12th November 1934. The engine is seen having backed down the siding adjacent to the bay to couple up with a second auto coach to strengthen the next service. BILL POTTER/KRM

Following on from the centre picture on the previous page, the youthful fireman of No. 1458 checks round the engine. Note that the cover of the left side tank is still open from taking water, the crane near the end of the platform and indeed the others around the station being supplied from the water tower in the background. On the right are the ex-GWR carriage sidings, although those on the Midland side were also used by the Western Region after Nationalisation. DON MANN

We step back into the mid-1950s again for this superb study of the footplate crew of No. 1441 coupling up to the auto trailer, whilst two young schoolboys watch the photographer with interest through the windows. The train has stopped slightly clear of the platform, which seems a little odd, and note the Starting signal for the Up Platform Line is 'off'. Information on the coach, which has 'TRAILER' painted in small yellow letters on the lower bodyside just to the left of the guard's compartment doors, has been provided by John Lewis. The vehicle is to Diagram E (No's 11 and 12) or Diagram F (No. 13) because of the way it looks like it has two compartments next to the guard's, although they were actually a small saloon. In fact this is almost certainly No. 12 because No's 11 and 13 had Collett 7ft bogies fitted and this trailer has not. The former were also condemned in 1954 but No. 12 lasted until December 1955. The lack of a number this end would probably be because it was repainted into BR colours early in 1949 before right-hand numbers became the rule and it had not been repainted since. It does show that the the BR red and cream livery did not suit some GWR coaches unless the lining under the roof was omitted! Another of the Bassingdale colour slides – and there are still more to come! – this almost certainly therefore gives us a summer 1955 date for the picture. No. 1441, which entered service at Horton Road on 10th April 1935, spent its entire career in Gloucestershire, frequently sub-shedded at Chalford or Lydney. It was stored in July 1959 and withdrawn in June 1960. Note the clinker dropped on the two Up lines where locomotives stood when taking water. J.T. BASSINGDALE/LAURENCE BROWNHILL COLLECTION

RIGHT: No. 1453 in the process of coupling up to trailer No. W234W in a view looking across all four through lines from Platform No. 1 on 3rd October 1964. The 63ft trailer was built in August 1951, Lot No. 1736 to Diagram A38, with the second lot constructed, in 1954, being the last GWR style auto trailers produced. The first two built were given the names *Thrush* and *Wren* and it was announced that the rest would also be given the names of birds but this was never carried out. Like the locomotives which hauled them, these auto trailers were also about to become redundant with the ending of these services. NPC

ABOVE: A fine close up study of No. 1453 taken on the same day as the previous picture. The driver is in the cab, whilst two men are at track level behind the engine – was there a minor problem perhaps with the control gear, with the fireman watching a fitter from Horton Road shed attempting to fix it? The train is on the Up Platform Line rather than the bay, with the ramp down from the platform just visible between engine and trailer. New into stock on 23rd July 1935, this was another of the '14XX' Class which only came to Gloucester late on in its life, in July 1962, for its final two years in service. JOHN GRANGER

LEFT: Trailer No. W234W again but this time behind 0-4-2T No. 1424 on 8th September 1963. This Bill Potter slide had been one swapped with R.C. 'Dick' Riley and arrived with me after being disposed of from his collection. New in November 1933 and going first to Goodwick in far West Wales on 18th of that month, No. 1424's first allocation to Horton Road was in January 1942. It was to remain there, apart from visits to works, for the rest of its career, which was close to ending when this picture was taken, withdrawal taking place on 2nd December 1963. BILL POTTER/NPC

Coach No. W242W, one of the last batch of GWR design auto trailers built, in June 1954 (lot No. 1766 to Diagram A43), is seen here on 16th July 1964 heading away from Platform No. 6 behind No. 1472. Note that the Home arm of the bracket signal ahead is 'off' but the Distant beneath it was fixed as a permanent indicator of the caution required passing through the maze of signals ahead leading to Tramway Crossing and the junctions. New in April 1936, No. 1472 spent most of its career in West Wales, moving between Carmarthen, Goodwick and Newcastle Emlyn, before being sent to Newton Abbot in February 1956. It spent nearly four months in Southern Region stock at Weymouth in late 1958/early 1959, transferring then to Cheltenham on 22nd March 1959. Put into store on 4th August 1960, it came out eight months later and after a visit to Wolverhampton Stafford Road Works, was sent to Gloucester on 11th May 1961, lasting then until the Chalford auto service was withdrawn. We get almost a driver's eye view here of the route out of Central, past the goods yard and Horton Road shed on the left. COURTESY RAIL-ONLINE

On the same day, No. 1444 heads back in propelling trailer No. W237W past Gloucester East Signal Box, forming a return working from Chalford. The coach was another of the June 1954 final batch. The picture is interesting in confirming that the frequency of the service, operated almost on motor bus principles, required two sets working in tandem, one going out whilst the other was coming back.
COURTESY RAIL-ONLINE

Railcar No. W20W rattles into the Down Platform Line in the summer of 1955. This is one of the later railcars, Lot No. 1635, to Diagram A1, with original builders the Associated Equipment Company Ltd (AEC) supplying the engines and transmissions to the GWR, to be fitted at Swindon Works where the cars were now built. No. 20 entered service on 4th June 1940 and was originally based at Reading. Moving to Weymouth Radipole in November 1945, from where it spent nearly eight years mainly working services to Bristol (during which time it also became BR No. W20W), it then transferred up to Horton Road in August 1953. It was withdrawn in October 1962 but was saved in 1966 for preservation by the Kent & East Sussex Railway. This batch could seat 48 passengers in two saloons (16 smoking /32 non-smoking) and also had a large luggage compartment, here seen at the nearer end. They were powered by two 8.8 litre, 6 cylinder, direct injection, high speed diesel engines (AEC type A180) which gave a combined output of 210hp. No's 19 (which was also later stationed at Gloucester) and 20 were fitted with five gear, dual range gearboxes and could maintain a maximum speed of 65 mph on the level. The fuel consumption was 7 miles per gallon at maximum speed, giving a 700 mile range. Note the driver's side window open to provide some air flow on this hot day. J.T. BASSINGDALE/LAURENCE BROWNHILL COLLECTION

With the Up Starter signal having given the right away, No. 6835 *Eastham Grange* heads away from Central in what we have now fairly certainly established as the summer of 1955. The imposing ex-GWR goods shed, approximately 150 yards in length, forms the backdrop. New into service on 1st September 1937, No. 6835 was based at Bristol St. Philip's Marsh at the date of this view. It moved to Penzance in January 1962 but its stay there was brief, the engine moving all the way back up to Wolverhampton Oxley three months later. This was an even briefer allocation, for just three weeks, the final move being back to St. Philip's Marsh, from where it was withdrawn on 24th May 1963. The inscription painted on the lower cab side appears to read '*Tap in 8*'.
J.T. BASSINGDALE/LAURENCE BROWNHILL COLLECTION

Remaining in the 1950s, ex-GWR railcar No. W20W is seen again, heading to the Up bay platform on 27th May 1958, whilst WD 2-8-0 No. 90188 waits for the road. The passenger door is open on the railcar, so it is likely to be just coming off shed after servicing and entering the bay to form the next service, probably to Stratford-upon-Avon via Cheltenham and the Honeybourne line. The K&ESR preserved railcar has been non-operational since 1980 but is now nearing the end of what has been a major, long drawn out restoration at Tenterden. The 'Dub-Dee' was based at Cardiff Canton at the date of the picture, so could be heading east with coal or with iron ore empties. New in September 1943 as WD No. 7214, it moved briefly to Banbury in late 1960 but then returned to South Wales, to Newport Ebbw Junction shed. In December 1962 it went north to Mexborough in Yorkshire, then to Staveley Barrow Hill in January 1964 and was withdrawn in early April 1965. COLOUR-RAIL

A typical workaday scene at the east end of Central on 25th April 1964 but on this occasion with an unusual visitor in the form of ex-LM&SR Hughes-designed 'Crab' 2-6-0 No. 42900 of Saltley shed passing through with a long mixed freight heading for South Wales. Built at Crewe Works and entering service on 23rd August 1930 as No. 13200, the 'Crab' had spent most of its BR years at Saltley, apart from a few weeks at Kettering in mid-1955, until moving on to Birkenhead Mollington Street two months after this picture was taken. It then went to Stockport Edgeley in early March 1965 and was withdrawn from there seven months later. Its progress is being watched with interest by the young fireman of 9F No. 92241, standing 'Light Engine' on the Up Main. New into service on 6th October 1958, the 2-10-0 had spent most of its short career in South Wales but was at Southall shed at the time of this view, its final allocation prior to withdrawal in July 1965, a career totalling six years and nine months! No doubt it would have passed through Gloucester quite regularly in the three years it spent working from Cardiff but to appear here when based at Southall would have been much more unusual. DON MANN

Collett 0-6-0 No. 2245 looks rather careworn as it heads over the east end foot crossing and along the Down Main Line on 5th June 1962. The '22XX' had just come off shed and is carrying a 'Light Engine' lamp code so may be heading to the west end of the station to assist in banking a heavy freight up the hump over London Road Bridge. New into service on 25th April 1945, No. 2245 was withdrawn off Horton Road shed a year after this picture was taken, on 23rd May 1963. Note the 'Cordon' wagon on the left, to Diagram DD4 with nine short gas tanks stacked in two rows; a second type, Diagram DD5, had two long gas tanks mounted longitudinally. In the right distance, a 'Warship' diesel-hydraulic can be seen peeping round Gloucester East Signal Box. The foot crossing, incidentally, was for railway staff only, there were notices (one is part in picture on the extreme left) requesting passengers to use the footbridge. ALAN JARVIS

ABOVE: In contrast to its classmate in the previous picture, Collett 0-6-0 No. 2242 was clearly fresh from having a major overhaul and repaint at Swindon Works when seen on the same day. The engine was three weeks the senior of No. 2245, having gone into service on 4th April 1945. It was a regular on the Ross on Wye line services, having been based at Hereford shed from July 1957 to early November 1964, and there are several views of it on that route in Volume 1, *West Gloucester & Wye Valley Lines*. It is seen here having recently arrived from Hereford, heading to the Horton Road turntable for turning prior to making the journey back home. With passenger services between Gloucester and Hereford being officially withdrawn on and from 2nd November 1964, No. 2242 transferred to Horton Road for its last seven months in service. ALAN JARVIS

RIGHT: The List of Signal Boxes between Kemble, Gloucester and Beachley Junction, near Chepstow, from the *Working Time Table of Freight Trains, Gloucester District, 12th June to 10th September inclusive, 1961*. The table shown here is an amalgamation, as the original extends over two pages in the WTT. Beachley Junction, on the South Wales main line which is also covered in Volume 1, was the box provided in 1917 for the branch serving Beachley shipyard. The yard was an expensive failure and was closed by 1919 but the box remained as a block post, finally closing in March 1969.

K135

List of Signal Boxes—continued

Distance Box to Box		NAME OF BOX	TIMES DURING WHICH BOXES ARE OPEN					Whether provided with Switch
			Weekdays			Sundays		
			Opened at		Closed at	Opened at	Closed at	
			Mondays	Other Days				
KEMBLE, GLOUCESTER AND BEACHLEY JUNCTION								
5	42	Kemble	—	Open continuously		—	—	No
—	64	Coates	—	As required **M**		—	—	Yes
2	43	Sapperton Sidings	—	Open continuously		—	2. 0 p.m.**A**	Yes
						10. 0 p.m.		
2	1	Frampton Crossing	7.50 a.m.	6.40 a.m.	9.20 p.m.	—	—	Yes
1	40	Chalford	5.50 a.m.	5.50 a.m.	10.40 p.m.**L**	2. 0 p.m.	10. 0 p.m.	Yes
					11.45 p.m.**SO L**			
1	29	Brimscombe East	—	Open continuously		10. 0 p.m.	8. 0 a.m.**A**	Yes
—	20	Brimscombe West	11.40 a.m.	11.40 a.m.	1.30 p.m.	—	—	Yes
			6. 0 p.m.	6.0 p.m.**SX**	7.40 p.m.**SX**			
2	40	Stroud	—	Open continuously		—	—	Yes
2	70	Stonehouse (Burdett Road)	6. 0 a.m.	—		—	6. 0 a.m.**A**	Yes
1	63	Standish Junction	—	Open continuously		—	—	Yes
1	24¾	Haresfield	—	Open continuously		—	—	No
1	61	Naas Crossing	—	Open continuously		—	—	No
2	9¼	Tuffley Junction	6. 0 a.m.	—		—	5.50 a.m.	Yes
1	27½	Gloucester (South Junction)	—	Open continuously		—	—	Yes
—	27	Gloucester (North)	4.30 a.m.	—		—	8. 0 a.m.**A**	Yes
—	12	Gloucester (Tramway Junction)	—	Open continuously		—	—	No
—	—	Gloucester Mileage Yard Ground Frame.	—	Open continuously		—	—	—
—	22	Gloucester (East)	—	Open continuously		—	—	No
—	22	Gloucester (West)	—	Open continuously		—	—	No
1	33	Over Junction	4.45 a.m.	—		—	8. 0 a.m.**A**	Yes
—	30	Over Sidings	—	—		10. 0 p.m.	8. 0 a.m.**A**	Yes
B	—	Oakle Street	—	Intermediate Block Signals		—	—	No
5	37½	Grange Court	—	Open continuously		—	—	
C	—	Newnham	—	Intermediate Block Signals		—	—	
4	28	Bullo Pill East	5. 0 a.m.	—		—	6. 0 a.m.**A**	Yes
2	26	Bullo Pill West	5. 0 a.m.	—		—	6. 0 a.m.**A**	Yes
2	6	Awre Junction	—	Open continuously		—	—	No
D	—	Gatcombe	—	Intermediate Block Signals		—	—	
4	77	Lydney Junction	5. 0 a.m.	—		—	6. 0 a.m.	Yes
2	23	Lydney West	—	Open continuously		—	—	No
2	54	Woolaston	6. 0 a.m.	—		—	6. 0 a.m.	Yes
						9. 0 a.m.	5. 0 p.m.**E**	
3	56	Beachley Junction	4. 0 a.m.	—		—	6. 0 a.m.	Yes
						10.45 a.m.**E**	5. 0 p.m.**E**	

A—Or as ordered by Control.

B—Down I.B.S. Home 2 m. 70ch. from Over Sidings.   Up I.B.S. Home 2 m. 28 ch. from Grange Court.

C—Down I.B.S. Home 1 m. 79 ch. from Grange Court.   Up I.B.S. Home 2 m. 8 ch. from Bullo Pill East.

D—Down I.B.S. Home 2 m. 20 ch. from Awre Junction.   Up I.B.S. Home 2 m. 43 ch. from Lydney Junction.

E—During Engineers occupation of Severn Tunnel only.

L—Or after last Rail Motor has cleared.

M—Open to deal with 8.20 a.m. Freight Swindon to Gloucester.

No. 4564 appears again, heading into the Down Platform Line on 22nd August 1964. The engine is carrying a minerals or empties lamp code but this may be changed when it picks up whatever train it is heading for, as there would have been no goods wagons to collect from the west end of the station. The unidentified Class '94XX' pannier tank in the background, whose driver is catching up on the news whilst awaiting the signal to proceed, is probably at the head of some empty coaching stock, from a Hereford train perhaps, which will be returned to the carriage sidings on the right once there is a clear path to do so. MARK B. WARBURTON

A spotter in the right foreground notes down the number of Class '28XX' No. 3855 as it clatters past Gloucester East Signal Box with a train of open wagons on 16th July 1964. A war-time build, entering service on 1st October 1942, the 2-8-0 was based at Banbury shed at the date of this view, transferring to Oswestry three months later. It was withdrawn off Croes Newydd shed in August 1965. COURTESY RAIL ONLINE

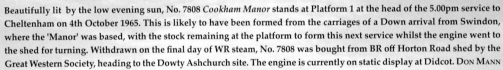

Beautifully lit by the low evening sun, No. 7808 *Cookham Manor* stands at Platform 1 at the head of the 5.00pm service to Cheltenham on 4th October 1965. This is likely to have been formed from the carriages of a Down arrival from Swindon, where the 'Manor' was based, with the stock remaining at the platform to form this next service whilst the engine went to the shed for turning. Withdrawn on the final day of WR steam, No. 7808 was bought from BR off Horton Road shed by the Great Western Society, heading to the Dowty Ashchurch site. The engine is currently on static display at Didcot. DON MANN

The fireman of work-stained '9F' No. 92117 of Kettering shed leans out of the cab whilst awaiting the road with a train of iron ore empties on 25th September 1964. He will need to keep an eye on the Up Starting signal, as the driver's position on the left-hand side of the cab meant that he could not see it. The 2-10-0 was withdrawn off Speke Junction shed in December 1967, after a service life of almost exactly eleven years. DON MANN

A contrast in tank engines on 29th April 1964, with '57XX' Class pannier tank No. 4624 on station pilot duties and '14XX' 0-4-2T No. 1474 in the bay at the head of the Chalford auto. Both based at Horton Road, the 0-6-0PT was withdrawn four months later, on 1st September. DON MANN

LEFT: Our last summer 1955 view courtesy of J.T. Bassingdale shows Collett 0-6-0 No. 2283 heading into the Down Platform Line whilst 2-8-0 No. 2879 waits at the Up Main Starter signal. The '22XX' is presumably at the head of a passenger working, a 'stopper' perhaps to Cardiff but was based at Neyland shed in West Wales, so was some distance from home. It was withdrawn off Severn Tunnel Junction in December 1963. The 2-8-0 transferred from St. Philip's Marsh to Severn Tunnel Junction in the four week period ending on 13th August 1955, so as we do not have an exact date for these pictures it is a toss-up as to which shed it belonged to when seen here! Weather charts for the year show the first three weeks of July as being very hot, which may point us to a mid-July date, when No. 2879 was still at Bristol. Incidentally, we tend to think it was in the early 1960s when the rot set in and the state of WR steam declined dramatically but both engines here are in filthy condition.

J.T. BASSINGDALE/LAURENCE BROWNHILL COLLECTION

ABOVE: A study in front ends on 23rd July 1965, with No. 6916 *Misterton Hall* having been given the 'off', whilst No. 92012 blows off steam on the Up Platform Line behind. The 'Hall', which had been new into service on 11th June 1941, belonged to Banbury shed and was withdrawn just over a fortnight later. The '9F' meanwhile had travelled far and wide during its short career, to March and New England sheds in Cambridgeshire, Annesley in Nottinghamshire, Newport in Monmouthshire, Rowsley in Derbyshire and Kettering in Northamptonshire before ending up at Carlisle Kingmoor in Cumberland, where it was based when seen here. It was withdrawn in October 1967. DON MANN

RIGHT: Class '5101' tank No. 4100 reverses out of the Up Platform Line on 1st September 1965. The 1935-built 2-6-2T had been based at Horton Road since early July 1957 and was probably engaged on station pilot duties when seen here, although these had reduced considerably since the cessation of most of the local passenger services. In fact, No. 4100's usefulness was about to come to an end, withdrawal taking place on Tuesday 26th October. On the right, ex-LM&SR '8F' No. 48468 of Stourbridge Junction shed waits for the road ahead. Built near the end of the Second World War and entering service on 16th March 1945, it was withdrawn off Rose Grove shed in late February 1968. DON MANN

'Grange' Class 4-6-0 No. 6846 *Ruckley Grange* of Bristol St. Philip's Marsh heads 'Light Engine' along the Down Main Line in July 1962. On the left, 'Hymek' diesel-hydraulic No. D7028 in the attractive two-tone green livery that many of the new diesels wore at this period, had arrived with an express from Cardiff. New into service from Beyer, Peacock on 5th April 1962, it was on its first posting, to Cardiff Canton shed but a short career of twelve years nine months ended when it was stored at Old Oak Common in November 1974, official withdrawal taking place on 1st January 1975. JOHN CHAMPION/COLOUR-RAIL

Seen heading to shed is 'Modified Hall' Class No. 6969 *Wraysbury Hall*, which was based at Didcot from February 1958 until withdrawal on 20th February 1965. In the background of this circa 1963 view, a 'Large Prairie' tank draws the ECS of a Hereford train out of the Up Platform Line to take it to the carriage sidings. NPC

LEFT: Celebrity ex-L&NER Gresley Class 'A3' 4-6-2 No. 4472 *Flying Scotsman* alongside Gloucester East Signal Box on 18th March 1964. The 'Pacific' was working a private special heading to a ceremony in Cardiff involving the Ffestiniog Railway Society and Alan Pegler, who as well as being the owner of No. 4472 was an officer of the FRS. NPC

BELOW: Two auto coaches are hauled into the Up Platform Line by '57XX' pannier tank No. 3775 on station pilot duties in October 1964. Note that the driving ends of both coaches are facing the 0-6-0PT, which was the normal orientation for these carriages at Gloucester, so that they could be driven back from Chalford with the locomotive propelling. New into service on 1st July 1938, the locomotive was at Horton Road from March 1961 until the end of December 1965, when steam working ceased on the Western Region of BR. It had spent the previous ten years working from Worcester shed. RAIL-ONLINE

Class '8F' No. 48475 ambles away from its stop at Gloucester with a freight on 16th July 1964. The 2-8-0 was a 'Western' engine in as much that it was one of a batch built late in the Second World War at Swindon Works, going into service as LM&SR No. 8475 on 8th June. It was 'Westernised' once again when transferred first to Newport Ebbw Junction shed, briefly, in June 1954, moving successively then over the rest of its career to St. Philip's Marsh, Tyseley, Stourbridge Junction, Tyseley and finally to Wolverhampton Oxley – all ex-GWR sheds! It was withdrawn from the latter in late October 1966. RAIL ONLINE

LEFT: A Gifford-esque glimpse, as an unknown 'Grange' 4-6-0 heads away east with a heavily loaded coal train on a cold day circa 1963. The almost continuous activity that the Gloucester railway scene provided meant that visits to photograph passing trains almost never went unrewarded, with the variety accorded by the steam era meaning that often there was the chance to capture something unusual. NPC

RIGHT: Another glimpse, with a 'Grange' about to head by again, with what is likely to be a part fitted express freight according to the lamp code, whilst a '9F' 2-10-0 takes water from the crane alongside the Up Main Line and a '14XX' waits in the bay with an auto working to Chalford. The semi-anonymous nature of the pictures on this page – none of the locomotives are indentified, the slides are not dated and we have no idea as to the identity of the photographer, apart from the clue that he was apparently a railwayman – actually serves to emphasise their charm, as they document what were everyday, common or garden scenes of the steam age railway at work, which would otherwise be lost forever. NPC

LEFT: No. 6945 *Glasfryn Hall* rumbles over the points as it makes its way west via the Down Main Line with a mixed freight bound for South Wales circa 1963. New into service on 8th September 1942, the 'Hall' was based at Cardiff East Dock shed from late September 1962 to withdrawal on 1st September 1964. Note the 'Peak' Class diesel-electric and the DMU peeking out from behind the East box. NPC

LEFT: No. 1444 heads off to the shed on 16th July 1964, whilst on Chalford auto duties. The bunker looks empty so the engine may be on its way for coaling or it might be coming 'off shift' to be replaced by another locomotive and crew. RAIL ONLINE

RIGHT: Auto-fitted Class '54XX' pannier tank No. 6437 blows steam from its cylinder drain cocks having just been given the right away for Chalford on 4th June 1960. New into service on 19th April 1937, the 0-6-0PT moved to Horton Road in May 1960 and is seen here in the slightly over the top but very attractive fully lined green passenger livery applied by BR Western Region. This is our first sighting of the engine in this volume but, for those collecting this series, it appeared in the last volume, 4B, working the Dursley Branch. It was withdrawn in July 1963. BILL POTTER/KRM

LEFT: Pristine Beyer, Peacock 'Hymek' No. D7002 entered service on 19th July 1961 at Bristol Bath Road, so this view of the engine in 'ex-factory' condition must have been taken very close to that date. Like the other diesel-hydraulic designs introduced by the Western Region – the 'Westerns', 'Warships' and even the small 'Teddy Bear' 0-6-0s – they were distinctive in appearance and had much more of a personality than many other of the diesel types brought in at this time. However, BR decided to go the diesel-electric route as standard instead and hence all of the diesel-hydraulic classes had relatively short careers. No. D7002 was withdrawn on 3rd October 1971. Overall, this was yet another poor return on the investment that was made in the railways in the 1950s and '60s. NPC

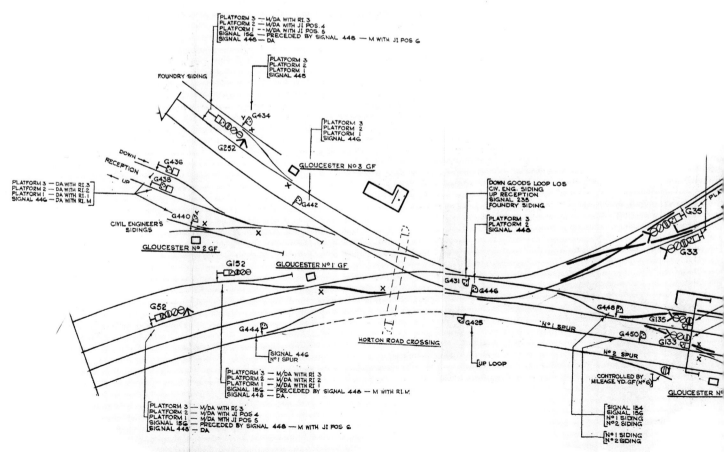

OPPOSITE PAGE LEFT AND RIGHT: Corresponding views looking west and east from the Down platform circa 1970. Both show useful detail beneath the canopies but colour photography within the station was never easy due to the lack of light. They do also illustrate other things of note, not least the healthy parcels traffic on the Up platform, which was no longer in use for passengers. The loss of most of the local and cross-country services saw the remaining passenger traffic concentrated on the Down platform, whilst the trackwork had also been simplified as a result, the four lines now comprising, from right to left: Down Main, Up Main, No. 1 Siding and No. 2 Siding. Both scissors crossovers had been taken out with a new crossover put in from the Up Main to the Down Main to allow Up trains to run into the platform. The work, carried out in 1968, is detailed on the MAS diagram below. At the same time, multiple aspect colour light signalling had been installed, replacing all of the semaphore signals (although the bracket jutting from the canopy over the parcels platform was still in place) and controlled from a new power signal box (PSB) on the south side of Tramway Crossing, which also allowed closure of all the mechanical boxes, apart from Mileage Yard Ground Frame and Barton Street Junction, California Crossing and Painswick Road Crossing, which were reduced to similar ground frame status. BOTH SEAN BOLAN

BELOW: Part of the 1968 Multiple Aspect Signalling (MAS) scheme for the Gloucester area, showing the section through Central station, the junction with the line to Eastgate, Horton Road Crossing and Tramway Junction. The plan covered all of the lines radiating from Gloucester, extending to Cheltenham, Standish Junction and Lydney. Track/connections shown in bold black were new. The revised layout only permitted one train at a time to use the platform but all of the local services had ceased and Eastgate was still open, with all north-south trains using that station, so the arrangement was not as restrictive as it at first seems. NPC

LEFT: The west end of the station shortly before rebuilding work commenced. 'Peak' Class '46' No. 46018 is seen departing west at the head of train No. 1V83, a Liverpool to Plymouth service, on Sunday 15th September 1974. The photographer noted on the slide mount that it had been due in here at 14.14 but was running around 40 minutes late and was bound for Severn Tunnel Junction, where it would reverse and cross back beneath the river, all of which would lose even more time but presumably there were Sunday engineering works on the ex-Midland main line to Bristol which had forced the pictureseque detour down the west bank of the Severn. New into service from Derby Works on 16th February 1962 as No. D155, the 'Peak' was based at Bristol Bath Road at the date of this view, moving to Cardiff Canton in October 1975. Withdrawn on 18th December 1983, it was cut up at Swindon in 1985. Note that relaying of the trackwork at this end of the station had seen the Down Main Line slewed away from the end of the platform, this shortening it by more than a coach length. NPC

LEFT: The demolition work in the late summer of 1975, looking west towards St. Peter's church. A rake of parcels vans in BR blue livery occupy the old Up Platform Line, with the Up Main now converted to a loop, whilst the two lines on the left, the erstwhile Down Platform Line and Down Main, were now the Down Main and Up Main respectively. However, the operational constraints that this introduced after the closure of Eastgate, coupled with the loss of all parcels traffic in the early 2000s, has seen the Up platform reopened for passengers and four track working through the station reintroduced once again. NPC

RIGHT: Looking east on the same day, with the main building in the process of being razed to the ground. There is little doubt that these attractive buildings could have been renovated and made fit for purpose in a more modern age but they contained far more accommodation than was required after the loss of so many service and staff roles, so a shiny new building was required. Predictably, this has not aged well nor stood the test of time as a design (although an arson blaze in the booking office in 2010 dod not help), so 45-plus years later, plans are now in place to rebuild it again. However, with the designation of the Up side platform for parcels traffic, there was little call to rebuild that, so much of that still survives as seen in these pictures, although it would – and also hopefully will – benefit from some refurbishment and renovation at the same time. NPC

Gloucester's new station building nearing completion but still surrounded by scaffolding on 8th June 1976, as No. D1010 *Western Campaigner* slows to a halt with a Cardiff to Paddington train. A tractor-hauled mail trolley waits in the foreground with sacks of mail to load in the guard's compartment, whilst parcels vans are being loaded at the old Up platform on the right – they will possibly form a parcels train to Swindon a little later. For the Up platform to be brought back into passenger use, a new footbridge had to be built, which now straddles the tracks about where the photographer was standing (he had nipped out from his office overlooking the station to take this and the following two pictures!). *Western Campaigner* had entered service from Swindon Works on 15th October 1962, originally in the maroon livery we saw demonstrated a few pages earlier, and was based at Plymouth Laira depot when seen here. It was repainted in BR blue livery on 15th August 1969 and was withdrawn from service on 28th February 1977. Happily, it is one of seven of the class which have survived to be preserved. Now owned by the Diesel & Electric Preservation Group and based on the West Somerset Railway, it has been returned to maroon livery but is currently non-operational awaiting transmission and bodywork repairs. Note that BR had dispensed with displaying train reporting numbers, which had largely been an aid to signalmen in mechanical boxes. As a result, many Western Region locomen took to using the headcode boxes to display the engine number, as here with 1010. STEPHEN TAVERNER

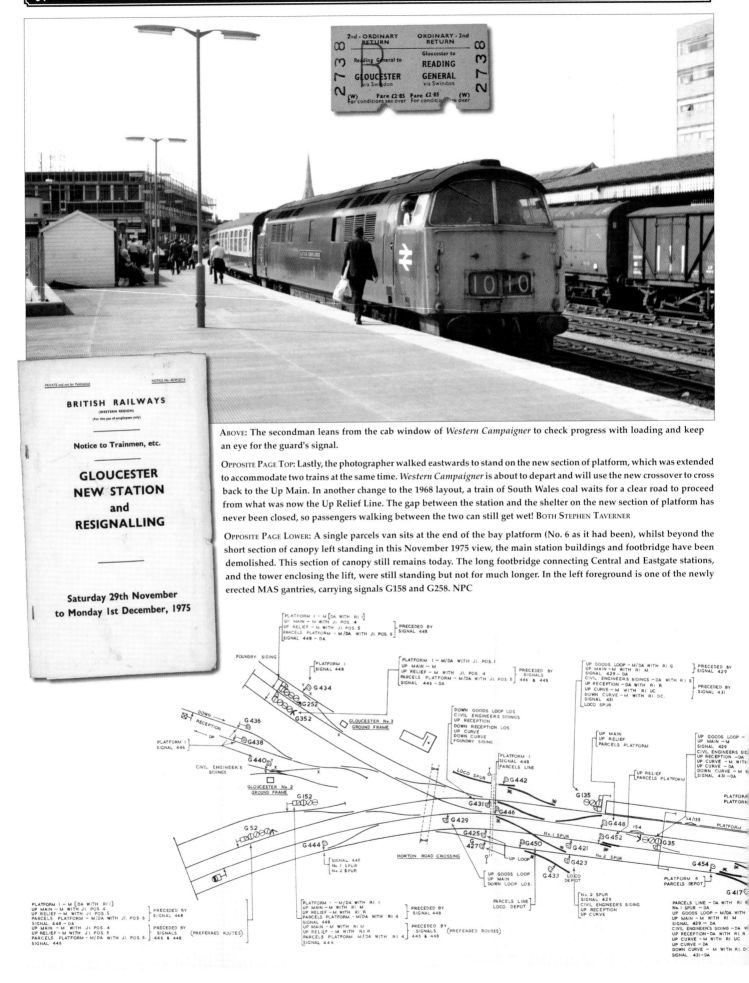

ABOVE: The secondman leans from the cab window of *Western Campaigner* to check progress with loading and keep an eye for the guard's signal.

OPPOSITE PAGE TOP: Lastly, the photographer walked eastwards to stand on the new section of platform, which was extended to accommodate two trains at the same time. *Western Campaigner* is about to depart and will use the new crossover to cross back to the Up Main. In another change to the 1968 layout, a train of South Wales coal waits for a clear road to proceed from what was now the Up Relief Line. The gap between the station and the shelter on the new section of platform has never been closed, so passengers walking between the two can still get wet! BOTH STEPHEN TAVERNER

OPPOSITE PAGE LOWER: A single parcels van sits at the end of the bay platform (No. 6 as it had been), whilst beyond the short section of canopy left standing in this November 1975 view, the main station buildings and footbridge have been demolished. This section of canopy still remains today. The long footbridge connecting Central and Eastgate stations, and the tower enclosing the lift, were still standing but not for much longer. In the left foreground is one of the newly erected MAS gantries, carrying signals G158 and G258. NPC

BELOW: The track rationalisation and MAS resignalling scheme of 1968 did not take into account the possible – likely even – closure of Eastgate, despite the reduction of that station to an island platform with single Up and Down lines running either side. Consequently, when it was finally decided that Eastgate would go – and with it all the level crossings on the Eastgate Loop – it was realised that a much greater strain would be put on the layout at Central and as a result, further track and signal alterations would be needed. The diagram below shows the work carried out in late 1975, with track in bold again being new. The four lines now became Down Main, Up Main, Up Relief and Platform 4 (Parcels), whilst the extended Down platform was split into 1 and 2 and the west end bay was resignalled for use by local passenger trains heading west, becoming Platform 3. NPC

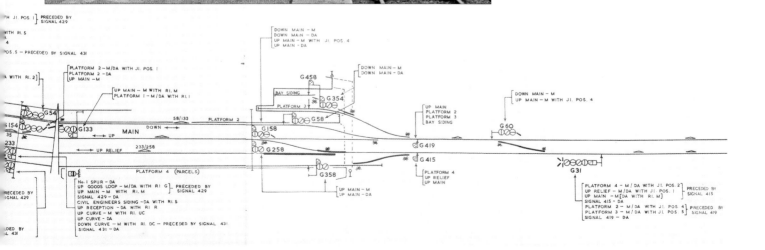

ABOVE: An April 1977 view from near the end of the recently extended platform which, at 1,977ft, was then the longest station platform in the UK. The extension became Platform 1, in which a DMU stands, probably on a local service to or from Swindon. The old GWR goods yard and shed on the right was now an NCL Parcels depot and a Class '08' 0-6-0 diesel shunter is seen moving a GUV van. RAOUL BEAMAN

LEFT: The view from the cab of a DMU approaching Gloucester station on 19th February 1976, with the remains of Eastgate on the left. NPC

We now start to move away from the passenger station and head past the yards towards Horton Road shed. We are also nearing the end of Western Region steam here, hence this view of '57XX' Class pannier tank No. 3675 bundling along the Down Main with an inter-yard trip freight, bound probably for the Llanthony Docks Branch, which sees the engine minus its cast brass cabside numberplates and with numerals crudely chalked on instead. The locomotive also appears not to be carrying any lamp code, although a lamp is visible on the footplate behind the tool box – were standards slipping in this area too? The 0-6-0PT entered service on 21st June 1940 and had moved to Horton Road from Bristol Barrow Road in January 1965; it was withdrawn on 31st December as WR steam ended. The wagons are all fitted and there is no brake van visible on the rear, whilst the first three opens contain what appear to be oil tanks. COURTESY RAIL ONLINE

A rather nice rear three-quarters study of No. 7820 *Dinmore Manor* heading off towards the carriage sidings in the late afternoon of Monday 20th April 1964. The locomotive was based at Shrewsbury at the date of this view and had almost certainly arrived here on a working from Hereford via Ross-on-Wye, which was a regular occurrence around this time for Shrewsbury's complement of these versatile, lightweight 4-6-0s; No. 7801 *Anthony Manor* had worked the service two days earlier on 18th April and then again on 31st October (the last day the passenger service operated), whilst No. 7800 *Torquay Manor* was seen at Gloucester on 22nd June 1964. It is likely that No. 7820 is in fact making its way to the ex-Midland turntable, so will pass to the right of the water tower; the turntable was just the other side but the engine would have to go right past it and then reverse in from the entrance to the Midland goods yard. In pre-Grouping and pre-Nationalisation days, this line was used for the transfer of traffic between the Great Western and the Midland. *Dinmore Manor* was one of nine of the thirty-strong class to make it into preservation and today resides not far from here on the Gloucestershire Warwickshire Railway. DON MANN

An unidentified 'Large Prairie' tank shunts empty carriage stock into the sidings next to the station. This is likely to have been a service from Hereford and the 2-6-2T will then head to Horton Road for servicing and awaiting its next trip. On the right, a pannier tank simmers gently in the two carriage sidings that ran behind East Box and terminated in the distance. The box itself is undergoing some routine maintenance – a lick of paint perhaps? The cabin was new in 1938, opening on 8th February and replacing two existing boxes: the old East Box, which had been sited a little further along, past the water tower, and Middle Box, perched high above the station at the south end of the footbridge. Measuring 53ft by 13ft with the operating floor at a height of 8ft, East Box had a 110 lever frame. However, its lifespan was just thirty years, closing on 2nd March 1968. The slide is undated but, from others that came from the same source (our unknown railwayman, was probably taken in 1963. NPC

The 'Manor's were a development of Churchward's highly successful Class '43XX' 2-6-0s, one of which, No. 6365 is seen here hauling carriages out of the sidings behind East Box on Tuesday 8th October 1963; engine and stock would shortly be forming a Down service to Hereford. New in October 1925, the 'Mogul' had been based at Horton Road since moving up from Exeter in July 1954 – apart from a brief stint at Wolverhampton Oxley in the early summer of 1955. Its career was very nearly at an end, however, withdrawal taking place just over two weeks after this picture was taken, on 21st October. We get a good view of the rear of Gloucester East Signal Box, showing that the three locking room windows had been bricked up at some stage. In the right background is the rear of Gloucester Passenger Stn box, whilst the water tower was also an ex-Midland structure. The relationship between the Midland and the GWR here at Gloucester was necessarily a close one, dating back to the earliest days of the railway and the boundary line dividing their territory here ran between the locomotive and the water tower. DON MANN

A 1965 view from the covered footbridge connecting Central and Eastgate stations, looking over the roofs of some parcels vans to the rear of East Box and the goods shed, as '9F' No. 92223 of Newport Ebbw Junction shed heads away 'Light Engine' having just taken water from the crane between the Up Main and Up Platform lines. It was probably on its way to Horton Road to turn on the table there. Don Mann

Nicely lit by a low afternoon sun, 2-6-2T No. 4109 waits for the off with a train probably bound for Cheltenham St. James in the spring of 1963. The previous year, on 13th October, this engine had had the dubious honour of hauling the last Kingham to Cheltenham passenger train – a line we shall explore in Volume 6 of this series. Note that it had also suffered quite a bash to the corner of the bunker and was the driver here filling out a time sheet or doing his football pools? Behind, one of Horton Road's BR-built 0-6-0 diesels shunts the goods yard; the number is not quite decipherable but starts 21 so is either D2137 or D2138. Both had arrived here new from Swindon Works in 1960 but only D2137 survived long enough to be renumbered under the 1974 TOPS scheme, becoming Class '03' No. 03137; sister No. D2138 was withdrawn in June 1969. NPC

RIGHT: An unidentified 'Large Prairie' tank is seen on its way to the carriage sidings to collect three or four coaches to form a service for Hereford in June 1963. The loaded coal wagons in the foreground are in the Midland yard but the bottom left corner of the picture is slightly greyed out, hence the cardinal sin being committed of another photograph overlapping and apparently obscuring some of the detail! Additionally, whilst this is not an outstanding picture in terms of composition, I love these incidental everyday scenes which provide a glimpse of the railway at work. Those on this and the next page are from the same cameraman, apparently a railwayman based here at Gloucester and quite a number of his views also featured in *Volume 3: Gloucester Midand Lines Part 1: North*. NPC

LEFT: Another technically poor view but one which provides us with another glimpse from an unusual angle, with the Midland turntable mentioned a few pages earlier featuring in the foreground. A 'Large Prairie' tank heads off bunker first to Cheltenham in the background. These engines were equally adept at working backwards or forwards so very rarely used a turntable. NPC

BELOW: Another unidentified 'Large Prairie' tank, this time returning to the station having collected three carriages for a Hereford service from the sidings, again circa 1963. The Midland water tower was a substantial building as can be seen and there is a glimpse of Horton Road shed in the right background. NPC

This view looking east from the covered footbridge running between the stations is taken on the same day as that which appears as a spread across pages 274-275 of *Vol. 3: Gloucester Midland Lines Part 1: North* (the 'Black Five' and wagons on the right are in exactly the same position). It is yet another (as is the one which follows) of the series of pictures of Gloucester taken by an unknown railwayman in the period 1962-64, this being one of those hugely interesting views which shows nothing in particular but is full of incidental detail. A 'Large Prairie' tank heads for the carriage sidings, perhaps to collect the stock to form a Hereford service, two further 'Light Engine's can be seen in the middle distance and steam emanates from another locomotive in Horton Road yard on the far left. The line the 'Prairie' tank is on curved round behind the brick-built yard hut in the centre right distance, to then join the siding leading to the Midland turntable, which can be seen just beyond the water tower. In BR years, Western engines also made use of this table for turning. Incidentally, it is not known exactly when, or indeed why, the WR started using the ex-LM&SR carriage sidings to store coaches, access to and from which was limited and with no obvious run round – observations on this would be welcome. To complete the scene, a DMU on a Worcester service sits in the Eastgate bay. A drone shot from this point today, 20ft up in the air above the junction of Bruton Way and Metz Way, would reveal that everything in this view has gone bar the main line on the left, which is hidden by trees bordering the Metz Way dual carriageway, which parallels the railway for a short distance. NPC

Another fascinating view from the footbridge, probably taken in 1963. On the main line in the background, a 'Peak' diesel heads out on an express passenger, whilst a DMU arrives with a service probably from Stratford-upon-Avon. The foreground is dominated by the two BR Camping Coaches. The coaches are in immaculate condition suggesting they may be parked here at the beginning of the season prior to be taken to their destinations: Andrew Macrae has suggested that they may be part of a longer rake destined for the several sites in South Wales still in use at this date: Lavernock, Ferryside, Manorbier, Sully, Saundersfoot and Tenby. Coach No. W9918W was converted from Corridor Third No. 2426 in May 1952 and painted crimson lake; it was probably repainted in brown and cream in 1957 or later. No. 2426 was a 56ft 'Toplight' Corridor Third built in January 1910 on Lot 1167. It had eight Third Class compartments and a lavatory at each end but at some stage the side had been covered in steel panelling hiding the toplights (the same goes for the adjacent coach). Amazingly, perhaps, it has survived to be preserved and is today on the Severn Valley Railway, where it is being rebuilt to its original condition. NPC

Whilst the 1935 plan presented within this volume on pages 32-33 and 86-87 gives a good impression of the GWR and later Western Region side of the railway at Gloucester, I decided a full plan of the railway in the centre of the city, showing the tracks of the WR and London Midland Region was now here worth including, to show just how much was there and how much has subsequently been lost. The map is based on the 1955 25 inch Ordance Survey and has been redrawn by Ian Pope, with the WR tracks in brown and the LMR lines in maroon. It is thus well worth studying this in conjunction with the photographs of Gloucester's railway system that also feature in Volume 1, Volume 3 and Volume 4A of this series.

RAILWAY MAP OF GLOUCESTER 1955

LEGEND:
1. Gloucester Central station entrance
2. Gloucester Central station platform 1
3. Gloucester Central station platform 2 and bay platform 3
4. Gloucester Central station parcels bay platform
5. Gloucester Central station platform 4
6. Gloucester Central station platform 5 and bay platform 6

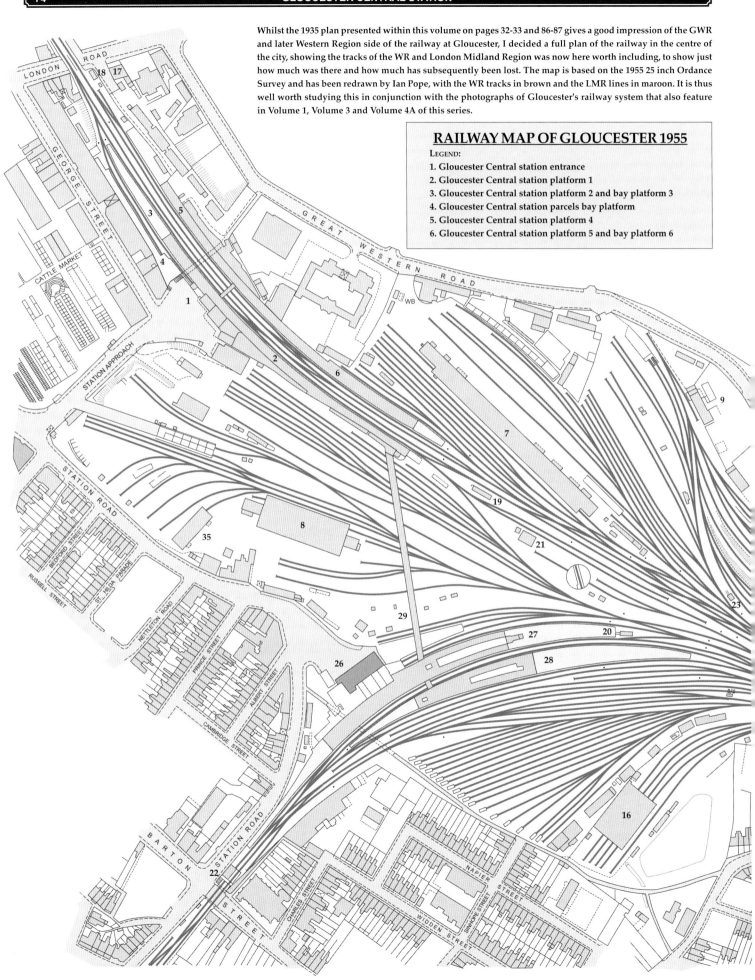

7. WR goods shed
8. LMR goods shed
9. British Road Services depot and siding
10. Horton Road 1855 shed, passenger engines
11. Horton Road 1872 shed, goods engines
12. Horton Road 1951 wheel drop shed (still standing 2021)
13. Engineer's Inspection coach shed (still standing 2021)
14. Coaling stage and water tank
15. Brick mess hut for footplate crews
16. Wagon repair depot
17. WR District General Manager's office
18. Gloucester West Signal Box (WR)
19. Gloucester East Signal Box (WR)
20. Gloucester Passenger Stn signal box (LMR)
21. Midland Water Tower
22. Barton Street Junction signal box (LMR)
23. Mileage Yard Ground Frame box (WR)
24. Tramway Junction signal box (LMR)
25. Gloucester Goods Junction signal box (LMR)
26. Gloucester Eastgate station entrance
27. Gloucester Eastgate bay platform 1 and platform 2
28. Gloucester Eastgate island platforms 3 and 4
29. Covered footbridge between Central and Eastgate
30. Midland water softening plant
31. Barnwood Sidings
32. Locomotive storage lines at the rear of Barnwood shed
33. Gloucester North signal box (WR)
34. Tate & Lyle depot

No. 5961 *Toynbee Hall* of Neath Court Sart eases its way off Horton Road shed in June 1963. The engine had entered service on 26th June 1936 and spent most of the BR years based at various sheds in South Wales. It was withdrawn from Newport Ebbw Junction on 6th August 1965. NPC

A fine panoramic view from the end of Eastgate's Up platform (the Midland was Up towards Derby from Gloucester and Bristol, as it did not run towards London from this area), this time showing classmate No. 3775 tripping a rake of bogie bolster wagons loaded with pipes on 27th November 1965. These are likely to have been collected from Over Yard or Docks Branch Sidings and are on their way to Barnwood, New Yard or T Sidings (depending on their final destination), where they will await being assembled into a longer distance freight. There is much else to see here as regards the general clutter and paraphernalia of the steam age railway, from gas lamps and water cranes, to the LM&SR asbestos panelled lamp hut in the left foreground. We also get a good end view of the goods shed. The vagueries of the GWR locomotive numbering system, particularly as regards the numerically huge '57XX' Class, means that despite apparently being a hundred numbers after No. 3675, No. 3775 was actually two years younger! BILL POTTER/KRM

RIGHT: Ex-LM&SR '8F' No. 48368 stands at the entrance to the WR goods yard, which was known as Gloucester Old Yard, on 1st September 1965. Built at Horwich Works and entering service in September 1944, the 2-8-0 was based at Burton-on-Trent at the date of this view, where it was shedded from the start of May 1964 to mid-September 1966. The locomotive was withdrawn off Newton Heath shed in Manchester at the end of June 1968. DON MANN

LEFT: An unusual view of Pressed Steel railcar No. W55020 coupled in a train at Gloucester at an unknown date. Sandwiched between a 4-wheeled container wagon and an ex-GWR 'Siphon G', the unit went new from Pressed Steel Co. Ltd's Linwood factory in Scotland to Southall in September 1960, transferring to Reading in July 1964. It looks very much like the unit is ex-works here, after overhaul and repainting with small yellow panels, probably in 1964 and carried out by the Gloucester Railway Carriage & Wagon Co. – but why not at Swindon? Could it have been a collision damage repair? Note the poster on the container on the 'Conflat' for Elkes Biscuits & Cakes of Uttoxeter. Their factory is still in operation today, although now as part of Fox's Biscuits. There is also branding on the 'Siphon G' which is not quite readable. NPC

RIGHT: No. 4109 again but here providing unusual motive power for the Stroud Valley auto in the summer of 1963. The 'Large Prairie' heads off to Chalford with a single trailer and although we do not have the exact date, the photographer noted that this was a Sunday service, with the 2-6-2T deputising for the more usual '14XX' 0-4-2T.
TONY BOWLES/COURTESY THE RESTORATION & ARCHIVING TRUST/REF. ARC00098

RIGHT: Standing around in freezing temperatures was often worth it because clear cold weather held the advantage of producing better steam and smoke effects, as here on 2nd January 1964. 'Mogul' No. 7318 is already a regular in these pages but was still based in South Wales at this date, on Neath Court Sart shed's allocation, and is carrying a fitted or partially fitted express freight code here. JOHN STRANGE/NPC

BELOW: BR 'Standard' Class '3' 2-6-2T No. 82040 poses alongside Mileage Yard Ground Frame box. The view is undated but the engine was only in use here for a very brief period, arriving from Exmouth Junction shed in early June 1965 and then being withdrawn on 2nd July. The box controlled entry to and exit from Horton Road shed and also to the goods yard; most stations had a mileage siding, with more at the bigger places. Wagon loads to/from mileage yards or sidings were charged to the customer by the mile and they were also responsible for loading/unloading. NPC

LEFT: Going new into service from Crewe Works on 13th February 1965, Brush Type '4' No. D1660 was named *City of Truro* by Dr Mabel Andrews, the Mayor of Truro, at a ceremony held at Truro station on 8th June 1965. This view is thought to have been taken a few weeks after that date, with the engine standing alongside Mileage Yard Ground Frame box. It was one of thirteen of the class given names in 1965, with five more following in 1966, most of which had either GWR connotations or were from ancient mythology and previously used on early L&NWR engines. Designated Class '47' under TOPS, the engine successively became No. 47076 in February 1974, No. 47625 in November 1984 and No. 47749 in November 1995; the name was retained until 1988 October 1988 and the locomotive remains in operational use today with GB Railfreight. NPC

RIGHT: In faded BR Rail Blue livery, 'Warship' diesel-hydraulic No. 858 *Valorous* heads a parcels train past the goods shed on 16th June 1971, by then in use by National Carriers Ltd as a parcels depot. NCL handled the railborne side of British Railways parcels traffic. Later becoming Lynx Express and then bought and absorbed by the American carrier United Parcels Services, all of this traffic has been lost to rail. The shed seems to have been demolished circa 1980 and a distribution warehouse was later built on its site but no use is made of the sidings which still lie mouldering alongside. Built by North British Locomotive and going new to Plymouth Laira depot on 15th December 1961, *Valorous* was based at Newton Abbot when seen here and was heading probably to Bristol with this parcels train. It was withdrawn less than four months after the picture was taken, on 3rd October 1971, just before reaching its tenth birthday. COURTESY RAIL ONLINE

LEFT: 'Western' Class diesel-hydraulic No. D1006 *Western Stalwart* departs with train No. 1Z40 on 27th November 1965. The 'Z' in the headcode denotes that this was a special, a part of BR Western Region's 'Last Steam Hauled Train From Paddington' rail tour. No. 7029 *Clun Castle* followed the GW Main Line to Bristol and then ran via Mangotsfield to Gloucester Eastgate, where No. D1006 took the train over for a trip to Cheltenham St. James and back to Gloucester Central. No. 7029 then took over for the run Up to Swindon, where it was taken off and two Type '3's, No's D6881 and D6882, returned the tour to Paddington. *Western Stalwart* is seen here coming out of Eastgate on its way to St. James at around 1.33pm. BILL POTTER/KRM

RIGHT: A Gloucester Railway Carriage & Wagon Company railcar passes Tramway Junction on 30th June 1967, on its way to Central station. Unit No. M55006, a Driving Motor Brake Second with Second Class only seating for 65 passengers, was new in May 1958. Later designated Class '122', it lasted in service until September 1993 but was saved for preservation upon withdrawal, initially on the Mid Norfolk Railway. Today the unit is to be found on the Ecclesbourne Valley Railway in Derbyshire. BILL POTTER/KRM

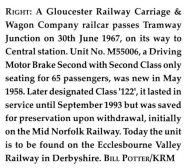

RIGHT: Glimpsed from the end of Eastgate's main Up platform through a forest of signal and lamp posts, '9F' No. 92236 heads west with a fitted freight circa 1963. Built at Crewe Works and new into service on 4th September 1958, the 2-10-0 had five allocations in its six year, seven month, seventeen day career. All were in South Wales being, successively, Pontypool Road, Newport Ebbw Junction, Cardiff Canton, Cardiff East Dock and finally Severn Tunnel Junction, from where it was withdrawn on 21st April 1965. Note the driver strolling alongside the tracks after coming off shift and also the ex-London & North Western Railway ground signal in the foreground, reused here by the LM&SR well away from its original point of placement. NPC

LEFT: Looking west through the gantry spanning the Midland lines on the approach to Eastgate in August 1964, as an ex-GWR 'Mogul' heads in with a passenger working, whilst in the background a pannier tank has just left the station for the run to Chalford. NPC

BELOW: Class '57XX' No. 4624 with two coaches on what is likely to be a Saturday service to Chalford. None of this class were ever fitted for auto working, so the 0-6-0PT will therefore having to run round the trailers at Chalford, where was still a loop in place which permitted this. No. 4624 looks very run down and was in fact withdrawn within days of the picture being taken, on 1st September 1964. NPC

A spirited getaway by 2-8-0 No. 3861 in October 1964, after the usual stop from water on the Up Main Line through the station. New from Swindon Works on 1st November 1942, the engine was on its final posting, to Newport Ebbw Junction shed, when seen here, withdrawal taking place nine months later on 21st July 1965. JOHN STRANGE/ALAN SAINTY COLLECTION

Like its classmate seen a couple of pages ago, BR 'Standard' Class '3' 2-6-2T No. 82039, was also sent up from Exmouth Junction shed in early June 1965 and withdrawn on 2nd July. Taken on 5th June, this must have been very soon after the engine first arrived at Horton Road. The headcode shows this to be a local passenger working, probably bound for Swindon. It is passing a gleaming Brush Type '4' standing outside the shed entrance. BILL POTTER/KRM

As we have also seen previously from the *Gloucester Midland Lines North* volume, this was a popular spot for photography with the signal gantry forming a centrepiece of any picture and the lines heading straight on to Central in the background or curving round left into Eastgate. Here we have a Midland engine on the Western lines in the form of 'Black Five' No. 44918 of Nottingham shed, hauling train No. 1M77, the 12.20pm service from Cardiff to Derby. The Crewe Works, December 1945-built 4-6-0 was based at Nottingham, where it spent almost its entire career up to March 1965, and with its tender piled high with coal, had probably just come onto the train here at Gloucester. It was withdrawn from Trafford Park shed in Manchester in January 1967. The unidentified (and unidentifiable) 'Hymek' facing is actually on the next line over so would be heading to Horton Road shed. The bracket signals on the right controlled the entrance to and exit from the locomotive yard and were worked from Mileage Yard Ground Frame box. NPC

This view westwards from near the level crossing at Tramway Junction is devoid of trains so is a good point to discuss some of the signals that appear in these pictures. The line in the immediate foreground was a siding serving the wagon repair shop and then alongside is the Down Siding, to which the signal with a route indicator on the left end of the gantry applied; it was worked from Gloucester Goods Junction signal box (MR). The next two signals, with distant arms for Barton Street Junction beneath, were the Home signals for the passenger lines, worked from Gloucester Passenger Stn signal box (MR). The signals on the right side of the gantry, seen from the rear, were the Home signals for Tramway Junction signal box (MR), the main arm relating to the running line towards Engine Shed Junction and the miniature arm allowing access to the Arrival Line to Barnwood. To the right of this ex-LM&SR/Midland Region gantry were the lines to Central station. The substantial bracket signal on the right, close to the walls of the engine shed, applied to trains coming from Central station and acted as both the Starting signal for Gloucester East Signal Box (GWR) and the home signal for Tramway Junction, the dual controls being effected here by the use of electric motors to work the signal arms – the motors were the devices fixed to the posts below the arms. The two bracket signals in the centre background controlled movements to and from Horton Road locomotive shed. NPC

A spectacular display of power as '9F' No. 92215 heads a convoy comprising two '8F's and another '9F' – all in steam note – past Horton Road shed at an unknown date but possibly early in 1965. No. 92215 was Tyseley-based from September 1963 to October 1966, so presumably the convoy was bound for Birmingham but the reason why so many locomotives required such a 'Light Engine' balancing move is not known. NPC

By the early 1970s, the eastern appoaches to the station were quite desolate in comparison, as demonstrated here by this view of 'Peak' Class '45' No. 68 *Royal Fusilier* arriving with train No. 1V89, a Birmingham to Cardiff express, past the line curving round to Eastgate. New into service on 5th October 1960 as No. D68, the 'Peak' was named on 21st January 1967 and is seen here in BR blue livery, having lost the D from its number but prior to being renumbered in February 1975 as Class '45' No. 45046. At the time of this circa 1971 view, the locomotive was allocated to the Nottingham Division, transferring to Cricklewood East in October 1974. It was withdrawn on 2nd August 1988. A classmate can just be glimpsed lurking in the centre left background. In the right distance there is a glimpse of the new Gloucester Power Signal Box, with its front corner window allowing signalmen to keep watch as they operated the Tramway Crossing barriers. NPC

LEFT: Photographed from Tramway Crossing, a pair of unidentified English Electric Type '3's power past the junction for Eastgate station (on the far left) with train No. 6M48, the Llandarcy to Rowley Regis oil tanks, in February 1970. Under TOPS, the Type '3's became Class '37'. Having been signalled in by the one remaining arm on the bracket in the foreground, a Brush Type '4' (later Class '47') makes its way into Horton Road depot on the right. CHRIS BALDWIN

RIGHT: Two unidentified English Electric Type '1' freight locomotives trundle past on the Up Main line, probably in the autumn of 1970. The class had started to become quite common in Gloucester by this date on coal freights from Toton and Washwood Heath. There is another glimpse of the goods shed in the left background, by then in use as a National Carriers parcels depot, and also of Mileage Yard Ground Frame cabin, which was to close on 2nd October 1970. Another Brush Type '4' can also be seen in the right background. CHRIS BALDWIN

LEFT: Moving on in time to August 1975 and looking from Horton Road, a Class '31' on an Up freight passes two more Class '20's. The photographer noted the '31' as No. 31225, which at this date was based at Finsbury Park in north London. However, blown up on screen the fourth number is definitely a 3, and is thus No. 31235 of Sheffield Tinsley depot. Built by Brush Traction and into service on 27th October 1960 as No. D5662, the '20' had moved to Tinsley in January 1974 and was to remain there for the rest of its working life, up until withdrawal on 26th May 2000. However, it was then bought for preservation and is today back in Gloucestershire, currently in store awaiting overhaul on the Dean Forest Railway. CHRIS BALDWIN

This hugely interesting aerial view of the railway at Gloucester was a late find on the Geograph.org website and after emailing the photographer, he kindly provided this scan for reproduction here. Taken on 16th July 1978, it shows the end of the transition period for the city's railway system, with the remains of Eastgate station in the centre and the rebuilt Central station – now renamed as simply Gloucester – bottom left. All that was left of Eastgate were the platforms, with the buildings having been razed, including the iconic signal box straddling the tracks, whilst the Midland goods yard and the carriage sidings had also been removed. The site of the station is now covered by a supermarket, whilst Park Road, to the right (south) of Barton Street crossing and Station Road to the left (north) are now Trier Way and Bruton Way respectively. The part of Station Road running to the right of the cross-shaped HM Land Registry building still exists, whilst the new Bruton Way dual carriageway follows the curve to run behind, between it and the rebuilt Central station. At the date of this view, the GWR goods shed, Old Yard and Horton Road were both still in use, as also were Barnwood Sidings by the gas holder top left. COLIN PARK

SECTION 2

GLOUCESTER HORTON ROAD SHED (85B)

A general view of the shed on Sunday 8th June 1958, with the usual varied selection of motive power on view, including two WD 2-8-0s on the left. At least one member of the class, No. 90149, was on the roster here at this date and others were regular visitors. In the centre, Collett 0-6-0 No. 3203 stands on the line leading to the turntable. Locomotives coming off shed via the Outgoing road (left) had to cross the double slip and then come back over it, over the diamond crossing and then onto the spur road in the right foreground, which ran almost all the way to the station. BILL POTTER/KRM

Gloucester Horton Road was undoubtedly one of the more important sheds of the steam age, one of the largest on the Great Western Railway and the Western Region of British Railways and yet was not even head of a division. It was actually part of the Worcester Division, Worcester shed being coded 85A under BR, with Horton Road 85B. This division also included the sheds at Hereford (85C) and Kidderminster (85D until 1961, then 85G), along with the smaller ones at Evesham and Honeybourne (sub-sheds to 85A), Leominster, Kington, Ross on Wye and Ledbury (sub-sheds to 85C), and Lydney, Cheltenham, Kingham, Brimscombe, Chalford, Cirencester and Tetbury, which were all sub-sheds to Horton Road. Kingham was a Worcester sub-shed under the GWR but transferred to Gloucester by BR, whilst that at Chalford was a railmotor shed which closed early in the BR era, in 1951. The GWR coded Gloucester GLO.

The development of locomotive accommodation at Gloucester is every bit as convoluted as that of the railway system in the city itself. A single through road broad gauge shed with a turntable at the east end was provided for the opening of the C&GWUR line in 1845. It was situated adjacent to the Midland terminus which the GWR first shared and parallel with the Midland's own two road shed. This shed closed temporarily with the opening of a new locomotive depot at Cheltenham St. James in 1847 but was then reopened again a year or so later. However, a better site was being sought and a new shed opened on the Horton Road site in 1854. There is some doubt as

to whether this was built as a two road shed, as initially planned, or as a four road shed, as shown by an amendment to a plan of 1855. Whatever the truth of that, the straight, high-roofed building nearest the main line which we see in these pictures is the old four road broad gauge shed shown on the 1855 plan. The shed measured 141ft 9ins in length by 69ft 6ins in height, whilst the four roads, all with long engine pits, were 132ft in length. The side walls were 20ft high and the height to the ridge of the roof was 41ft.

In 1872, Horton Road was significantly expanded when a new longer, twin-roofed, six road shed was constructed adjoining the original building on the north side. Arches were built into the communal wall allowing foot access between the two. Interestingly, although the newer building was longer and lower, its design otherwise very much mirrored that of the original shed, and used very similar coloured bricks. As the GWR plan on the following two pages shows, the most southerly of the six internal roads was slightly shorter than the others, being 178ft as against 206ft, and all again had long engine pits. Internally, the new building measured 217ft 6ins in length by 75ft in width, whilst the external walls were 15ft 9ins high and the height to the two roof ridges was 28ft. Following the expansion of Horton Road, the original building became the passenger engine shed, whilst the newer one was designated for goods engines, Gloucester having been from the outset a major centre for the sorting and exchange of freight traffic.

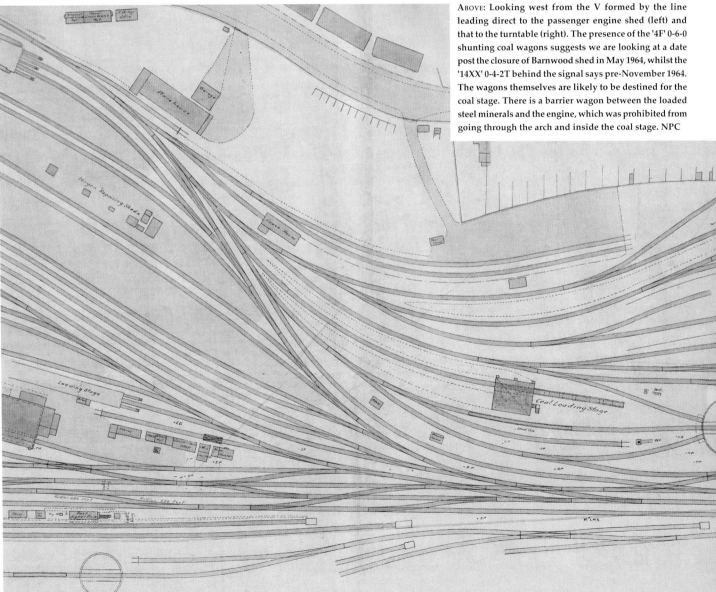

ABOVE: Looking west from the V formed by the line leading direct to the passenger engine shed (left) and that to the turntable (right). The presence of the '4F' 0-6-0 shunting coal wagons suggests we are looking at a date post the closure of Barnwood shed in May 1964, whilst the '14XX' 0-4-2T behind the signal says pre-November 1964. The wagons themselves are likely to be destined for the coal stage. There is a barrier wagon between the loaded steel minerals and the engine, which was prohibited from going through the arch and inside the coal stage. NPC

A small lifting shed, 49ft 6ins long by 26ft 3ins wide, was also built adjoining the north-west corner of the new shed. It was demolished in 1947 and replaced by a larger shed, 110ft long by 35ft wide and housing a wheel drop, which stands out from the other buildings in the photographs which follow by dint of its plain design and clean red brickwork. Interestingly, Gloucester-based photographer Peter Copeland took a couple of pictures of Horton Road in March 1948 which show the original lifting shop as having gone (it is still there in pictures he took in June 1947) but before construction had started on the new one, the date of which is unconfirmed. Permission was given in October 1948 for the '*provision of a new tarmac surface between the new lifting shop and store office ...*' but another reference mentions a date of November 1951 for the new wheel drop facility.

Other late 19th century facilities included a coaling stage, 43ft 6ins long by 37ft 4ins wide, with a single line running through it and a 76,000 gallon capacity water tank on top. A furnace was also built, providing dry sand for locomotive sand boxes, which could trickle sand onto wet and greasy rails to assist with grip. Two turntables were also installed, one of 42ft diameter in the middle of the engine yard and one of 45ft diameter on a headshunt at the north-west corner of the yard. The former was removed in March 1899 but then replaced by one of 55ft diameter in 1900, after which the second turntable was removed. The table seen in the pictures following is one of 65ft diameter, which was installed at the end of 1918.

The other major change leading to the version of Horton Road shown in these pictures was the replacement of the coaling stage in 1921 with one of standard Churchward design, fed by means of an earth ramp up which laden coal wagons were shunted. This siding ran right through the building to terminate on a series of supporting brick arches the other side. Locomotives could be coaled from both sides of the structure, which again included a water tank on top, of slightly smaller capacity at 74,250 gallons. Further developments in the 1930s included increased office accommodation and extra

sidings on the north side of the yard. Meanwhile, electric lighting inside the sheds was finally installed in September 1951.

At the start of the 20th century, Gloucester's allocation comprised fifty-four engines but this number was to fluctuate over the decades, dropping to forty in January 1914, before climbing again to fifty-six (which included three steam railmotors) in 1926. The peak total was sixty-six (including a diesel railcar) in 1947, after which numbers dropped gradually under BR, with sixty locomotives still on the allocation in 1952. As steam declined in the early 1960s, Gloucester's popularity as a railway centre was maintained by the shed still having a healthy fleet totalling thirty-nine engines in December 1964, the third highest number on the Western Region at that time. This included a small number of ex-LM&SR locomotives transferred over following the closure of Barnwood shed on 4th May 1964.

The shed was never at the forefront of express motive power and in GWR days had only one regular Paddington turn, most London-bound expresses being exchanged at Swindon. Under BR, it did have an allocation of 'Castle' Class engines to cover express services to the Capital. As such its allocation was generally the more workaday classes, in BR days ranging from 'Halls', 'Granges' and 'Manors' to 'Mogul' 2-6-0s, Collett 0-6-0s, pannier tanks, '45XX' and 'Large Prairie' tanks, and of course the '14XX' 0-4-2Ts for the auto services, although other types and classes did feature.

A larger shed such as Horton Road also required a large staff, which would have fluctuated a little over the years depending on the number of locomotives allocated. In 1927, when the number of engines allocated totalled fifty-four, the shed had a staff of 261, headed by the Loco Shed Foreman, with 162 footplate crew split equally between drivers and firemen. The rest was made up of the usual assortment of cleaners, boilerwashers, coalmen, firelighters and droppers, cranemen, etc and from this we can extrapolate that the maximum number of staff here would have been around 290 at the end of the GWR era and probably still around 275 in the early

(continued on page 94)

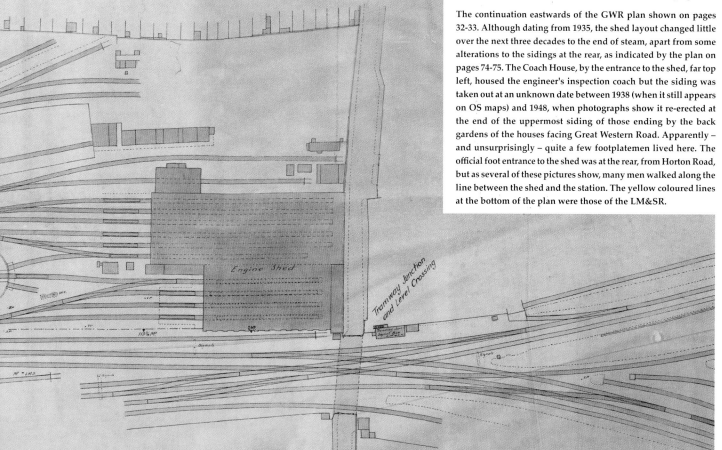

The continuation eastwards of the GWR plan shown on pages 32-33. Although dating from 1935, the shed layout changed little over the next three decades to the end of steam, apart from some alterations to the sidings at the rear, as indicated by the plan on pages 74-75. The Coach House, by the entrance to the shed, far top left, housed the engineer's inspection coach but the siding was taken out at an unknown date between 1938 (when it still appears on OS maps) and 1948, when photographs show it re-erected at the end of the uppermost siding of those ending by the back gardens of the houses facing Great Western Road. Apparently – and unsurprisingly – quite a few footplatemen lived here. The official foot entrance to the shed was at the rear, from Horton Road, but as several of these pictures show, many men walked along the line between the shed and the station. The yellow coloured lines at the bottom of the plan were those of the LM&SR.

The main route to and from Horton Road for engines going on or coming off shed was via the lines running between Mileage Yard Ground Frame box and the coaling stage, which led to a headshunt at the north-west corner of the yard; the line nearest the rear of the box was the Ingoing road, with the Outgoing road next on the right and running to the right of the signal which controlled exit from the shed yard. From the end of the headshunt, locomotives ran to and from the shed along the lines on the opposite side of the coal stage from here. Interestingly, we do not have a date for the opening of Mileage Yard Ground Frame but the *GWR Signal Box Nameplate Ordering Register* notes that the nameplate was ordered on 2nd October 1899. The diminutive box measured 13ft 6ins by 8ft 3ins, with the operating floor at a height of 7ft 9ins. The GWR stud frame containing 13 levers at 5¼ins centres dated from May 1929 and the box was closed on 2nd October 1970. This view is undated but may well have been taken in early January 1966, shortly after the shed had closed to steam. There is a general air of decay, little sign of any activity and the three locomotives in front of the coal stage are all minus name and numberplates. The brick hut built against the end of the arches carrying the coal stage siding was a mess hut used by footplate crews. NPC

No. 3822 is on the next line over from the Ingoing Road for the shed, so could be waiting here to collect some wagons from the goods yard or the Mileage Yard, having just just come from coaling (the tender is piled high) on 3rd September 1963. New into service on 25th April 1940, the 2-8-0 was based at Neath Court Sart at the date of the picture, so could be here having brought up coal for the yard in any case. It was withdrawn off Cardiff East Dock shed on 15th January 1964. There is a rare glimpse in the left background here of the extensive ex-Midland yard on the Down or east side of Eastgate station. This included five loop sidings on the east side of the two through goods lines and then a bank of nineteen sidings which fanned out from the outer loop. The large shed at the far end of the yard was not a railway building, despite its appearance, in fact being part of Barton Foundry engineering works. Just out of picture to the left on the eastern edge of the yard was a large wagon repair depot with a further five sidings. NPC

A low evening sun turns No. 4985 *Allesley Hall* copper brown as it sits at the head of a train of coal wagons at the entrance to the pair of fenced off sidings just to the north of the lines leading to the shed and coal stage. These were known as the Corporation Sidings and had been used for coal deliveries for Gloucester Corporation but probably not for a few years by the early 1960s. The view is undated but was probably taken in June or more likely July 1964, during a four week period when the 'Hall' was briefly allocated here. New in January 1931, it had previously been at Pontypool Road from early 1963 and after its short time here at Horton Road moved on to Neath Court Sart, from where it was withdrawn two months later on 29th September. Also, at the head of the line of stored engines on the next road is '57XX' Class 0-6-0PT No. 3693; new on 3rd March 1941, it was withdrawn on 24th July but may already have been placed here out of use. The 'Hall' may therefore have brought the coal wagons up from Neath and is perhaps parked here for the weekend prior to a Monday morning return – the presence of two railway photographers wandering the yard suggests this may be a Sunday. This was the route in for engines heading on shed, although the older of the two buildings, the lofty passenger engines shed, could be accessed more directly without the need to run right round the coal stage complex. On the right stands a wagon that has been filled with ash by the crane. NPC

There is a glimpse of the Mileage Yard sidings in the left background here, as No. 6872 *Crawley Grange* stands on the Ash Road, as it was known, having the clinker raked from its firebox on 24th April 1965. The shovel on the bufferbeam suggests the smokebox will be next but there is no sign of anyone at work so it must have been tea break time! The engine had reversed to this point having completed coaling, with the picture being taken from the lower slopes of the line leading up to the coal stage. New from Swindon Works on 31st March 1939 and based at Cardiff East Dock shed at the time of this picture, No. 6872 was withdrawn two months later on 21st July but was then reinstated to service at Worcester on 6th August, where it remained until the demise of WR steam at the end of the year. The route onto shed was via the headshunt at the north-west corner of the yard, where a green Brush Type '4' can be seen coming in. The 'Standard' Class '3' tank stored in the coal sidings on the right is likely to be No. 82036 of Bristol Barrow Road shed, which the Shed Bash UK website notes as being here at Horton Road a week later on 2nd May 1965. It may never have returned to Bristol, being officially withdrawn on 25th July and sent to Cashmores of Newport for scrapping. NPC

LEFT: No. 6957 *Norcliffe Hall* being cleaned out on the Ash Road in January 1965, with more engines stored out of the way in the right background. The furthest is No. 6942 *Eshton Hall*, which had been withdrawn a few weeks earlier on 14th December 1964, having been reallocated from Pontypool Road in the June. No. 6957 meanwhile was to move on to Oxford in early March 1965, from where it was withdrawn on 26th October. New on 1st April 1943, the engine had been one of the 'Halls' converted for oil burning in April 1947 and renumbered as No. 3952. It was converted back and given its old number again in March 1950. Colour views of the Great Western goods yard here have not been seen, so these glimpses of the Mileage Yard sidings are invaluable. NPC

RIGHT: No. 4564 now, posing in a similar position in 1964. This engine has already featured several times and will make a few more appearances after this but I have not been able to get to the bottom of the apparent damage to the side tank which, as the picture on page 51 shows, was in fact in the same place on both sides of the engine. Presumably this happened during its time at Gloucester but I have been unable to find any pre-1964 pictures of No. 4564 to work out if this was the case (a picture found on line purporting to be at Gloucester in 1961 is unlikely to be correct, as the engine was allocated to Shrewsbury at that date). Note the withdrawn 'Mogul' in the background still has coal piled in its tender. NPC

1950s. Thereafter, the total gradually declined, although there was a brief rise in 1964 when Barnwood closed and some locomotives and crew transferred over. However, with the end of steam by then actively being planned for, few of these stayed long and the number employed was down to less than 150 when steam finished.

Horton Road lost its steam allocation officially on 31st December 1965 (some sources quote 1st January 1966), when the Western Region completed its wholesale move to diesel (mainly diesel-hydraulic) traction. By this date, the old sheds were some way past their best, particularly internally as some of the pictures that follow will show, whilst the yard was neglected and filthy, covered in a muddy mixture of coal, ash, oil and grease, with plants growing through in many places – in short, an anachronism in BR's shiny new age. The two steam sheds were demolished and although I have been unable to ascertain the extact date, it was certainly by the autumn of 1967.

The site remained in use as diesel depot, with a small allocation of diesel shunters and as a signing on point, whilst also providing stabling for larger locomotives including classes '31', 45', '47', '50' and 'Westerns'. Facilities for fuelling had been provided when the first diesels were allocated here in 1960. The early 1950s wheel drop building was retained for use as a maintenance shed but this closed in 1991 and BR ceased using Horton Road as a stabling and signing on point in 1993. The site was then dormant until a lease was taken out on it by the private freight and locomotive spot hire company Cotswold Rail in 2006 but that company went bankrupt in 2010 and the site has been derelict since. The engineers carriage shed and the wheel drop building still stand today, although now in imminent danger of demolition with the site earmarked for housing. An attempt to save the latter in 2017 by a reborn Gloucester Carriage & Wagon Company and establish a museum, workshops and steam centre failed.

There was a short siding between the south side coal stage line and the line from the Outgoing Road to the turntable which, latterly at least, was used for the storage of redundant and withdrawn locomotives awaiting disposal. The long line of '14XX' 0-4-2Ts gives the clue as to the date, the picture being taken on Sunday 1st November 1964, the day after the Chalford and Sharpness auto services ceased running, although the official date of withdrawal is recorded as Monday 2nd November. In the line-up here are No's 1453, 1458, 1472 and 1420, of which No's 1458 and 1472 had worked the previous day on the final Chalford autos, along with 0-6-0PT No. 6412. The Chalford and Berkeley Road-Sharpness services were not quite the last Western Region auto workings as is sometimes stated, that honour falling, somewhat ironically, to the auto-worked shuttle on the ex-Southern Railway line between Yeovil Junction and Yeovil Town. BILL POTTER/KRM

RIGHT: A fine side on study of No. 1420 on 15th November, sitting in late autumn sunshine awaiting its fate. If this engine looks a little more sprightly than the others, perhaps it already knew that it did in fact have a future, being sold by BR in running order to the newly formed Dart Valley Railway, where it arrived a year later in October 1964. In tandem with pannier tank No. 6435, also bound for the DVR, on 17th October the pair were scheduled to haul an SLS special originating from Snow Hill, taking it over at Worcester for the leg to Bristol, which would assist in moving them south to Devon. However, No. 1420 was taken off at Gloucester and replaced by No. 5029 *Nunney Castle*, which later worked the tour back to Birmingham on its own, No. 1420 subsequently rejoining the pannier tank at Bristol to carry on to the DVR. Pictures of this tour feature in the *Gloucester Midland Lines* volumes. BILL POTTER/KRM

OPPOSITE PAGE TOP: Photographed on 4th April 1965, Class '61XX' 2-6-2T No. 6128 had also just been withdrawn, a week earlier on 26th March. New in October 1931, it first arrived at Horton Road in April 1964 but then moved to Southall for the last two months of the year before coming back. The 'Manor' behind, devoid of nameplates, is almost certainly No. 7808 *Cookham Manor*, which as we saw earlier was latterly paired with a Collett 4,000 gallon tender and which was still in service, lasting until the end of the year. A second nameless 'Manor' is in steam on the right.
BILL POTTER/KRM

OPPOSITE PAGE BOTTOM: No. 6924 *Grantley Hall* was photographed at the end of the siding on 16th October 1965. It was based at Oxford shed but may have failed here at Gloucester and is recorded as being officially withdrawn ten days later, on 26th October. BILL POTTER/KRM

ABOVE: No. 1420's classmate No. 1453 was not so fortunate, its final journey being to the Newport scrapyard of John Cashmore & Sons. The engine's last day in service, 31st October, had been spent working the Berkeley Road-Sharpness auto shuttles, which also finished on that date. BILL POTTER/KRM

RIGHT: 'Large Prairie' tank No. 4100 and ex-LM&SR Class '4F' 0-6-0 stored on the same siding. The 2-6-2T, which we saw previously on station pilot duties, had been withdrawn on 26th October 1965, whilst the '4F' is probably No. 44264, which had been reallocated from Bristol Barrow Road to Horton Road in June 1965 and was also withdrawn on 26th October. It had been built at Derby Works in October 1926, so had completed just over thirty-nine years in service. NPC

Another mixed array of engines were photographed alongside the coal stage on 24th January 1965. In the foreground is ex-Midland Railway '4F' No. 43887, built at Derby Works in 1919 and based at Gloucester Barnwood throughout the BR era up until that shed closed. Moving over to Horton Road, it was subsequently sent down to Bristol Barrow Road for three months in the autumn of 1964, returning in early October and had just been withdrawn when seen here. Behind is ex-GWR 'Castle' Class No. 5055 *Earl of Eldon*, which had been taken out of service the previous September and which we shall see again shortly. On the right is ex-LM&SR '8F' No. 48187, still in service and some way from home, with the shedplate on its smokebox door matching its class designation – 8F Wigan Springs Branch shed! New from the North British Locomotive Company, Glasgow in April 1942, it was to last in service until early January 1967. Note the elderly condemned wooden-bodied open wagon up on the coal stage siding arches. DON MANN

RIGHT: An unidentified 'Mogul' 2-6-0 steams off shed towards the station, quite possibly to head up a Hereford-bound train. The date is likely to be 1963, probably in the spring. A withdrawn 'Large Prairie' tank, minus its numberplates, stands near the coal stage; this could be No. 5173, a '5101' Class 2-6-2T new in December 1930, ownership of which had flipped between Newport Ebbw Junction and Horton Road sheds between October 1952, when it first arrived at the former, and September 1961, when it returned to the latter for the second and final time. It was withdrawn from service in August 1962 but remained in store here until sold in September 1963 to Cashmores of Newport for scrapping. NPC

LEFT: A general view of the lines leading directly to and from the passenger engines shed in August 1964, with a pannier tank sandwiched between a 'Hall' and a 'Mogul' on the stored engines siding. NPC

RIGHT: Our first sighting of the other side of the coal stage which, latterly at least, seems to have been the side used for coaling, either mostly or completely. Standing over the ash pit on 7th February 1965 is No. 44766, one of two 'Black Fives' that was experimentally fitted with a double chimney when built at Crewe Works in 1947. The other, No. 44765, appears in *Volume 4A*, hauling a holiday relief between Haresfield and Standish Junction. Saltley-based at the time of this view, once servicing had finished No. 44766 would head to the turntable for turning to face in the right direction for heading back to Birmingham. The 4-6-0 lasted in service until October 1967, when it was withdrawn from Wigan Springs Branch shed. The brakes on the steel mineral wagons in the background would have been full on to prevent them running away down the slope, although the open doors hanging down show that they were empty. DON MANN

It wasn't all grime and rust! On 24th August 1962, gleaming No. 7814 *Fringford Manor* stands on the Ash Road proudly sporting its 89C Machynlleth shedplate on the smokebox door. This clearly puts the engine a long way from its home in the far west of mid-Wales and although nearly two years later it became part of Horton Road's stud, the 'Manor' would have been an unusual sight here at this date. There is no obvious explanation as to how the locomotive had found its way here – no rail tour ran on this day, for instance – so it can only be surmised that it had been at Shrewbury, where the shed foreman had then sent it south to Hereford, from where it had then been pressed into action again to run to Gloucester via Ross. Were there ever occasions I wonder when shed foremen thought to themselves "*I'll send this engine over there, it will make a change and a surprise for them!*". We also get a good view here of the earthen ramp up to the coal stage and the cast iron notice advising 'CAUTION ENGINES MUST NOT PASS THIS ARCH'. NPC

The '16XX' Class 0-6-0PTs were a smaller, lighter design of pannier tank built at Swindon Works by British Railways as a direct replacement for the ageing '2021' Class engines which had reached the end of their lives, these having been constructed over a nine year period between 1897 and 1905. New into stock in November 1954, No. 1650, seen here on 3rd September 1963, was the first of the final batch of twenty built, the last two emerging in May 1955. The lines in the Forest of Dean had been worked for decades by various members of the '2021' Class, both in their original saddle tank form and later when converted as pannier tanks, so it was no surprise that Gloucester had a complement of the '16XX' Class engines. Many were regularly sub-shedded at Lydney but others travelled down from Gloucester to work the Forest of Dean Branch to Cinderford. No. 1650 had gone new to Plymouth Laira on 30th November 1954, moved to Exeter in August 1960 and then arrived at Horton Road in October 1961. It spent most of its final two and a half years in service out-stationed at Lydney, being withdrawn on 26th February 1964, a week before that shed closed on 2nd March. The two steel mineral wagons have been positioned where they are to load ash, which was usually done by means of the crane seen in other pictures, but the side doors of both hang down so presumably it was being 'hand-balled' with shovels. NPC

Black liveried 0-4-2T No. 1440 was photographed in the yard on the same day. New in February 1935, most of its career was spent based at Exeter and Tiverton Junction, hauling Exe Valley trains. It first arrived at Horton Road on 10th May 1961 but was loaned to Oswestry on 5th July and then moved to Banbury on 15th November. It was back at Gloucester for the month of April 1962, then back to Banbury and then into store. Reinstated at Gloucester on 1st April 1963, four days later it went into Worcester workshops, coming back to Horton Road on 23rd April but only to then go into the workshops at Cheltenham on 2nd May. Problems seemingly solved, it was back at work on 24th May but was withdrawn on 28th December and cut up at Swindon Works six weeks later. There is a rare sighting, particularly in colour, of a Mechanical & Engineering department 'Enwheels' open wagon on the right, lettered 'LOCO WHEELS ONLY'. NPC

LEFT: No. 6349 being cleaned out on the Ash Road in early August 1964, with its lined green livery just about showing through the layers of grime. New in May 1923, the 'Mogul' had been stationed here for five years from late 1952 to late 1957, returning in September 1963 for what was to be its final posting, withdrawal in fact being just days away when seen here, on 10th August. Facing it is 0-6-0PT No. 4624, which was not to survive much longer either, being withdrawn on 1st September. JOHN STRANGE/NPC

ABOVE: One of the large pannier tanks of the '94XX' Class, No. 9453, paused in the yard between duties in 1964, whilst the footplate crew have a chat; the fireman seems to be counting something off on his fingers. Considered the tank engine equivalent of Collett's '22XX' 0-6-0s, only the first ten were built by the GWR, in 1947, a further 200 then being built under BR between 1950 and 1956 but all by sub-contractors, No. 9453 by Robert Stephenson & Co. in July 1951. It moved to Gloucester in March 1960 and apart from a stint at Bromsgrove in the summer of 1964 as a Lickey banker, remained here until withdrawal on 6th November 1964. These engines were quite heavy, so were generally restricted to yard, trip or main line work. Horton Road had several in its allocation in the late 1950s/early 1960s and often used one on the Gloucester to Cheltenham locals. They were capable even of taking a Paddington express on the last leg to Cheltenham St. James. NPC

OPPOSITE PAGE BOTTOM: Class '57XX' No. 3759, looking both filthy and very rusty on 29th August 1965, managed to survive another four months, until the end of WR steam. It had entered service on 4th December 1937. On the stored out of use line behind is 'Standard' Class '3' tank No. 82039, which we saw a little earlier on prior to its withdrawal on 2nd July, with a Collett 0-6-0 minus its numberplates in front, probably either No. 2242 or 2287, which had both been withdrawn on 21st May. BILL POTTER/KRM

One of the later BR-build 'Castles', coming new from Swindon Works on 1st August 1950, No. 7034 *Ince Castle* spent its first ten years based at Bristol Bath Road, moving to St. Philip's Marsh when Bath Road became a diesel depot in 1960. Transfer to Gloucester followed on 16th September 1961. The big 4-6-0 is seen here in one of the back sidings at Horton Road on 25th July 1965, exactly a month after it had been taken out of service. By the end of the year it was no more, broken up by Hayes of Bridgend. The career of 1927-built '4F' No. 44422 in the right background had ended on 3rd June. NPC

LEFT: The first of two rather dark slides but taken under challenging lighting conditions, which are included for their interest in showing stages in the coaling of No. 5042 *Winchester Castle* in May 1965. Here the fireman hangs from the cab whilst keeping an eye as the coal is tipped in from above. Entering service on 5th July 1935 at Old Oak Common shed, No. 5042 was well acquainted with Horton Road, first being allocated here from Worcester on 27th May 1939. Nearly twenty years later, on 2nd February 1959, it went back to Worcester but was then moved quite frequently over the next five years, which also included two short periods in store, at Newton Abbot and Llanelly. It finally came back 'home' to Horton Road when moved across from Hereford on 20th July 1964. The engine's filthy condition here is an indicator that the end was nigh, withdrawal taking place a few weeks later on 25th June 1965. NPC

RIGHT: Viewed from the other side of the engine, the driver gives the fireman some instruction as to what he wants done next whilst a member of the maintenance staff is about to climb onto the running plate of No. 5042. Many of these top ex-GWR express locomotives ended their days in this sort of sad neglected condition, bereft of name and numberplates, and covered in grease and grime. Its demise after withdrawal was perhaps mercifully quick, cut up by Hayes of Bridgend in October 1965. NPC

LEFT: Many of photographer Don Mann's slides have suffered, sadly, from poor storage and the film of many is either deterioratating or is covered in mould spots. I have done my utmost to get the best out of those that I wanted to use but as can be seen, this was one of the worst. I have included it, however, as it provides a clear view of the yard crane, which was more normally used for ash disposal, being employed to coal No. 6956 *Mottram Hall* from a pile of coal lying between the tracks on 7th February 1965. Was this a common occurrence I wonder? It seems odd to be using such a time-consuming method right next to the coal stage. New into service on 28th March 1943, No. 6956 spent most of the 1950s working from Shrewsbury and Wolverhampton Stafford Road, moving to Gloucester in late September 1961, where it would have become quite well known to local spotters and enthusiasts, as it stayed until early July 1965. Its final move to Oxford saw it remain in service until the last day of WR steam. DON MANN

LEFT: Collett 0-6-0 No. 2253 was shedded at Horton Road from February 1959 to December 1963, when it moved a little way north to Worcester. This undated view was probably taken a little before that, in the summer or autumn of 1963, with the engine coaled up and ready for its next turn of duty, standing in front of one of the fuel tanks provided when the shed began housing its first diesels. The engine was withdrawn off Worcester shed on 8th March 1965. NPC

RIGHT: Withdrawn Class '94XX' No. 8402 sits forlorn on one of the sidings at the north-west end of the site on 24th January 1965. The British Road Services depot bordered the locomotive yard and, indeed, had a small rail-served goods shed which was accessed off the head shunt. Hawksworth designed No. 8402 was one of a batch built for BR by W.G. Bagnall of Stafford, entering service on 30th September 1949 at Newport Pill shed. After allocations to Aberbeeg and Cardiff Canton, in early August 1956 it was sent to Bromsgrove as a Lickey banker, where it stayed for eight years. Heavy freights climbing the long steep bank between Bromsgrove and Blackwell sometimes required three of these sturdy tank engines assisting from the rear. It was withdrawn in early November 1964, six weeks after transferring south to Gloucester. It is still carrying its Bromsgrove 85D plate, the code for that shed from 1961 to 1964. DON MANN

LEFT: As can be seen, in its final years Horton Road became something of a dumping ground for withdrawn engines, in large part no doubt because it was a useful storage point en route to South Wales, where most of these engines were destined. Also photographed on 24th January 1965, 'Castle' Class No. 5063 *Earl Baldwin* was never allocated here, its final allocation, as the 2B shedplate indicates, being to Wolverhampton Oxley, where it moved on 9th September 1963. Somewhat bizarrely, however, it did not go from Gloucester to South Wales for scrapping, for although bought by John Cashmore & Sons Ltd, they returned it to the West Midlands and scrapped it at their Great Bridge yard in May 1965. No. 5063 had entered service on 22nd June 1937 as *Thornbury Castle* but was renamed a week later on 2nd July. Part of the British Road Services depot is again glimpsed in the background. DON MANN

No. 1426 stands in front of the 1872 shed on 27th December 1960. New into service at Southall on 27th November 1933, the engine spent most of its career in the Home Counties, first arriving in Gloucestershire on 15th September 1958 when it moved to Lydney. It was sub-shedded there working auto services across the Severn Bridge, to and from Berkeley Road, until put into store on 6th January 1960. The engine was given a heavy intermediate overhaul at Caerphilly in March 1960 and then went briefly to Swindon and Bristol Bath Road before returning to Lydney on 16th August 1960. No. 1426 then transferred to Gloucester in April 1961, moving over to Barnwood from the 28th of that month to work the Sharpness Branch after the Severn Bridge was damaged. It was withdrawn on 3rd April 1962. NPC

Classmate No. 1454 was photographed on the back road on the same day. New into stock on 23rd July 1935, its early career was spent at Yatton, sub-shedded from Bristol St. Philip's Marsh, followed by a ten year stint from 1942 to 1952 at Weymouth. It was then based at Bristol Bath Road until moving to Gloucester on 17th July 1959. Its time in service here was brief, with the 0-4-2T in fact having been withdrawn four days before this picture was taken and it was cut up at Swindon in early September 1961. NPC

LEFT: The sidings originally laid in the late 1930s at the north end of the shed site for the delivery and storage of coal were latterly used instead for the storage of withdrawn engines awaiting the call of the scrapman. Here, on 21st October 1962, '14XX' 0-4-2T No. 1473 was parked out of the way having been withdrawn ten weeks earlier on 10th August. The engine remained here for the best part of a year, until sold for scrap to A. King of Norwich on 19th June 1963. Its numberplates had been removed but its number was chalked on the smokebox door. The 'Large Prairie' behind has its number chalked on the cylinder cover, so we know it to be No. 5173, which had been withdrawn on 17th August. NPC

RIGHT: Although Horton Road ceased to be a home for working steam after 31st December 1965, as we shall see, the yard was to play host to numerous 'dead' steam locomotives over the next two or more years, being dumped here whilst waiting to proceed to one of the scrapyards in South Wales. On 9th January 1966, No. 7816 *Frilsham Manor* presents a sad sight, with its name and numberplates removed and the pre-1948 'G W R' letters showing through the dirt on its tender. It was bought for scrap by Cashmores of Newport.
BILL POTTER/KRM

LEFT: Along with No. 7816 above, No. 7808 *Cookham Manor* was the other member of the class to remain in use at Horton Road up until the end of WR steam. Pictured on the same day, the engine stands at the rear of the yard following withdrawal on 31st December 1965, still coupled with the larger 4,000 gallon tender with which it is seen in previous pictures. Purchased for preservation off Gloucester shed around the time this picture was taken, it was quickly reunited with a more visually suitable 3,500 gallon tender – was that sourced from here from a '22XX' 0-6-0 perhaps? A picture of the engine at Dowty Ashchurch in September 1966 shows it in freshly applied lined green livery, having apparently arrived in steam from Horton Road coupled with a smaller tender. Interestingly, although first coupled with the 4,000 gallon tender in the summer of 1964, photographs from early 1965 show it with a 3,500 gallon tender again, so it clearly swapped a couple of times at least.
BILL POTTER/KRM

An unusual view from the end of the sidings by Horton Road at the north-east corner of the shed yard on 10th March 1963, as the 'Big Freeze' (as the winter of 1963 came to be known) came to an end. These three sidings, running parallel to the rear of the terraces fronting onto Great Western Road, were known as the coal stacking ground when they were added in the late 1930s. By the late 1950s they were apparently covered in stacks of coal but one of the shed clerks maintained that he never saw any of it used and that it was later all taken away. As can be seen, they were still covered in chunks of coal and by a layer of coal dust afterwards. There is a glimpse of the 'Black Shed' for the engineer's inspection coach behind the rows of withdrawn and stored engines, which was moved from the other end of the yard probably in the 1940s. Also note that partially in picture on the left is the grounded body of a Dean 40ft Brake coach, which was placed here in September 1943 for use as a clothing store. GERALD DANIELS/COURTESY THE RESTORATION & ARCHIVING TRUST/REF. GD630219

LEFT: Despite looking in absolutely pristine condition, the missing nameplates of No. 5017 *The Gloucestershire Regiment 28th 61st* are the indicator to the fact that it had also just been withdrawn when photographed here on 21st October 1962. Taken out of service exactly a month earlier, we saw this engine previously, on page 30, posed in the station in the mid 1950s. Clearly spotlessly maintained right to the end, the Horton Road shed staff must have been quite downhearted when it was withdrawn. No time was wasted in scrapping the engine either, by Cashmores at their Newport yard two months after this picture was taken. One of the nameplates now resides in the Soldiers of Gloucestershire Museum at Gloucester Docks. NPC

RIGHT: Back to some happier pictures now of locomotives still in use. Ex-GWR Class '28XX' 2-8-0 No. 2836 rests quietly in front of the 1951 wheel drop shed on 8th June 1958, with just a wisp of steam escaping from the whistles. The rather spartan cab is the clue to the fact that this otherwise modern looking steam locomotive was in fact quite an ancient beast, having entered service in September 1912. The long lives enjoyed by most of the class were a testimony to their simple but highly capable design. Based at Oxford shed at the date of this view, the engine was eventually withdrawn off Severn Tunnel Junction shed on 15th June 1964, two and a half months shy of fifty-two years in service. BILL POTTER/KRM

LEFT: A fine study of one of the 'Grange' Class 4-6-0s in tidy condition in the shed yard on 27th June 1965. No. 6859 *Yiewsley Grange* was allocated to Cardiff East Dock shed at this date but also moved to Severn Tunnel Junction, two months later and three months prior to its withdrawal. It had entered service on 4th December 1937 and previous BR allocations included Birkenhead Mollington Street, Bristol St. Philip's Marsh, Newton Abbot and Oxford. BILL POTTER/KRM

Pannier tank No. 8745 stands amidst the muck and puddles on 25th July 1965. New in June 1931, the engine was built by Bagnalls of Stafford as part of a much wider Government initiative to stimulate the economy by ploughing money into industry and infrastructure. Moving from Bath Green Park shed to Horton Road in early October 1964, it was withdrawn exactly a month after this picture was taken. BILL POTTER/KRM

'Large Prairie' tank No. 6113 also had just a month left in service when photographed on 16th October 1965. Two months younger than No. 8745 above, its last year was spent here at Gloucester, withdrawal taking place on 18th November. BILL POTTER/KRM

RIGHT: No. 6947 *Helmingham Hall* was sporting a homemade smokebox numberplate when photographed in the yard in August 1964 and was also coupled with one of the slab-sided, 4,000 gallon Hawksworth tenders. Entering service on 7th December 1942 but not named until November 1946, presumably due to the Second World War, the 'Hall' was stationed here at Gloucester from early October 1962 to early March 1965. Moving on then to Oxford, it was withdrawn on 18th November 1965.
JOHN STRANGE/ALAN SAINTY COLLECTION

LEFT: No. 5055 *Earl of Eldon* again but in more cheerful circumstances than when last seen on page 98, in steam and apparently stopped behind Milage Yard Ground Frame box, on the Outgoing Road from the shed, in April 1964. The turntable could be accessed from here, which may be where the engine was coming from, as it was based at Hereford at the date of this view, so has been turned ready for its return journey. The 'Castle' was withdrawn on 28th September 1964, having been stored and reinstated three times in the previous two years. There was to be no fourth reprieve, however, for an engine which had originally entered service on 9th June 1936 as *Lydford Castle*, a name it carried for just over a year before becoming *Earl of Eldon* on 20th August 1937. Note that the engine had lost its numberplates, with the number now stencilled on in place instead.
JOHN STRANGE/ALAN SAINTY COLLECTION

RIGHT: An unidentified '28XX' 2-8-0 in the yard in August 1964, with a 'Large Prairie' tank and a 'Western' diesel-hydraulic behind and an ex-GWR 'Mogul' in the left background. None of the locomotives are positively identifiable – Gloucester did not have any of the 2-8-0s on its allocation – but the Western nameplate, under heavy magnification and by a process of elimination, could be that of No. D1048 *Western Lady*, which was based at Cardiff Canton at this date. NPC

RIGHT: Another 'Castle' to swap its originally allotted name for that of an Earl was No. 5056 *Earl of Powis*, which entered service on 17th June 1936 as *Ogmore Castle*. This was all part of a move by the GWR to impart the names of these exalted personages on rather grander engines than the little 4-4-0s for which they were at first intended. The displaced names were subsequently reused later on in the class, although the *Ogmore Castle* name had more of a troubled time than most. Next given to No. 5080, it was removed for a second time when that engine was renamed *Defiant* in January 1941, finally ending up with BR-built 'Castle' No. 7035. Seen here in February 1964, No. 5056 was at this date based at Cardiff East Dock, moving to Hereford on 13th April and then on to Wolverhampton Oxley on 14th June but it was then withdrawn on 21st November. The driver gives the photographer an encouraging grin and note the chalked inscription on the cabside '*All out 30/1*' – to what does that refer one wonders? JOHN STRANGE/NPC

RIGHT: We saw No. 2836 a few pages ago, in fine condition outside the wheel drop shed in 1958, but here it is again in the yard in April 1964, two months prior to withdrawal. This picture is included because here the locomotive is accompanied by a couple of interesting items of rolling stock. The van on the right is lettered M&E Swindon Works Workshop Van but does not equate to any of the GWR-built Workshop Vans in Atkins, Beard & Tourret's *GWR Goods Wagons* opus and may therefore be a BR rebuild of a Permanent Way Brake Van. Behind the engine is a GWR Mark 2 4-wheeled, 6-ton crane. A total of nineteen of these were built at Swindon, in small batches between 1893 and 1904, in three number series – 240-252, 443-446 and 456-457. JOHN STRANGE/NPC

OPPOSITE PAGE BOTTOM: Withdrawn Class '4F' No. 43387 features again in the left foreground of this frosty January 1965 view, showing the line curving round to the turntable, with the shed forming a backdrop. DON MANN

LEFT: No. 5979 *Cruckton Hall* was captured on shed on 10th May 1964. New on 8th September 1938, this engine had been a long term resident of Reading shed, from November 1948 until transferring to Horton Road at the end of March 1963. This was another engine near the end of its working life, with a move to Cardiff East Dock in September 1964 preceeding its withdrawal two months later on 6th November. JOHN STRANGE/NPC

One of the shed cleaners had polished some of the soot covered metalwork on the smokebox door of No. 4104, which is otherwise seen here in typically work stained condition not long after withdrawal on 14th May 1964. The engine had arrived here in March of the previous year. The '14XX' behind is not identified and Eastgate station can be seen in the left background. NPC

Ubiquitous 2-6-2T No. 4564 with its apparently damaged side tanks features here one last time, standing on the headshunt alongside the passenger engine shed in August 1964, with 'Hymek' diesel-hydraulic No. D7080 parked behind. The 'Prairie' tank has a bunker full of coal, so had presumably come off shed and, along with the Hymek, was waiting to reverse out; the headshunt was generally used for this purpose, as it prevented locomotives from being able to run straight out onto the main line from the shed. No. D7080 was new from Beyer, Peacock on 14th December 1963, so was not yet a year old. It was based at Cardiff Canton until July 1965, moving then to Old Oak Common. Returning to Cardiff in October 1966, it stayed then until January 1972, when it made its final move to Bristol Bath Road, from where it was withdrawn on 7th November 1972. The picture includes good detail of the shed's construction and shows the original colour of the bricks, a few of which had managed to avoid being covered in layers of soot and grime. JOHN STRANGE/NPC

Although the raised siding at the end of the coal stage provided an obvious viewpoint of the shed, seemingly few photographers were able to gain access to it. This slide is undated but there are enough clues here to suggest that our unknown photographer had managed to climb the steps and stand on the walkway jutting out either side of the supporting brick arches because the coal stage was now redundant and out of use. I rather think we may be in early 1966, after the shed had closed to steam, with Type 'I' diesel shunter No. D3993 in the process of hauling three dead '57XX' pannier tanks, of which Horton Road still had at least five allocated in December 1965, away to one of the storage lines. Another steam engine can just be seen in the doorway immediately to the left of the 'Peak' diesel. New on 22nd September 1960, No. D3993 became '08' No. 08825 under TOPS and finished its service on 30th June 2005. Bought for preservation, it is now on the Chinnor & Princes Risborough Railway which, in 2019, returned it to service in Network South East red, blue and white livery. The tall tower in the background with a water tank on top housed the pumping equipment for the shed, supplying the coal stage tank and the various water cranes. NPC

OPPOSITE PAGE TOP: A final glimpse of No. 5055, again in August 1964, facing 'Mogul' No. 7318 and a couple of '57XX' pannier tanks which are sandwiching a wooden bodied open wagon. No. 7318 was new in December 1921 and spent its BR career based at sheds in South and West Wales, only moving to Gloucester in June 1964. It then appeared regularly on the line to Hereford (see *Vol. 1 West Gloucester & Wye Valley Lines*), including on 31st October, the last day of those services, after which, with its work having gone, it was withdrawn a week later on 6th November. We also get a good close up of the water crane, one of six scattered around the shed yard, whilst one of the shed's senior drivers strolls past. NPC

OPPOSITE PAGE BOTTOM: We also saw No. 5056, No. 5055's immediate successor in the 'Castle' number series, a couple of pages ago but here is a rather fine front end study of *Earl of Powis* blowing steam from its cylinder cocks outside the shed in February 1964, in the company of No. 4564. JOHN STRANGE/NPC

ABOVE: Pannier tank No. 3745 was based at Horton Road from October 1962 until withdrawal on 14th December 1964. It had previously spent eight years on the allocation of Stourbridge Junction shed, having entered service on 9th October 1937. Engine and driver pose here in the shed yard probably in the summer of 1963. NPC

ABOVE: A third sighting of No. 5055 *Earl of Eldon*, taken in August 1964 and included partly because it gives a clue as to the sequence of events leading up to its withdrawal on 28th September. The engine still has its name and numberplates (although not the one on the smokebox door) but also a 'NOT TO BE MOVED' pressed steel sign on its front bufferbeam and there is rust visible on its wheel tyres. It also appears to have a tender full of coal. It would seem likely therefore that No. 5055 had suffered some possibly minor problem which saw it taken out of service temporarily here at Gloucester pending a decision on its future which, given what was happening with Western Region steam in particular, was only really going to have one outcome – not worth repairing, so condemned and officially withdrawn on the date noted above, although as this picture shows, without having worked in fact for at least six weeks prior to that date. The sighting of No. D1048 *Western Lady* on the left may confirm that this indeed is the identity of the 'Western' seen in the bottom picture on page 111. JOHN STRANGE/NPC

Looking west from in front of the passenger engines shed on Sunday 17th October 1965, with a pair of '9F's either side of the turntable. Both are in steam but neither appear to be wanting to use it. Nearest is No. 92131, which was new into service on 31st May 1957 and five months into its final allocation, to Birkenhead Mollington Street shed, at the date of this view. The engine spent all of its career based first at sheds in the East Midlands, then the North East and finally the North West, so would have been quite a rare 'cop' here. It was withdrawn in September 1967. On the other side of the turntable is No. 92224 of Banbury shed, which entered service on 16th June 1958 and was withdrawn off Warrington Dallam shed, also in September 1967 – a combined total of just over nineteen and a half years in service for the two engines. Both were Crewe Works builds. This was obviously the occasion of an official depot visit, with a camera wielding enthusiast crossing the lines on the right and a couple more in discussion far left; I wonder if the very young lad with them has any recollection at all of this visit, two and a half months before the shed closed to steam. NPC

'Dub-Dee' 2-8-0 No. 90491 might have just come off the turntable in this 24th January 1965 view. New from Vulcan Foundry in August 1944 as WD No. 8706, successive changes saw it renumbered 78706 (WD), 3170 (L&NER) and 63170 (BR), before becoming No. 90491 in September 1949. It was based at Staveley Barrow Hill shed at the date of this view and from where it was withdrawn in September 1965. Note the BR 'Standard' Class '4' 2-6-0 on the right, minus its rear set of driving wheels. DON MANN

Another 'Dub-Dee' 2-8-0, No. 90572, also belonging to Staveley Barrow Hill, by the turntable on 3rd October 1965. Again built by Vulcan Foundry but in October 1943, it was WD No. 7115 when new and then WD No. 77115, before renumbering by BR in October 1950. It moved on to Langwith Junction shed a couple of days after this picture was taken and was withdrawn on 10th February 1966. DON MANN

ABOVE AND BELOW: Two views of Tyseley-based '9F' No. 92118 being turned on 3rd October 1965. In the first picture, the driver watches intently as he inches the big 2-10-0 onto the table, whilst the fireman holds the wheel and will give him the all clear when the front pony truck is on. The wheelbase of a '9F' measured 55ft 11ins, whilst the length over buffers of the engine and tender was 66ft 2ins, so there was not a great deal of clearance to play with on Horton Road's 65ft turntable. In the lower picture, the footplate crew put their backs into turning locomotive and tender which together weighed a shade under 142 tons. The task was all about weight distribution – if the locomotive was positioned nicely in the centre of the table it would turn with relative ease. Built at Crewe Works and entering service on 31st December 1956, No. 92118 was withdrawn off Carnforth shed in May 1968. BOTH DON MANN

As mentioned in the Introduction, your author is building an N gauge model railway which will be a reasonably accurate portrayal of Grange Court Junction but will also include a 'light' version of Horton Road. One of the locomotives that will run on this layout is a Bachmann Farish 'Castle' converted to run as No. 7003 *Elmley Castle*, a late GWR build entering service on 13th June 1946 and seen here looking smart in its BR lined green livery coming off the turntable circa 1961. The engine was allocated to Horton Road shed from 16th June 1960 up until its withdrawal on 10th August 1964, apart from a few weeks at Bristol St. Philip's Marsh between 13th April and 22nd June 1964. My parents moved us from North Devon to Worcestershire in the late summer of 1958, to a farm at Netherton, a mile from the village of Elmley Castle where I subsequently attended the primary school from 1960 to 1965. Etched brass plates were thus ordered so I could replicate this engine in miniature. The picture is another gem from the camera of a lovely man who we sadly lost in 2020. ROY DENISON

A splendid portrait of '43XX' Class 'Mogul' No. 4358 and crew at Horton Road on 8th June 1958 appeared as a frontispiece in *Vol. 1 West Gloucester & Wye Valley Lines* and here we have the corresponding view of the engine coming off shed a short while later, bound for the west end of Central station to head up a service to Hereford. We are fortunate to have two such fine colour studies of this engine, as it only had fourteen months left in service, withdrawal taking place on 11th August 1959. At the date of this view, Horton Road shed was still a haven for steam, as the array behind and to the left of No. 4358 shows, unspoilt by the arrival of any diesels. In fact the shed's allocation in March 1959 still comprised all ex-GWR types, as this list shows: '16XX' 0-6-0PT – 9; '54XX' 0-6-0PT – 3; '64XX' 0-6-0PT – 1; '94XX' 0-6-0PT – 9; '14XX' 0-4-2T – 7; '56XX' 0-6-2T – 2; '22XX' 0-6-0 – 5; '43XX' 2-6-0 – 8; '51XX' 2-6-2T – 10; '45XX' 2-6-2T – 3; '61XX' 2-6-2T – 1; '28XX' 2-8-0 – 3; 'Hall' 4-6-0 – 6; 'Castle' 4-6-0 – 3; 'Manor' 4-6-0 – 4; Total – 79. BILL POTTER/KRM

Ex-Somerset & Dorset line '4F' No. 44560 poses in front of the wheel drop shed during Don Mann's visit of 24th January 1965. Built for the Midland Railway by Armstrong, Whitworth in April 1922, the 0-6-0 was based at Bath Green Park at the start of the BR era, moving on to Templecombe in April 1960 and then arriving here at Horton Road in November 1964 for its last few months in traffic, withdrawal occurring on 25th August 1965. Don Mann

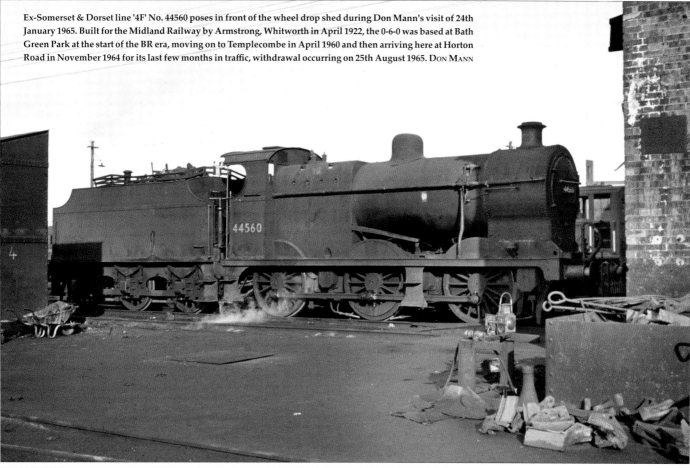

Class '8F' No. 48134 near the turntable on 1st August 1965. New from Crewe Works in April 1941, the 2-8-0 was withdrawn off 6C Croes Newydd shed in early January 1966. The engine would also have been another unusual sight at Horton Road but the reporting number gives a small clue as to how it got here, the 'X' denoting an inter-regional excursion, military or special train. In the right background is 0-6-0 diesel shunter No. D2196, new from Swindon on 8th June 1961. Later Class '03' No. 03196, it was withdrawn on 112th June 1983 but was preserved and is now with West Coast Railways at Carnforth. Don Mann

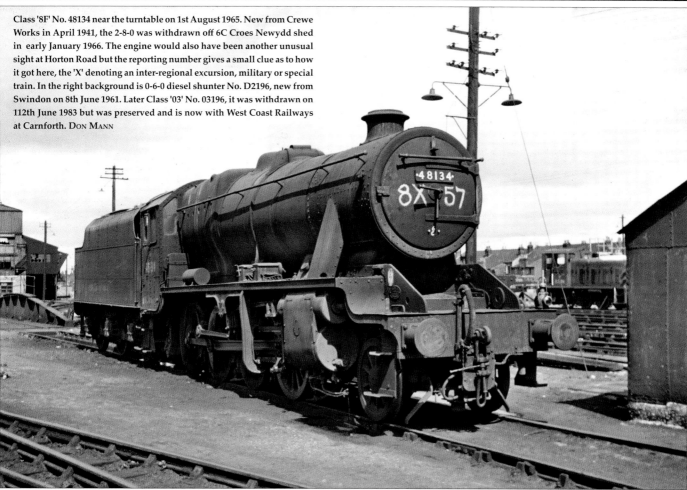

The glow of a warm summer evening bathes an assortment of tank engines gathered in front of the 1872 shed in hues of red and gold in this lovely view from July 1964. Identifiable are '57XX' Class 0-6-0PTs No's 4614, on the left, and 3737 in the centre. No. 4614 had entered service on 27th February 1942 and had spent its years under British Railways based in Worcestershire, alternating between Kidderminster and Worcester sheds, until allocated to Gloucester Barnwood in early August 1961, which was now under Western Region control. From there it was sent out to work both the branches from Ashchurch – to Evesham and Upton-on-Severn – as depicted in *Vol. 3 Gloucester Midland Lines Part 1: North*. The engine then transferred across to Horton Road in July 1962, by which time the line to Upton-on-Severn had lost its passenger service. It was withdrawn soon after this picture was taken, on 24th July. No. 3737 meanwhile, which had appropriately for its number entered service in 1937, on 6th September, moved from Treherbert to Horton Road in August 1963 and was also facing imminent withdrawal when seen here, on 1st September. The 'Large Prairie' tanks in front of No. 4614 will be two of No's 4100, 4104, 5184 and 6128, all allocated here at this date. NPC

All goods engines outside the 1855 passenger engine shed in June 1963, including '57XX' No. 4611 and 2-8-0 No. 3825. New on 21st February 1942, No. 4611 had only a brief acquaintance with Horton Road, from March to December 1963. No. 3825 meanwhile was a Banbury engine in 1963, so only here probably on an overnight stay. NPC

On a wet and miserable Saturday 16th October 1965, No. 3745 steams gently in the drizzle as the shed lights fail to do more than pierce the gloom of the interior in the background. The new order in the form of a green liveried 'Peak' diesel features on the left. BILL POTTER/KRM

Study of the selection of pictures presented here of Horton Road would seem to indicate that the demarcation line between the passenger engine and goods engine sheds became quite blurred in the BR era, with even the 1958 view on page 112 showing pannier tanks lined up in front of the former, whilst here we have passenger locomotives in front of the latter circa 1964. On the left is No. 6816 *Frankton Grange*, which had entered service on 17th December 1936. The engine was based at Bristol St. Philip's Marsh from late September 1960, moving the short distance to Barrow Road in June 1964, when it then departed the city for a move to Worcester; it was withdrawn in June 1965. The mobile crane on the left used for lifting tasks around the wheel drop shed probably dated from the mid-1930s. CHRIS WALKER

A second view of 'Large Prairie' No. 6113, standing at the entrance to the 'taller passenger engines shed. The engine is in much the same condition as in the view on page 110, although when seen there in August 1965 had lost the route availability 'D' in a blue circle that it carries on its cabside here, so this picture is clearly a little earlier. No. 6113 arrived here from Radyr shed in late September 1964, so this picture may have been taken soon after that, but it then moved down to Bath Green Park for three weeks in the November, so equally we could be looking at a spring 1965 date. Again this close-up study of the brickwork shows that 110 years of smokey engines in and around the older shed and ninety-plus years for the newer shed on the left had covered the red bricks with layers of soot. By May 1965, the shed's steam allocation had halved from the 1958 figure, with ex-LM&SR and BR types now breaking the domination of ex-GWR classes: '94XX' 0-6-0PT – 1; '57XX' 0-6-0PT – 9; '22XX' 0-6-0 – 3; LMS '4F' 0-6-0 – 2; BR '2MT' 2-6-0 – 3; '51XX' 2-6-2T – 1; '61XX' 2-6-2T – 1; 'Castle' 4-6-0 – 4; 'Hall' 4-6-0 – 4; 'Manor' 4-6-0 – 1; BR '5MT' 4-6-0 – 3; BR 9F 2-10-0 – 3. Total 35. CHRIS WALKER

LEFT: With its green livery hidden by a thick layer of water-streaked grime, No. 7926 *Willey Hall* stands outside the shed on 15th November 1964. This BR-built 'Modified Hall' entered service on 12th October 1950 and was allocated to Horton Road. It stayed through the 1950s and into the '60s, moving to Worcester in September 1962, then on to Reading in April 1964, to Swindon in the July and finally back to Horton Road in the September. It had six weeks left in service when seen here, being withdrawn on 26th December 1964. BILL POTTER/KRM

ABOVE: A side on view of the 1855 shed entrance, with No. 6832 *Headbourne Grange* standing outside circa 1963. New into stock from Swindon Works on 9th September 1937, the engine was based at Newport Ebbw Junction shed when seen here, from where it was withdrawn in January 1964. Just in view on the road behind is the cab of 2-8-0 No. 3832 which, depending on exactly when the picture was taken, was either also an Ebbw Junction engine, where it was allocated from February 1957 to March 1963, or Neath Court Sart to where it then moved and from where it was withdrawn in April 1964. NPC

RIGHT: A poor quality general view, also circa 1963 and included because it provides another view of the depot's GWR Mark 2 6-ton crane and its attendant Match truck, which looks of reasonably ancient origin but again does not equate with any GWR designs in Atkins, Beard & Tourret. NPC

Grass growing around the turntable approach line and in the pit in June 1963. Detail such as this is very useful for any modellers of the British Railways scene of the 1960s. There is a glimpse inside the open doors of the wheel drop shed on the far left and then we have 2-8-0 No. 3812 of Severn Tunnel Junction shed (but shortly to transfer to Newport Ebbw Junction), a '14XX' 0-4-2T and finally Neath Court Sart's No. 5961 *Toynbee Hall* behind the turntable. NPC

A 1963 view across to the shed from the end of Eastgate's island platform, with a fine array of motive power on display. Eastgate was more popular with spotters because they could see almost everything going in or out of both stations, whilst also having a splendid view of Horton Road shed. The more mischievous would dare each other to run off the end of the platform and try to reach the signal post between the tracks on the right but risked being banned from the station if caught! NPC

RIGHT: Shed interior views, whilst invariably not taken under the best of conditions, particularly for colour photography, are invaluable, hugely atmospheric and full of useful detail for the modeller. We are fortunate therefore that several of our intrepid cameramen ventured within the dark, cavernous confines of Horton Road and the results of their endeavours are presented over the next few pages. This first view, looking out from the entrance to the 1872 shed, is undated but the presence of '45XX' 2-6-2T No. 5518 on the left enables us to narrow it down, as the engine was only here from September 1963, when it moved up from St. Blazey shed in Cornwall, to withdrawal on 6th May 1964. The snowplough is attached to the front of one of the three Collett 0-6-0s that were allocated to the shed at this time but the smokebox numberplate is missing so we cannot be sure which one and there is a 'Hymek' just sneaking into the picture on the right. NPC

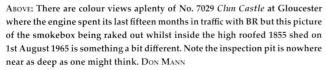

ABOVE: There are colour views aplenty of No. 7029 *Clun Castle* at Gloucester where the engine spent its last fifteen months in traffic with BR but this picture of the smokebox being raked out whilst inside the high roofed 1855 shed on 1st August 1965 is something a bit different. Note the inspection pit is nowhere near as deep as one might think. DON MANN

ABOVE: Collett '22XX' No. 2287 inside the shed with the snowplough fitted on 24th January 1965. These two interior views provide good detail of the wooden ducting that extracted the smoke emanating from engines inside, although it could never remove all of it. The pictures also show the tools, parts and other bits and pieces that were found around the floor of a busy steam shed. DON MANN

An unidentified BR 'Standard' Class '5' 4-6-0 gently simmers inside the shed on 3rd October 1965. It is not No. 73091, which had been resident here from May 1964 after trasnferring over from Barnwood when it closed, as that engine was withdrawn in May 1965, so must be a visitor from elsewhere On the right is a rear view of the tender of one of the two 'Manors' allocated to Horton Road at this time, No. 7829 *Ramsbury Manor* which is also seen from the front, below, after the Class '5' had moved out of thr way. DON MANN

No. 7829 *Ramsbury Manor*, the last of the class to be built, was one of two of the class still on Horton Road's allocation at this time (No. 7816 *Frilsham Manor* was the other). No. 7829 was a BR build, going into stock on 29th December 1950 but not getting its first shed allocation, to Neath in South Wales, until 22nd February 1951. It moved around a bit subsequently, to Shrewsbury, Carmarthen, Llanelly, Reading, Swindon and Didcot in that order, before finally ending up here at Gloucester in July 1965. Not one of the more photographed members of the class, this view of it, albeit in pretty careworn condition as the engine neared the end of its days, is thus welcome. Withdrawn along with the rest of Horton Road's steam complement on 31st December 1965, it was sold to Cashmores of Newport for scrapping. DON MANN

Colour film, handled well and then subsequently manipulated correctly using the latest computer software, can be every bit as dramatic as black and white photography and this wonderfully evocative study of steam on Horton Road shed in April 1964 ranks up there with the very best of the acknowledged masters of the latter medium. Sadly the original slide came with no provenance attached, so I cannot credit the taker of this magnificent study. With a low late afternoon sun lighting up its motion, No. 7003 *Elmley Castle* faces out from just inside the entrance of the 1872 shed, its gaze focussed on BR '9F' No. 92216. We saw the 'Castle' a little earlier, coming off the turntable, but No. 92216 is a new 'cop' for us – no surprise as the 2-10-0 was based at Southall at the date of the picture. Of all the '9F's we have seen so far, this one had by far the shortest career. It entered service at Cardiff Canton from Swindon Works on 31st December 1959 and was withdrawn off Severn Tunnel Junction on 26th October 1965, after a paltry five years and ten months in traffic. NPC

ABOVE: A rare view inside the 1951 wheel drop shed on 1st August 1965, with BR 'Standard' Class '4' 2-6-4T No. 80041 being attended to. The engine has its connecting rod removed, presumably so that one of the wheelsets can be dropped for attention. The locomotive was one of a batch built at Brighton Works, entering service on 5th July 1952 at Bletchley shed. Its next three allocations, starting in December 1959, were all to Southern Region sheds, successively to Ashford, Tonbridge, Exmouth Junction and finally Templecombe (S&D) in June 1965. Somerset & Dorset line engines needing attention to their wheels had been sent to use the wheel drop at Barnwood but when that shed closed in May 1964 they came here to Horton Road instead. No. 80041 was withdrawn off Templecombe when that shed closed on 7th March 1966. Again this interior view provides useful detail of the tools and equipment to be found inside this shed. DON MANN

ABOVE: We complete our tour of Horton Road shed in the steam era with this Great Western Railway notice to be found bolted to one of the shed walls, forbidding any untrained or unauthorised member of the shed staff from moving an engine in steam. Despite the dire warning, however, it was not unknown for 'others' to be allowed to move a locomotive when no one in authority was about. NPC

LEFT: On 12th December 1965, less than three weeks before the end, Don Mann took this now historic and valuable close-up colour shot of the G W R initials clearly showing through on the tender of No. 7816 Frilsham Manor, some seventeen years after they had first been painted over. Elements of the gold with which the letters were painted can be made out, whilst the red shading on the W in particular was still very strong, protected as it had been to an extent behind the transfer carrying the BR emblem. DON MANN

A rather bleak view on 9th January 1966, with the life seemingly sucked out of the depot after it had closed to steam despite there being a couple of locomotives still in view amongst the complement of diesels. The depot still had the task of turning and playing host to those steam engines that continued to arrive here via the Midland main line from Birmingham, with many goods trains being steam worked, a practice which only ceased towards the end of 1966. As we shall see, Horton Road also played host to withdrawn steam engines on their way to South Wales for a couple of years, although they were stored away from the sheds. NPC

Another historic picture, with Don Mann, who took this photograph of '8F' No. 48681 on 23rd August 1966, noting that it was the last live steam that he saw on Horton Road shed. Built by the Southern Railway at Brighton Works under war-time orders and going into service in January 1944 as LM&SR No. 8681, the engine gained its BR number in February 1950. It was allocated to Burton-on-Trent when seen here but transferred to Northwich a month later and was withdrawn in July 1967. DON MANN

The 'D95XX' Class 0-6-0 diesel-hydraulics are now held in great affection, although their time with British Railways was short and their reputation for reliability was poor. Famously nicknamed 'Teddy Bears' (or 'Yogi Bears' in the Forest of Dean), they were a late addition to the ranks of replacement WR motive power, which had not initially been allocated any Type 'I' diesels. By the time the first of the class, No. D9500, emerged from Swindon Works on 24th July 1964, much of the work for which they were intended was drying up, the coal industry being in decline, whilst small goods yards were closing and freight was being lost wholesale to road transport. Although intended to run on the main line, which they did on occasion, their liability to fail at any sort of speed saw their duties becoming even more restricted. The last of the class, No. D9555, entered service on 22nd October 1965 but BR had withdrawn all sixty-five engines by the end of April 1969; one, No. D9531, completed just two years and ten months in service. Happily, most found a second life in industry and nineteen have survived into preservation, including last built No. D9555 on the Dean Forest Railway. Here, on 6th November 1965, No's D9521 and D9502 pose in Horton Road yard looking resplendent in their two tone green livery. The former was new on 20th November 1964, based at Bristol Bath Road when seen here, withdrawn on 3rd May 1969 but then went to the National Coal Board at Burradon, County Durham and is now also preserved at Norchard on the DFR. No. D9502 meanwhile, entered service on 27th July 1964 and was also a Bristol Bath Road engine. Withdrawn on 3rd May 1969, it went to NCB Ashington and is now preserved on the East Lancashire Railway. BILL POTTER/KRM

It seems few photographers were attracted by the new diesels arriving at Horton Road in the early 1960s, most preferring to concentrate on capturing the fast disappearing steam scene. Happily, Bill Potter was an exception, as further demonstrated by this exceptionally fine study of 'Peak' Type '4' No. D38 on shed on 29th August 1965. New from Derby Works on 13th July 1971, after four years of use the green livery with the light grey lower body stripe, whilst attractive, was starting to look a little tired. The locomotive was based at Bristol Bath Road from 10th September 1961 until transferred to the Line Power Controller, Derby in January 1966. It became Class '45' No. 45032 under TOPS in February 1975 and was withdrawn from Leeds Holbeck depot on 21st September 1980. Scrapping at Swindon Locomotive Works took place exactly three years later. Also of interest in this picture is the glimpse of an ex-GWR Toplight coach body on the left, in use perhaps as a mess or stores hut. BILL POTTER/KRM

LEFT: '8F' No. 48376 of Wellingborough shed was a visitor on 30th May 1965 and is seen here facing the turntable, with '9F' No. 92000 stored out of use alongside. Horton Road's role as one of the last WR steam sheds to remain operational up to 31st December 1965 saw it increasingly used as a storage point for withdrawn engines awaiting their final journey. New from Crewe Works on 31st January 1954, the 2-10-0 had arrived here in early March 1965 but saw little use and was not to turn a wheel again in traffic, official withdrawal taking place on 2nd July. No. 48376, built at Horwich Works and entering service in November 1944, made three quick transfers in 1965, to Leicester Midland in June, Coalville in late July and then Westhouses by the end of October. It was withdrawn from Buxton shed in July 1967. DON MANN

RIGHT: Horton Road's final role of the steam age was as a storage point for withdrawn ex-Southern Region engines heading for the scrapyards of South Wales. Their journeys were routed this way because 'dead' engines were prohibited from being towed through the Severn Tunnel. Some of the slides are not annotated in any way but, fortunately, issues of *The Railway Observer* for 1967-68 carried details. Seen here alongside the coal stage in this first view are rebuilt 'West Country' 4-6-2s No's 34100 *Appledore* and 34103 *Calstock*, both from the later batch built under BR. They were apparently detained whilst on their way for scrapping so they could feature at the Bristol Bath Road Open Day of 21st October 1967, arriving here at Gloucester afterwards on 25th October. The picture is useful in confirming that the engine shed buildings had been demolished by this date. NPC

LEFT: A closer look at No. 34100 *Appledore*. New from Brighton Works in December 1940, the air-smoothed 'Pacific' had been rebuilt in September 1960, to the form seen here with its streamlining removed, and was withdrawn from Brighton shed in early Febraury 1967. It was ultimately bound for Cashmores Newport scrapyard. *The Railway Observer* notes that the other engines temporarily stored here between 25th October and 10th November were Ivatt 2-6-2T No. 41312, BR 'Standard' Class '4' 2-6-4Ts No's 80015, 80016 80085, 80133, 80139, 80143, 80146 and 80152, and BR 'Standard' Class '3' 2-6-2Ts No's 82019 and 82029. The three 2-6-2 tanks can be seen in the background, and No. 82029 again on the left of the picture above. NPC

RIGHT: A close-up of BR 'Standard' Class '3' tank No. 82019. Built at Swindon Works and entering service at Exmouth Junction on 26th September 1952, the 'Prairie' was withdrawn on 9th July 1967 – some sources say off Eastleigh shed but SLS data almost certainly correctly states it as Nine Elms. Facing is classmate No. 82029, also built at Swindon but more than two years later, going new to Darlington shed on 13th December 1954. The locomotive stayed in the North East until September 1963, when it transferred south to Guildford. Withdrawal from Nine Elms depot also occurred on 9th July 1967, which strongly suggests that that was where No. 82019 had also been shedded (since November 1962 according to the SLS) and was therefore withdrawn from too. NPC

LEFT: Rebuilt 'West Country' Class No. 34013 *Okehampton* stored on the coaling road in late summer/early autumn 1967. New from Brighton Works in October 1945 as No. 21C113, the 'Pacific' was rebuilt in October 1957 and had been withdrawn off Salisbury shed in early July 1967. It is recorded as being scrapped by Cashmores of Newport in October 1967 but the length of its stay here at Gloucester and subsequent onward movement to South Wales seems to have escaped the notice of any RCTS observers. NPC

RIGHT: The March 1968 issue of *The Railway Observer* noted that four more ex-SR rebuilt 'Pacifics' had been sold in January to Cashmores of Newport for scrapping. They included 'West Country' No. 34036 *Westward Ho* and 'Battle of Britain' No. 34052 *Lord Dowding*, which are seen here en route to South Wales probably in early February 1968. The other two, both 'West Country' Class, were No's 34093 *Saunton* and 34095 *Brentor*. At the rear in this view, however, are two BR 'Standard' Class '5' 4-6-0s, No's 73020 and 73092, also on their way to Newport for scrapping, having been bought off Weymouth shed. NPC

On Sunday 3rd September 1967, ex-Southern Railway 'West Country' Class 'Rebuilt Light Pacific' No. 34002 *Salisbury* was detached at Coaley Junction from another scrap train heading for South Wales via Gloucester, after suffering a hot box (see Vol. 4B *Gloucester Midland Lines South Part 2*, page 279). Pete Berry takes up the story: *"Two weeks later the loco was brought to Gloucester and positioned on one of the northern sidings at Horton Road shed, close to the engineer's carriage shed (left). For enthusiasts brought up on copper cap chimneys, this strange streamlined engine became an immediate magnet. The shed staff were just as excited about the visitor and tolerated the endless bunking by local spotters, probably more lenient as it was well away from the shed running lines. Spontaneously, one or two of us started cleaning the cabside, revealing the number, glorious green livery and wonderful lining. After that, with more helpers (and oily rags and cotton waste from the shed foreman) the side casing and tender were all cleaned to bring our celebrity loco back to (in our eyes) ex-works condition. Even the local Citizen newspaper did a splendid article, with a photo showing all of us hard at work, with 85B oil drums and ladders used to reach the top of the boiler casing, etc. Just four short days after arrival, the foreman advised us that Salisbury would soon be collected for its final journey to Cashmores at Newport. Early on the morning of its departure (24th September) I used the tins of paint I bought from Woolworths and started highlighting the smokebox area. All I had to go on was photos of unrebuilt West Country's in the magazines but it looked great to me! There was just time to paint the nameplate red with white letters and crest and scroll, and I was still painting the 'West Country Class' words on the scroll when the Class '47' arrived. Photos were taken by everyone, including the shed staff. The sun shone on our very own Bulleid as the Class '47' buffed up and took Salisbury to the centre road at Gloucester Central, where No's 34047, 34008 and 80145 were waiting. Within a week, No. 34002 was reduced to scrap, but we were all proud that we gave our 'West Country Pacific' a dignified final journey. Co-incidentally, many years later I found out that a friend of mine photographed it in the scrapyard and was baffled as why it was all polished up on just the one side".* PETER BERRY

RIGHT: Before taking our final leave of Horton Road, we will take a brief look at the site in the early 1970s and its role as a diesel depot. This first picture shows North British Type '2' No. D6310 here on 29th June 1970. Despite appearances to the contrary, the locomotive had not been withdrawn and was not being scrapped. Based at Bristol Bath Road, it was a regular visitor here at this time. New into service on 5th January 1960, No. 6310 was withdrawn on 27th March 1971 and scrapped at Swindon Locomotive Works in May 1972. NPC

A near classmate of the 'Peak' we saw a couple of pages ago, No. D21, pictured here at Gloucester on 10th March 1968, was also built at Derby Works, entering service on 3rd March 1961. Based in Leeds from new, first at Neville Hill and then moving to Holbeck, it too had then transferred to the Line Power Controller at Derby, in October 1967. It moved on to Nottingham Division in June 1968, finally returning back to Leeds Holbeck in October 1971, where it remained until withdrawn on 7th April 1986. Under TOPS it had become Class '45' No. 45026 in February 1975. Scrapping by MC Metals at their Springburn, Glasgow yard was carried out in February 1989. The first ten members of what became known as the 'Peak' Class, No's D1-D10, were all named after English and Welsh mountains and were later designated Class '44' under TOPS. Those built subsequently at Derby, No's D11-D137, had a lower motor gearing, which reduced their tractive effort but also the risk of flashovers, from which the initial ten suffered. These became Class '45', whilst a further fifty-six built at Derby up to 1963, No's 138-D193, were given Brush generators and traction motors, and became Class '46' under TOPS. Note the 'Z' headcode again; No. D21 may have taken an unfitted military train to Ashchurch. BILL POTTER/KRM

Although this 11th June 1975 view is post TOPS, Class '47' No. 47365 (previously Brush Type '4' No. D1884) is still carrying two tone green livery. New from Brush Traction at Loughborough on 6th July 1965, the locomotive was based at Crewe diesel depot but moved to Toton four months after this picture was taken. Coincidentally, No. 47365's long career ended back here at Horton Road, having been purchased from the withdrawn locomotives pool by Cotswold Rail in September 2004. It was moved here in February 2006 after CR took over the abandoned depot but was then sent to Booth Roe's scrapyard at Rotherham six months later, presumably having been robbed for parts first. 'Peak' No. 45042, previously No. D47, built at Crewe Works and new on 29th June 1963, was allocated to London Division when seen here. It was withdrawn on 29th April 1985 and scrapped by Vic Berry of Leicester in January 1987. NPC

Two weeks later, on 25th June 1975, Class '31' No. 31193 and Class '25' No. 25032 were photographed in the same spot. The '31', which was based at Bristol Bath Road, started life on 19th May 1960 as Type '3' No. D5617. In later became No. 31426 (1983), No. 31526 (1990) and finally No. 31426 again in 2001, although it had been stored withdrawn since 1st May 1995. It was finally scrapped in November 2006. No. 25032 was Type '2' No. D5182 when new on 19th March 1963 and was a Cardiff Canton engine when seen here. It was withdrawn on 10th March 1986 and cut up in December 1988. NPC

Whilst this this circa 1975 overall view of the Horton Road site does not have the cachet of the steam age panoramas of a decade or so previously, this line of of diesel motive power nevertheless presents quite an impressive sight. From left to right we have Class '47' No. 47033, 'Peak' Class '45' No. 45034, 'Peak' Class '46' No. 46049, Class '25' No. 25266, Class '25' No. 25166. The locomotives all carry 'Z' headcodes (the hidden Class '45' may do so too), again for special, military or excursion trains. Their depot spread was also quite extensive: No. 47033 was based at Pymouth Laira, No. 45034 at Leeds Holbeck, No. 46049 at Cardiff Canton, No. 25266 at Wigan Springs Branch and No. 25166 also at Cardiff Canton and it may be that this unusual gathering was what had attracted our unknown photographer. Also in the picture, between the two 'Peaks', is a Plasser & Theurer USP 5000C Ballast Regular, almost certainly No. DB966011 (Works No. 250 of 1974), which was stationed here at Gloucester. ED RENNIE COLLECTION

RIGHT: As they neared the end of their time in service, many of the 'Western' diesel-hydraulics became very neglected, as demonstrated here by rust bucket No. D1022 *Western Sentinel*, which was photographed parked on a short siding alongside the Down Main Line and opposite Horton Road probably in 1976. One of the Swindon-built examples, going new to Old Oak Common shed on 16th July 1963, No. D1022 was, like many of the class in their final years, based at Plymouth Laira, from where it was to be withdrawn on 18th January 1977. It was cut up at Swindon Locomotive works in December 1978. COURTESY RAIL ONLINE

ABOVE: Type '1' diesel shunter No. 4119 faces an unidentified 'Western' in January 1973. Both locomotives are standing on one of the roads of the former 1872 goods engines shed, whilst the 1951 wheel drop shed was the only building which remained of the steam sheds, retained for use as a maintenance depot. New from the old Lancashire & Yorkshire Railway's Horwich Works on 22nd February 1962, No. 4119 became Class '08' No. 08889 under TOPS in May 1974 and was withdrawn on 6th March 1992. It was cut up by Gwent Demolition (Margam) two years later. Note the engineer's inspection coach visible in the left distance. JOHN STRANGE/NPC

LEFT: Tatty looking No. D1041 *Western Prince* in the depot sidings circa 1976. New from Crewe Works on 10th October 1962, the locomotive was based at Plymouth Laira depot when seen here, from where it was withdrawn on 23rd February 1977. No. D1041 is today one of seven of the seventy-four strong class to have survived into preservation, being owned by the Bury Hydraulic Group and based on the East Lancashire Railway. COURTESY RAIL ONLINE

An interesting overall view of the depot looking west on 31st July 1976, with No. D1013 *Western Ranger* in the centre, an unidentified 'Peak' on the left and a Class '37' hiding in the maintenance shed. New from Swindon Works on 13th December 1962, No. D1013 was again Plymouth Laira-based and just seven months away from withdrawal, on 28th February 1977. However, *Western Ranger* was bought for preservation by Richard Holdsworth of the Western Locomotive Association, who placed the locomotive in their care. Based on the Severn Valley Railway, No. D1013 hauled the first train, a load of sleepers, onto the then newly acquired Kidderminster station site in 1984. Taken out of use in 2009, the engine is currently nearing the end of an extensive overhaul at the SVR's Kidderminster diesel depot. In the right foreground is an ex-LM&SR Cowans & Sheldon 6½/ or 10-ton hand crane of early 1940s vintage, one of the last still in use with British Railways at this time; several examples have, however, been preserved. STEPHEN TAVERNER

To complete this section before we head off towards Stroud, we have the first of two overall views of the depot, this one on 8th June 1976, with No. D1013 standing in front of the maintenance shed. Of note here are the red backed name and numberplates that *Western Ranger* is carrying. Seven 'Westerns' were turned out in green livery when new with red plates but the rest of the class had black ones, including No. D1013. When repainted into Rail Blue, these seven had their plates painted black to match. However, in April 1976, Laira depot designated *Western Ranger* as the 'official' rail tour engine for the class and painted the plates with red backgrounds, along with white wheel rims and silver buffer heads, headboard clips and screw couplings. These embellishments were carried until the locomotive was withdrawn, although were not always carefully maintained. Also in view in the yard are a track machine, a Class '20' and a breakdown coach, whilst on the left, the tank wagons were delivering fuel for the depot. Just glimpsed over the top of these tankers is the roof of the shed for the engineers coach, which is also still (just) standing today. With the main sheds demolished, there was a clear view of the gas holder and the old pin factory on Horton Road. STEPHEN TAVERNER

This final panorama of the depot, taken in April 1977, shows a somewhat crowded scene with at least eight locomotives on view, plus a couple of maintenance vans and rakes of tank wagons delivering diesel fuel. Although none of the locomotives are positively identifiable, from left to right we have two Class '31's, a Class '50', a 'Peak', a Class '47', another Class '31' and at least two Class '08's, so again there was still plenty of variety for the enthusiast to savour. RAOUL BEAMAN

SECTION 3

TRAMWAY JUNCTION to STANDISH JUNCTION (and the GLOUCESTER TRIANGLE)

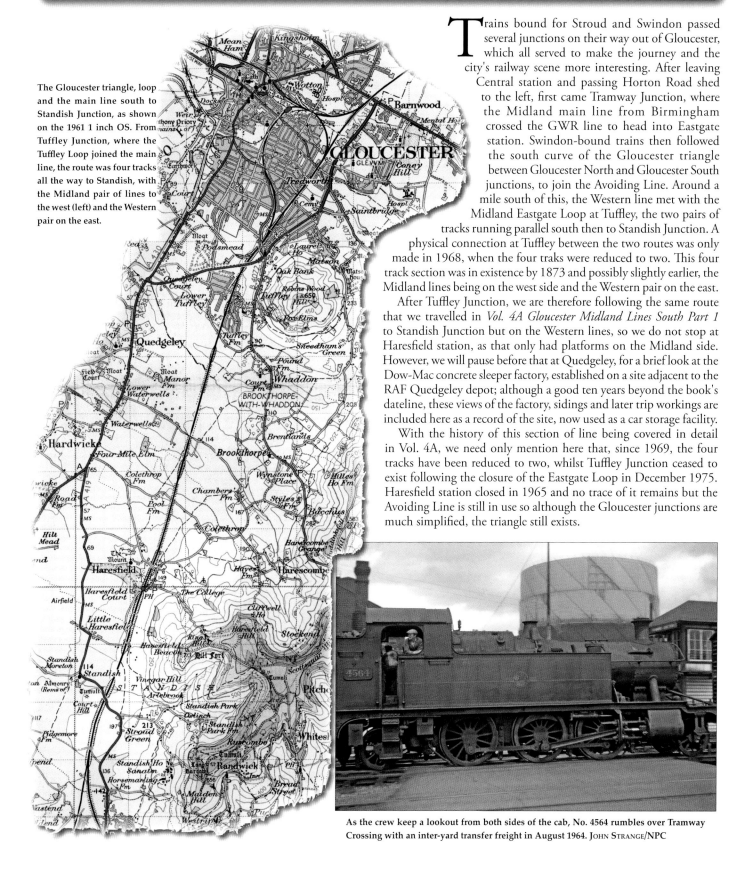

The Gloucester triangle, loop and the main line south to Standish Junction, as shown on the 1961 1 inch OS. From Tuffley Junction, where the Tuffley Loop joined the main line, the route was four tracks all the way to Standish, with the Midland pair of lines to the west (left) and the Western pair on the east.

Trains bound for Stroud and Swindon passed several junctions on their way out of Gloucester, which all served to make the journey and the city's railway scene more interesting. After leaving Central station and passing Horton Road shed to the left, first came Tramway Junction, where the Midland main line from Birmingham crossed the GWR line to head into Eastgate station. Swindon-bound trains then followed the south curve of the Gloucester triangle between Gloucester North and Gloucester South junctions, to join the Avoiding Line. Around a mile south of this, the Western line met with the Midland Eastgate Loop at Tuffley, the two pairs of tracks running parallel south then to Standish Junction. A physical connection at Tuffley between the two routes was only made in 1968, when the four traks were reduced to two. This four track section was in existence by 1873 and possibly slightly earlier, the Midland lines being on the west side and the Western pair on the east.

After Tuffley Junction, we are therefore following the same route that we travelled in *Vol. 4A Gloucester Midland Lines South Part 1* to Standish Junction but on the Western lines, so we do not stop at Haresfield station, as that only had platforms on the Midland side. However, we will pause before that at Quedgeley, for a brief look at the Dow-Mac concrete sleeper factory, established on a site adjacent to the RAF Quedgeley depot; although a good ten years beyond the book's dateline, these views of the factory, sidings and later trip workings are included here as a record of the site, now used as a car storage facility.

With the history of this section of line being covered in detail in Vol. 4A, we need only mention here that, since 1969, the four tracks have been reduced to two, whilst Tuffley Junction ceased to exist following the closure of the Eastgate Loop in December 1975. Haresfield station closed in 1965 and no trace of it remains but the Avoiding Line is still in use so although the Gloucester junctions are much simplified, the triangle still exists.

As the crew keep a lookout from both sides of the cab, No. 4564 rumbles over Tramway Crossing with an inter-yard transfer freight in August 1964. JOHN STRANGE/NPC

Few views were taken showing the rear of Horton Road sheds and this is the only one I have seen in colour. On 7th June 1965, No. 3759 heads 'Light Engine' over Tramway Crossing on its way back to the shed after a shift spent on shunting and inter-yard trip duties. The road today is open, bright and airy, not the dark and dingy thoroughfare depicted here, with the soot-stained sheds towering over vehicles and pedestrians below. The lean-to portion at the rear of the shed (it was not a later addition) originally housed the offices when first built but this changed when the goods engines shed was added in 1872 and they became instead mess rooms – that for the fitters was nearest the line, for the boiler washers in the center and the mess room for the cleaners at the far end just before the gable roof marking the end of the later shed. Beyond the water tower was a wall separating the rest of the depot from Horton Road and the main staff pedestrian entrance was via a gate in this wall. ROY DENISON

As a Midland Railway cabin, Tramway Junction signal box was illustrated in Volume 3, *Gloucester Midland Lines Part 1: North*, but it also oversaw the passage of all Great Western and latterly Western Region trains through the junction and over the level crossing. Pictured here in July 1966, it was a Midland type 4d box, opened on 30th August 1896, replacing an earlier box of 1884, and was equipped with a 40-lever frame. The junction took its name from the old Gloucester & Cheltenham Railway, a horse-drawn tramroad whose rails were the first to reach the city in 1811. The later Birmingham & Gloucester, Cheltenham & Great Western Union and Bristol & Gloucester railways had thus to negotiate the G&CR's line, which crossed here diagonally on the level, the route being marked by the pathway on the left, which then heads to the right of the gas holder; the tram rails were lifted in 1860-61. Tramway Junction box closed over the weekend of 25th-26th May 1968 as part of the Gloucester area MAS resignalling project but the level crossing remains, overseen by the new power box. NPC

The fireman keeps a look-out from the footplate of the '14XX' 0-4-2T as the driver, ensconced in the driving end of the trailer, brings a Chalford auto working back into Gloucester on 7th September 1962. Note the gatekeeper standing on the left facing the crossing gate. Level crossing gates were required to close the railway off completely from road traffic but that was not possible here due to the width of the crossing, hence the requirement for a gatekeeper and also a hut, on the left. The keeper would be notified by a bell from the signal box when the gates were released, so he could then emerge to open them. Horton Road was very much a backwater at this period, so often the gates would only be reopened for road traffic if there was anything that needed to cross. B.J. ASHWORTH

The Chalford auto headed by a '64XX' pannier tank trundles over the crossing on its way to the Stroud Valley in August 1964. Note the Gloucester Engineers Department handcart between the tracks by the crossing. The line in the right foreground was variously known as the Wagon Works Siding or Loop Line. The miniature arm signals were all worked from Tramway Junction box but were also slotted (dual controlled) from Gloucester North (WR) and Gloucester Goods Junction (LMR boxes). JOHN STRANGE/NPC

A fine view looking east at Tramway Junction at just before 3 o'clock in the afternoon of 27th November 1965, as No. 7029 *Clun Castle* heads away back to Swindon with British Railways' 'Last Steam Hauled Train From Paddington' rail tour. The 'Castle' had started out from the Western Region's London terminus at 9.18am but, as noted earlier when we saw No. D1006 *Western Stalwart* working the tour leg from Gloucester Eastgate to Cheltenham St. James and back, No. 7029 was booked to come off the train at Swindon on its return journey and Type '3's No's D6881 and D6882 then returned it to London. The main lines to Cheltenham and points north can be seen heading away beneath *Clun Castle*'s tender, whilst that curving to the left just in front of the engine is the Down Gloucester GW Line, which allowed LM trains to access the Western lines to Central. The shed in the centre right distance was part of the Gloucester Engineers' depot, situated in the triangle of lines here, the bufferstops in the V being at the end of a couple of the depot's sidings. BILL POTTER/KRM

'Black Five' No. 45410 comes off the Down Gloucester GW Line seen just ahead of *Clun* in the previous picture, heading into Gloucester with a mixed goods on Saturday 12th June 1965. Built for the LM&SR by Armstrong, Whitworth in September 1937, No. 45410 spent its career in the North West up until April 1961, when it transferred from Liverpool Edge Hill to Bescot. At the start of April 1965 it moved across Birmingham to Saltley shed, where it was based when seen here, but the engine then returned to Bescot a few days later. Its final allocation was a move back to Saltley in March 1966, from where it was withdrawn six months later in early September. Behind the engine on the left is part of the extensive bank of ex-Midland sidings forming Barnwood Yard. ROY DENISON

I had acquired several undated slides showing No. 6201 *Princess Elizabeth* and No. 35028 *Clan Line* at Gloucester, clearly in the 1970s but exactly when and why were not clear. Fortunately, the redoubtable Pete Berry then came up with some of his own, for which he had a date and background but he has since winkled out the full story of what was going on, much of the information coming from Roger Bell, who had purchased No. 6201 direct from BR. Both locomotives featured in the 1975 Cavalcade that was part of the Stockton & Darlington Railway 150th anniversary celebrations. Afterwards, on 1st September, both worked south from Shildon, in common with numerous other steam locomotives, as a result of which obtaining water on a waterless BR became a problem. Eric Ellis, *Princess Elizabeth's* locomotive engineer for decades, recalled waiting hours in York for water. It may be that *Clan Line* either did not bother or did not take on much, as by the time the pair reached Gloucester, the 'Merchant Navy' 'Pacific' was running very low. The engine can just be seen in the right background here, coupled to two support coaches, one of which belonged to No. 6201. The coach had apparently not been attached to the ex-LM&SR 'Princess Royal' Class 'Pacific' on its journey south, as it was always intended that the engine would be turned on the Gloucester triangle, so it could head back a few miles north to the Dowty Sidings at Ashchurch, its then home. PETER BERRY

Complete with 'Atlantic Coast Express' headboard, No. 35028 then made its way into Gloucester but hauling just its own support coach, having left the other in the loop by Barnwood Junction (the renamed Engine Shed Junction) for No. 6201 *Princess Elizabeth* to collect before heading back to Ashchurch. As we shall see in Follow-Up 2 at the end of this volume, *Clan Line* was in fact bound for Eastgate station, where the tender would be refilled from a fire hydrant. This unplanned event resulted in this Southern Railway 'Merchant Navy' Class locomotive becoming the very last steam engine to visit Eastgate, a fact which I suspect very few enthusiasts are aware of today – it was certainly surprise news to me! There is a Class '31' hauled freight waiting in the Down Loop. On the left is the end of Barnwood Sidings and Pete Berry recalled: *'The raised ground acted as buffer stops for much heavy-handed hump shunting – the wagons would be shoved at speed and often hit the raised ground with a thump, sometimes even derailing! Local spotters also used this higher ground as a perfect vantage point where you would watch the trains and play football or cricket at the same time to while away the summer evenings'*. PETER BERRY

Before *Clan Line*'s move into Eastgate, No. 6201 *Princess Elizabeth* was sent round the triangle so it could collect its support coach and head off to Dowty Ashchurch. The 'Pacific' is seen here reversing round towards Gloucester South Junction, where it would then change direction again to head north along the Avoiding Line. The line on the extreme right was a long siding extending to the Wagon Repairs Ltd depot. NPC

A different aspect at Tramway Junction, as the Chalford auto heads through on 1st February 1961. The tiny hut just in front of the 0-4-2T's buffer beam was originally provided as shelter for numbertakers recording the number of each wagon exchanged between the GWR and LM&SR, a vital role prior to the Nationalisation of the railways. The line in the foreground is the extension south-eastwards of the Loop Line, which carried on round to serve the Emlyn Ironworks, the Gloucester Co-op siding and the premises of Wagon Repairs Ltd. A short siding also kicked back off this just to the right to serve a Signal & Telegraph depot. ROY DENISON

A rare colour view of Gloucester North signal box looking back towards Tramway Crossing and Horton Road shed circa 1963. Opened in April 1901, it was a medium sized box, measuring 33ft 6ins by 13ft, with the operating floor at a height of 9ft, housing a 47-lever frame; until circa 1945-46, it was named Gloucester Goods Yard North Box. Situated in between the Up and Down Main lines behind it and the Up and Down Goods lines to which the box faced, it had windows all round apart from where the brick chimney stack rose to the roof at the rear, and was closed on 25th May 1968. The two tracks branching off the Up and Down Goods lines by the box steps were the Up and Down Goods Relief lines. Class '42XX' No. 5220 is standing on the Down Goods Line in the foreground. New in May 1924, it transferred from Cardiff Canton to Cardiff East Dock in late August 1962 and was withdrawn on 28th December 1963. NPC

A view further round the curve from one of the carriages behind *Clun Castle* on 27th November 1965. The shed housing Wagon Repairs Ltd can be in the right distance, with the wagons on the right standing in the sidings at the entrance to their depot. Ahead of the engine is part of Gloucester New Yard. Courtesy Rail Online

An unusual aspect, as No. 7034 *Ince Castle* heads through New Yard on 4th January 1965. The photographer spent some time around here on this day and we shall see more of this engine a little later on. Here it is passing by on the Up Goods Relief Line, whilst the view is looking in a south-westerly direction across the Up and Down Goods Lines. The water tank behind the engine was positioned next to the long siding serving the repair depot, whilst the building and gantry were part of the Emlyn Iron Works factory site. The two rectangular sets of railings mark the route of a subway running beneath the railway, which connected a short cul-de-sac off Alfred Street with the footpath that crossed the line via the footbridge by the old T station. The footpath and subway have now gone, whilst the cul-de-sac is now a small housing development called Ayland Gardens. DON MANN

Class '28XX' 2-8-0 No. 2891 stands on the Down Goods Line on the curve past Gloucester New Yard on 22nd July 1964. The lines running in front of Gloucester North Signal Box divided as they passed it, with the Up and Down Goods Relief Lines curving right to run parallel with the Up and Down Main Lines, whilst the other pair ran through New Yard to form the Up and Down Goods Lines. There were goods sidings on both sides of these, plus a bank of ten sidings forming the New Yard on the Up side, with an additional pair of sidings angling off that were used for cripples and by the Carriage & Wagon men for repairs, and finally a pair of long sidings on the Down side that ran parallel with the Up Main Line – the Hawksworth coach on the right is parked in one of these sidings. This is an interesting vehicle in itself, a double-ended Slip coach, of which there were three, produced by altering three Brake Composites of Diagram E164 during 1958. Diagram F25 should have been issued to illustrate them but may not ever have been done and when the use of Slip coaches ceased in 1960 they had their slip hooks removed and were retired to branch line services as non-gangwayed Brake Composites. The vacuum tanks can be seen above the underframe trussing and the coach has the yellow First Class band in the eaves towards the left-hand end. The building behind the rake of wagons on the left housed the yard inspector's office, as well as a goods guards room, washroom and WCs. No. 2891 entered service on 11th April 1938 at Cardiff Canton shed, where it was still based in August 1950. By the time it was seen here, however, the engine had moved over to Cardiff East Dock shed, from where it was withdrawn on 23rd October 1964. DON MANN

Returning to what had by now become Horton Road Junction, 'Hymek' No. D7032 is seen in July 1970 backing train No. 6B40, a nuclear flask trip from Berkeley, into Barnwood yard, probably to insert a barrier wagon before heading back north. In the background, No. D1003 *Western Pioneer* waits in the Down Loop with train No. 6V79, the Rowley Regis to Llandarcy empty tank wagons. New into service on 5th May 1962, the 'Hymek was based at Bristol Bath Road when seen here but transferred to Old Oak Common before the end of the year. It was withdrawn on 6th May 1973. *Western Pioneer* had entered service on 14th April 1962 and was based at Swansea Landore. It was withdrawn from Laira depot on 5th January 1975. Note the levers and white painted cabinet of Gloucester No. 1 Ground Frame in the right foreground. CHRIS BALDWIN

Four years later, on 24th August 1974, 'Peak' No. 45001 heads in towards Eastgate with train No. 1V88, the latter-day working of the old cross-country 'Ports to Ports' express, the 10.15am from Newcastle to Cardiff. New from Derby Works on 5th November 1960 as No. D13, the 'Peak', which became Class '45' under the 1974 TOPS scheme, was based at Leeds Holbeck depot, from where it was withdrawn on 20th January 1986. NPC

No's 20197 and 20162 head a freight away from Gloucester in April 1975. The 1969 resignalling scheme had seen the track layout here rationalised, with the four lines remaining on the north curve now reading, from left to right, Up Loop, Up Main, Down Main and Down Loop, the latter pair joining up just before Tramway Crossing. Both engines had come new from English Electric's Vulcan Foundry, No. 20197 as No. D8197 on 25th February 1967 and No. D20162, still in a faded green livery here, as No. D8162 on 19th September 1966. Both based with Nottingham Division, they were withdrawn on 1st January 1973. NPC

'Black Five' No. 44761 heads round the curve on the Up Main line past the then recently closed Barnwood shed circa summer 1964, at the head of train No. 1N84, a Bristol to York service which will have called at Eastgate station. This slide was acquired after *Vol. 3 Gloucester Midland Lines Part 1: North* was published but would have featured within if it had been to hand. However, I am using the excuse of travelling all three legs of the Gloucester triangle to include it here. The ex-GWR tank engine in the left background is standing on the Down Gloucester GW Line (see page 145), which joined with the WR main line into Central station; in the foreground immediately to its right is the Down Goods Line, which was removed during the 1968 resignalling scheme. New in September 1947, No. 44761 was based at Crewe North so would probably come off the train at Birmingham. It was withdrawn off Lostock Hall shed in early April 1968. NPC

RIGHT: At the north-east corner of the triangle was Engine Shed Junction, which was overseen from 22nd February 1942 to its closure on 24th May 1968 by this utilitarian Air Raid Precaution design signal box. When the line between Gloucester and Cheltenham was quadrupled during the Second World War to cope with the huge increase in freight traffic, six of these boxes were built to control it – the others were at Elm Bridge, Churchdown, Badgeworth, Hatherley Junction and Lansdown Junction. Whilst they would not have survived a direct hit, they were designed to be blast proof, to survive the more likely scenario of a bomb falling nearby. Lansdown Junction box at Cheltenham is still just clinging on to existence, albeit derelict and hidden in the undergrowth. Engine Shed Junction was renamed Barnwood Junction following the box's closure as part of the 1968 resignalling. The view is looking south-east from the exit from Barnwood shed, across the lines to Cheltenham, with Chosen Hill in the background and the Avoiding Line running behind the box. DAVID STOWELL

LEFT: Photographed from a southbound train on 29th May 1964, 'Jubilee' Class No. 45593 *Kolhapur* heads away from Engine Shed Junction and over Barnwood Road Bridge with an Up express. Note the gas holder in the far right background – the one behind Horton Road shed. New from North British Locomotive Co. in December 1934, *Kolhapur* was based at Burton-on-Trent when seen here. It was withdrawn from Leeds Holbeck shed on 15th October 1967 but was bought for preservation by the Standard Gauge Steam Trust in January 1968, which subsequently acquired the Tyseley shed site. The engine is now part of the collection there and, in 2021, was awaiting an overhaul and return to service. JOHN RYAN

RIGHT: No. 7024 *Powis Castle* on the Avoiding Line near Engine Shed Junction whilst at the head of a Paignton to Wolverhampton holiday relief on 1st August 1964. It would appear that No. 7024 had been held at the junction waiting for another train to clear, with the crew watching for the signal to proceed. This was one of the BR-built 'Castles', entering service on 30th June 1949 at Old Oak Common shed, where it stayed until moved to Wolverhampton Stafford Road on 18th August 1961. It then moved across town to Oxley shed on 9th September 1963, from where it was withdrawn on 13th February 1965. NPC

LEFT: In early October 1971, five of the New Yard sidings were lengthened, so that they extended through the footbridge; the shunt spur at the end of No. 19 siding was also lengthened to run behind the red brick relay room, built in 1968 as part of the new power signalling scheme and which is still in existence today. In this circa 1975 view, a 'Peak' heads by the extended sidings with an express that was not scheduled to call at Gloucester. NPC

BELOW: The first of two views showing developments at Barnwood Junction, as it had now been renamed. In the first picture, below, D7512 and an unidentified classmate head train No. 8V69, a Washwood Heath to Stoke Gifford freight, along the Avoiding Line in July 1970. The picture was taken from the footbridge next to the old, long closed, broad gauge Gloucester T station, which I have been unable to find a colour view of to include here. Sadly, it was demolished to make way for the extended sidings shown in the picture right, having survived as a residence lived in by a succession of railwaymen and their families. No. 19 siding in the left foreground had been extended at its north end over the weekend of 25th-26th February 1967, work that included connecting it to the WR Up line by means of a facing crossover and which was carried out in advance of the 1968 resignalling This meant that arrivals at and departures from this end of the otherwise south facing WR sidings were now possible and it was accordingly signalled for bi-directional use. Based with Nottingham Division at the time of this view, the lead engine became Class '25' No. 25162 under TOPS and was withdrawn from Crewe Diesel depot on 31st May 1981. CHRIS BALDWIN

An unidentified Brush Type '2' rumbles by in July 1970 with train No. 8V68, a Manvers Main colliery to Exeter Riverside working carrying coal for Exeter gas works, which would cease gas production the following year. Note here that a southbound goods train stands in the bi-directional No. 19 siding. CHRIS BALDWIN

'Peak' No. 46004 powers past the extended sidings on 25th June 1974, at the head of train No. 1V92, the 10.06am Edinburgh to Plymouth express. New from Derby Works as No D141 on 17th November 1961, the engine was heading home, being based at Laira depot, from where it was to be withdrawn on 26th June 1983. The sidings still held plenty of interest at this time, with two Class '37's amongst the wagons and an '08' diesel shunter just visible at the far end. NPC

Class '20' No's 20071 and 20069 about to head beneath the footbridge with a loaded coal train that includes a few empty wagons at the front in July 1974. Separated by just one number, the two locomotives began life at almost the same time, both built by Robert Stephenson & Hawthorn Ltd, No. 20069 going into service on 30th June 1961 as No. D8069 and No. 20071 two weeks later, on 10th July, as No. D8071. Unsurprisingly they were both with Nottingham Division when seen here, so this is likely to be Nottinghamshire coal heading south. The Class '20's were useful and capable freight engines, and many have had long careers, a few still continuing in use today with the Harry Needle Railroad Company. No. 20071 was withdrawn on 27th July 1993 and scrapped in March 1995 but No. 20069, which had been withdrawn on 20th May 1991, was bought for preservation, and is today privately owned and based on the Mid Norfolk Railway at Dereham. NPC

We are today used to seeing pictures of No. 7808 *Cookham Manor* in pristine condition following withdrawal and preservation, although it is currently on static display at the Great Western Society's Didcot base, awaiting a major overhaul. It is therefore a change to see it here on a workaday freight heading along the Avoiding Line on 4th January 1965. We have seen this engine a few times already but this is the first time showing it paired with a Churchward 3,500 gallon tender, rather than the non-standard Collett 4,000 gallon tender it is seen with in the other views and which it had acquired again by the time it was withdrawn. Behind the engine is No. 19 siding, which was always longer than the other T or New Yard sidings, prior to its being extended further to form a bi-directional loop siding in 1967. Commercial property and road developments mean that this area is unrecognisable today from the view here. Don Mann

RIGHT AND BELOW: Two poor quality views of 'Britannia' Class No. 70053 *Moray Firth* with a Saturdays Only Wolverhampton to the West Country express on the Avoiding Line circa 1964. These are Bill Potter duplicates but Kidderminster Railway Museum have not been able to locate the originals. However, they are interesting in showing a 'Brit' using this section of line and also giving a glimpse, below, of Gloucester South Junction in steam days. The box, which also features in a similarly distant view in *Gloucester Midland Lines Part 1: North*, can just about be made out in the right background. The buildings behind *Moray Firth*, right, are part of the Royal Air Force records and pay centre established here in 1941, which relocated to RAF Innsworth in 1975. BILL POTTER/KRM

BELOW: A fine study of second of the class No. 20001, waiting in one of the extended loop sidings on 20th May 1974. Construction of the Class '20s' was split between Vulcan Foundry and Robert Stephenson & Hawthorn, albeit both were part of the English Electric group, with the first batch No's D8000-8019, coming from the former in 1957-58. A total of 228 were eventually built, with the type gaining the nickname 'Choppers' from enthusiasts. No. 20001 was new as No. D8001 on 8th July 1957, based with Nottingham Division when seen here (probably waiting to head back with coal empties) and was withdrawn on 20th April 1988. It too has made it to preservation, now owned by the Class 20 Preservation Society, based at the Midland Railway Butterley but currently on loan to the Epping Ongar Railway. New commercial and industrial units now cover the site of the RAF buildings. NPC

LEFT: Moments after the picture on page 150, this is the view south from the footbridge on 4th January 1965, as No. 7808 *Cookham Manor* heads by shrouded in steam on this bitterly cold day. The New Yard or T Sidings behind the engine comprised two banks of sidings and marshalling loops, one set parallel with the Avoiding Line and the other with the GWR main line curving round from Gloucester Central station. We also get another glimpse of Wagon Repairs Ltd's shed in the background here. DON MANN

RIGHT AND BELOW: Later on the same day but from trackside a little further south, Gloucester-based No. 7034 *Ince Castle* was photographed whilst stood here with the local breakdown train, which had been based at Barnwood up until it closed. The train comprised an assortment of elderly vehicles, a tool van with sagging clerestory roof (possibly a panelled over Royal Mail carriage of circa 1907 vintage that had been withdrawn from regular service circa 1951), a box van and another ancient Midland bogie coach of unknown origin. Two further views of it at Berkeley Road station can be found in Vol. 4B *Gloucester Midland Lines Part 3: South*. No. 7034, which was just entering its final six months in traffic, was seen on Horton Road shed earlier on, after it had been withdrawn from traffic. DON MANN

Class '47' No. 47240 in the New Yard or T Sidings, looking towards Gloucester Yard Junction (as South Junction had been renamed in May 1968) on 13th June 1975. The leading wagons are probably loaded with steel coil, which has been sheeted over. As can be seen, the yard was still busy with wagonload traffic at this date, although wagon variety had declined a fair bit since steam days. The locomotive entered service as Brush Type '4' No. D1917 on 3rd December 1965, becoming No. 47240 under TOPS on 13th November 1973. On 28th January 1987 it was reclassified as '47/4' No. 47663 and then on 23rd February 1989 reclassified again as '47/8' No. 47818. It saw more local use after being bought by Cotswold Rail in May 2003, who intended to name it *Joe Strummer*, after the deceased lead singer of the punk rock band The Clash but the name was switched to classmate No. 47828 instead, as No. 47818 was not available on the planned date. At the time of writing, the locomotive is owned by Arlington Fleet Services and based at their Eastleigh Works depot. NPC

RIGHT: Class '22' diesel-hydraulic No. D6331 was one of four based at Gloucester in July 1970, sub-shedded from Bristol Bath Road. The engine is seen here in that month backing into the New Yard sidings with a trip working from Lydney Junction, comprising two coal wagons and a Berry Wiggins tank. In 1967, Berry Wiggins had moved their depot from Whimsey, near Cinderford to Lydney Junction, bringing about the final closure of the Forest of Dean Branch. This depot in turn was closed in 1971, when the company moved their operations to Cardiff. No. D6331 entered service on 26th July 1960 and was withdrawn on 27th March 1971. CHRIS BALDWIN

ABOVE: Gloucester Yard Junction and the south end of the T Sidings as seen from the footbridge through a telephoto lens circa 1978. A Class '47' heads north onto the Avoiding Line with a container train from Avonmouth Docks to Birmingham. It is worth comparing this picture with that on page 218 of *Vol. 3: Gloucester Midland Lines Part 1: North*, taken from a similar viewpoint circa 1963. NPC

LEFT: A similar view but this time a southbound express is seen heading off the Avoiding Line behind what looks to be a 'Peak' Class. In the intervening four decades or so since these pictures were taken and with the demise of wagonload freight, most of the New Yard has fallen out of use and been removed, so the land could be redeveloped. The aforementioned A302 Metz Way link road now bisects the triangle, with the site of the Gloucester engineers depot now buried beneath a supermarket and other commercial property. From Horton Road Junction (previously Tramway Junction) round to Yard Junction is now plain double track apart from one short stub disappearing into undergrowth beneath the Metz Way flyover. The sidings alongside the Avoiding Line remain but see little use, with one having been severed to allow positioning of a new gantry in any case. NPC

LEFT: An unmarked slide but I think that this is *Clun Castle* again, on 27th November 1965, heading through Gloucester South Junction. A footpath passes through the arch on the left and the roofs of the wagon repair depot buildings can be seen in the left background. NPC

BELOW: Class '94XX' pannier tank No. 9471 heads away from Gloucester South Junction with a pair of trailers forming what is probably a Saturday auto service to Chalford circa 1963. The engine was not auto-fitted, so unlike the '14XX' 0-4-2Ts and '64XX' 0-6-0PTs that normally worked the service, it would have to run round the carriages at Chalford and haul them back bunker first. No. 9471 was built for BR by Robert Stephenson & Hawthorn Ltd and entered service at Horton Road on 30th April 1952. Apart from visits to works for repairs and overhauls, the engine spent its entire career based here, being withdrawn on 7th September 1964, shortly before the end of all the local passenger services. The train has just crossed over Chequers Bridge (GWR Bridge No. 113) spanning the east end of Barton Street; unfortunately, the Up side brick parapet has largely obscured another glimpse of Gloucester South Junction Signal Box in the distance beyond. The box closed on 25th May 1968 and South Junction was renamed Gloucester Yard Junction. PAUL RILEY/COURTESY THE RESTORATION & ARCHIVING TRUST/REF. PR1702

LEFT: On a map, the line between South and Tuffley junctions appears almost straight, so it is interesting to see the curve introduced in the background here by the use of a telephoto lens. On Wednesday 18th March 1970, No. D1064 *Western Regent* powers towards Tuffley Junction with train No. 1V70, the Down 'The Cornishman'. This name was applied by British Railways to the 9.15am from Wolverhampton Low Level to Penzance in 1952 but, by the late 1960s, a combination of line and station closures had seen its route much changed, whilst it was also extended north to start from Bradford; in May 1967, departure from Bradford Exchange station was at 7.06am, arriving Penzance at 17.55pm – a near 11 hour journey! Today, the Great Western Railway train operating company uses the name for a Paddington to Penzance express. *Western Regent* entered service from Crewe Works on 24th May 1963 and was withdrawn off Laira depot on 11th December 1975. CHRIS BALDWIN

RIGHT: Photographed from the footbridge spanning the line near Tuffley Junction, Class '47' No. 47128 was seen on 5th July 1975 with train No. 4B01, a Gloucester to Swindon parcels working. New as No. D1719 on 25th February 1964, the engine was based at Cardiff Canton when seen here, moving to Bristol Bath Road in May 1988. Renumbered twice more, as No. 47656 (on 22nd September 1986) and then No. 47811 (on 4th August 1989), the '47' is still in existence, owned by Locomotive Services Ltd at Crewe but used as a spare parts donor for others of the class in their fleet. NPC

BELOW: An unidentified 'Peak' on train No. 1V65 at the same location on Sunday 1st June 1975. This is likely to be the SuO 9.15am Birmingham New Street to Bristol Temple Meads, passing Gloucester at 10.37am. The row of houses above the train, which feature in all these pictures, are on Hartland Road. BILL POTTER/KRM

A fine panoramic study of the two bridges at Tuffley on 17th April 1965, with the Eastgate Loop just glimpsed coming in beneath Black Bridge on the left, as '9F' No. 92230 rumbles beneath the graceful red brick arch of the footbridge spanning the Western lines on the right. Entering service from Crewe Works at Banbury on 1st August 1958, the engine had seven further allocations in its brief seven years and five months career, including a seven month stint at Bromsgrove in 1964 as a Lickey banker. No. 92230 was based at Newport Ebbw Junction when seen here but spent its final two months in traffic allocated to Horton Road, becoming a victim then of the final cull of Western Region steam at the end of 1965. The lineside here today is heavily wooded but the arch remains albeit with iron railing parapets. COURTESY RAIL ONLINE

Heavily lime-stained '9F' classmate No. 92108 of Birkenhead Mollington Street shed produces a spectacular column of steam as it storms towards Stroud Road Bridge with a trainload of coal on 17th October 1965. As we shall shortly see, the photographer was here for the SLS Special but in common with a fellow 'photter' standing near the lineside on the south side of the bridge, was unable to resist the spectacle of No. 92108 passing by working very hard. TREVOR OWEN/COLOUR-RAIL

On a warm summer's day circa 1963, Horton Road shed's 'Large Prairie' No. 4100 steams towards Tuffley Junction with what is probably a Gloucester to Swindon three-coach 'stopper', the locomotive sporting an ordinary passenger lamp code. Whilst the Western and Midland pairs of lines met at this point, there was no physical connection between them until Standish Junction and that only permitted GWR/WR trains to run to and from the Bristol direction. However, in October 1964 a new crossover was laid in at Standish to allow Swindon line trains – specifically diesel-hauled expresses between Paddington and Cheltenham – to run via Eastgate, thus negating the need for a reversal or engine change at Gloucester, which ended steam-hauled passenger workings to/from Cheltenham. PAUL RILEY/COURTESY THE RESTORATION & ARCHIVING TRUST/REF. PR1724

As we saw in *Vol. 4A Gloucester Midland Lines Part 2 South*, a new junction providing a direct connection between the LMR and WR lines was put in at Tuffley in 1968, with the work commencing over the Bank Holiday weekend of 4th-6th May, when the Eastgate Loop was temporarily closed to allow the laying in of a point on the Midland Up line and a diamond crossover on the Down. The new junction opened when the connections on the WR side were completed in August 1968, with the route southwards then being reduced to two tracks. Photographed from Stroud Road bridge on Saturday 5th May, an unidentified green liveried 'Peak' heads past the works with train No. 1V80, the southbound 'The Devonian', which would normally have travelled via Eastgate and the loop line. In another sign of the transition taking place on the railways, the train is made up of four carriages in maroon and four in the new corporate blue and grey livery. Note too that the footbridge had already had its brick parapets replaced by railings by the date of this picture. CHRIS BALDWIN

'Peak' Class '45' No. 45072 heads an express through the junction. Taken in June 1976, this picture is out of date sequence with the following view and in fact shows the junction after the Eastgate Loop had closed. The signals by the junction are in fact those newly provided in December 1975 as a result of this. Built at Crewe Works and going new to Derby on 15th November 1961 as No. D127, the 'Peak' was based at Toton when seen here, having moved from Cricklewood East the previous month. Its service career ended on 26th April 1985 and it was scrapped by Vic Berry of Leicester in December 1986.
MIKE SQUIRE
COURTESY THE RESTORATION AND ARCHIVING TRUST
REF. MSZZ4295

Slightly out of date sequence as mentioned, this view, another gem from the camera of master photographer Bill Potter, shows a double-headed coal train carrying reporting No. 6Z97 heading through Tuffley Junction on 7th June 1975. Note that the new layout retained one Midland and one WR line. The pilot engine is 'Western' diesel-hydraulic No. D1069 *Western Vanguard*, whilst the train engine is Class '47' No. 47247 of Cardiff Canton depot. In common with most of the rest of the class, *Western Vanguard* was on its final allocation based at Plymouth Laira, from where it was withdrawn four months later on 6th October. It had entered traffic from Crewe Works at Cardiff Canton on 21st October 1963. By contrast, the Class '47' behind is still apparently in existence today, albeit quite where is something of a mystery which Google was unable to solve. The locomotive entered service as No. D1924 on 20th December 1965, becoming No. 47274 in December 1973. It subsequently became No. 47655 on 10th September 1986 and finally No. 47810 on 23rd February 1989, and has also been named three times: *Porterbrook* on 27th March 1996, *Captain Sensible* on 10th February 2007 (again reflecting the CEO of then owner Cotswold Rail's passion for punk rock music) and finally *Peter Bath MBE 1927-2006* by Direct Rail Services (DRS), who disposed of the engine circa 2018. The headcode indicates this to be a fully fitted block train (6) but not a regularly time-tabled one (Z), whilst the destination is a guess but quite probably Didcot Power Station, as these coal trains from South Wales were often routed through Gloucester instead of the Severn Tunnel. Bill Potter/KRM

RIGHT: No. 5971 *Merevale Hall* heads 'Light Engine' through Stroud Road Bridge at Tuffley Junction on Friday 30th July 1965. In the foreground is the connection to the Hempsted or New Docks Branch. The engine was new from Swindon Works on 17th April 1937 and had moved from Oxford shed to Worcester in early January 1965. It then transferred to Bristol Barrow Road during the four week period ending on 8th August, which may well be reason for the 'Light Engine' move we are seeing here. Withdrawal came at the end of December. DON MANN

ABOVE: This is another picture that would have been included in the previous volume if it had been to hand then, as it shows an LMR train on the Midland lines but using it here gives us a chance to see this end of the LM&SR ARP design signal box that controlled Tuffley Junction. 'Jubilee' Class No. 45608 *Gibraltar* heads past in October 1964, with what is likely to be a Bristol to Leeds express, the engine being based at Leeds Holbeck shed. The yellow strip on the cabside was a visual notification that the locomotive was prohibited from running beneath overhead electrification wires south of Crewe. New from Crewe Works on 13th July 1934, No. 45608 was withdrawn off Holbeck shed on 1st September 1965. JOHN CARTER/NPC

LEFT: We have seen the SLS 'GWR Cavalcade' rail tour of 17th October 1965 in previous volumes but this impressive view of 0-6-0PT No. 6435 and No. 7029 *Clun Castle* bursting through the arch of Stroud Road Bridge is well worth including here. NPC

Whilst waiting for the SLS Tour to pass by, No. 92108 was also photographed by the unknown cameraman who took that picture, who had trespassed down the bank almost to lineside to capture these shots. The same train seen four pages ago in Trevor Owen's picture, he is no doubt one of the photographers now peering over the parapet at the right-hand end of the bridge and there are others dotted around. Also built by Crewe Works but entering service at Wellingborough on 13th October 1956, the 2-10-0 had moved to Birkenhead from Leicester Midland shed in early April 1965. It was withdrawn in November 1967, after completing just over eleven years of revenue earning service. The steel mineral wagons are likely to be loaded with house coal and the train bound for London via Swindon and the Great Western Main Line. NPC

No. 1424 rattles past Tuffley Junction signal box with an auto service for Chalford circa summer 1963. The date is unlikely to be much later than this, as the 0-4-2T was withdrawn from Horton Road shed on 2nd December 1963. The box opened on 7th December 1941, replacing an earlier timber box of 1898 vintage, and was closed over the weekend of 10th-12th August 1968, after which the remaining points and signals here were power worked from the new Gloucester box. However, a ground frame was also provided here at the same time to operate an emergency trailing crossover, which is shown in the next picture; the frame was only in use for just over seven years, with point motors then being installed on the crossover so that it could be worked from Gloucester PSB. This was part of the December 1975 resignalling, after closure of Eastgate station and the Loop line. The Hempsted or New Docks Branch, seen here on the far side and which closed on 14th January 1971, was lifted at the same time. PAUL RILEY/COURTESY THE RESTORATION & ARCHIVING TRUST/REF. PR1703

LEFT: Class '37' No. 37228 heading 'Light Engine' through the remains of Tuffley Junction on 21st August 1976. By this date the only remaining connection here was for Quedgeley Depot Siding, heading south beneath Cole Avenue Bridge to serve the Dow-Mac works. The closed ground frame also appears to be still in place in the left distance, although the crossover it controlled was now power worked. Built at English Electric's Vulcan Foundry and new into service at Swansea Landore depot as No. D6928 on 28th February 1964, the engine had been transferred to the North Eastern Region in October 1967. It returned to South Wales in early February 1974, to Cardiff Canton where it was based when seen here. It became No. 37696 in 1986 and had a late adventure after coming into English, Welsh & Scottish Railway (EWS) hands after the rail privatisation of the 1990s, when it spent a year working in France in 1999-2000. It was finally withdrawn by DRS on 18th November 2014 and cut up by C.F. Booth, Rotherham a week later. NPC

RIGHT: Class '47' No. 47074 heads under Cole Avenue Bridge and through the site of the junction with the docks branch at the head of a northbound mixed freight on 27th May 1975. The lead wagons match those seen on page 167 and appear to be 50ft steel carriers of the type introduced by BR in 1973. The Brush type '4' was new on 12th February 1965 as No. D1658 and also entered service at Swansea Landore depot. Based at Cardiff Canton when seen here, it transferred to Bristol Bath Road two months after this picture was taken. It was renumbered twice more, as No. 47646 on 8th April 1986 and then No. 47852 on 7th February 1990, and was withdrawn on 1st March 1991. NPC

LEFT: Looking south from the bridge on Saturday 5th July 1975, as Class '47' No. 47083 *Orion* approaches with a freight, train No. 7V91, the Fridays only 22.12pm from Norwood to Severn Tunnel Junction. This was clearly running late but had also been diverted away from its normal route through the Severn Tunnel, presumably closed for maintenance over the weekend, so the train had most likely been delayed waiting for a path from Swindon to Gloucester. Going new into service from Crewe Works at Cardiff Canton on 13th March 1965 as No. D1668, the name *Orion* was bestowed in October that year by which time the engine had transferred to Swansea Landore depot. Back at Cardiff Canton when seen here, the locomotive was renumbered as No. 47633 in December 1985 and withdrawn in December 1991. On the right is Quedgeley Depot Siding to the Dow-Mac works. NPC

QUEDGELEY DOW-MAC FACTORY

Whilst I have generally tried to maintain the upper timeline for these books at 1975, for reasons explained in the Introduction, there are odd instances where coming forward a few more years is justified. In 1963, Dow-Mac Concrete Ltd opened a works at Quedgeley on a small part of the abandoned First World War munitions factory site (near Naas Crossing), for making precast concrete sleepers. The northern end of this site had been re-opened in 1941 as RAF Quedgeley, the home of No. 7 Maintenance Unit and had its own internal rail network, colour views of which remain elusive. Both were served via the long siding from Tuffley Junction, left in after the four tracks were reduced to two in 1968, which was termed the Quedgeley Depot Siding. The series of late 1980s views on the next two pages show the Dow-Mac factory, their locomotive and trips from Gloucester serving it.

ABOVE: Class '08' No. 08799 was photographed on 6th July 1989 with a long train of bogie flats, passing under Stroud Road Bridge. The 1975 resignalling and the opening of the new Gloucester Power Signal Box had seen the nomenclature for the lines change again. The fringe between Gloucester PSB and Bristol PSB was Charfield, so the train is crossing over from what was now the Down Charfield to the Up Charfield prior to accessing the Depot Line. The crossover is today motor worked from Gloucester PSB and now forms the end of bi-directional working from Gloucester station. Built at Derby Works and new into service as No. D3967 on 4th June 1960 at St. Blazey shed in Cornwall, the 0-6-0 was renumbered under TOPS in February 1974. No. 08799 became part of the EWS fleet in 1996. It was withdrawn circa 2015 and is now privately preserved on the East Kent Railway. JOHN SEARLE

ABOVE: No. 08836 had just gained the Depot Line when seen here circa 1987 with another lengthy train comprising five ex-LM&SR Tube opens at the front followed by a long rake of bogie flats. The '08' was new from Derby Works on 12th November 1960 as D4004 and is still at work today, with Great Western Railway as depot shunter at Reading. Milepost 95 is reading from from Derby and the signals were now numbered accordingly – DC (Down Charfield) or UC (Up Charfield) and then the milepost number, with A, B, C, etc appended for multiple signals inbetween mileposts. JOHN SEARLE

RIGHT: A view with no details, although this could well be No. 08836 again, tripping back to Gloucester having just passed beneath Cole Avenue Bridge. The train comprises three bogie bolster wagons loaded with concrete sleepers and two brake vans, providing extra braking power. The bridge was built in 1959, completing the final link in the city's southern ring road. JOHN SEARLE

LEFT: On 29th May 1986, the Dow-Mac works shunter collects three ex-LM&SR Tube wagons from the loop at the end of the Depot Line. The locomotive, a Class '165DE' 0-4-0 manufactured by Ruston & Hornsby (Works No. 418602 of 1958), will reverse past the main line signal and then propel the wagons into the works site. The white board in the distance may have been a 'do-not-proceed-past' indicator for the depot shunter. A hand-painted notice at the entrance to the works sidings that was still in existence in 1985 stated that Class '08's were allowed to enter to collect wagons and Class '35's ('Hymeks') were also permitted onto the shed road to pick up loads of concrete sleepers. JOHN SEARLE

ABOVE: By 1967, when various types of large pre-cast concrete units were being manufactured here, the factory had a workforce of 240 people but this number dwindled in later years. Here, on 27th February 1989, the works shunter draws wagons beneath the sleeper loading gantry. Dow-Mac acquired the engine from Stapleton Road Gas Works in August 1971, after it closed and where it had been since new. The locomotive was scrapped some time after the works closed around 2006 and the site is now a car storage facility. JOHN SEARLE

RIGHT: Class '37' No. 37237 passes the factory on 14th April 1987 with a Gloucester to Swindon ballast train, with driver Peter Jones and secondman John Hastings standing behind both leaning out of the cab for the photographer. New from English Electric's Vulcan Foundry on 13th May 1964 and entering service at Cardiff Canton as No. D6937, the locomotive was given its new TOPS number in September 1974. On 2nd October 1987, it was renumbered again as No. 37893, in which guise it lasted in service until being officially withdrawn in December 2009, having been stored since September 2007. It was cut up in April 2012. JOHN SEARLE

A light load for No. 5936 *Oakley Hall* about to head beneath Dunn's Bridge (MR Bridge No. 94), just to the north of Haresfield station, with a short freight bound for Swindon on 26th June 1963. Interestingly, the GWR named two of its 4-6-0s, of different classes, after country houses called Oakley and coincidentally, we will see the other one a couple of pages further on, at exactly the same location! Oakley Hall was and is a magnificent Queen Anne mansion on the borders of Shropshire and Staffordshire, whilst Oakley Grange is a large house near Corby in Northamptonshire. No. 5936's train comprises an oil tank wagon, an ancient looking wooden bodied coal wagon (possibly an ex-private owner), a Loriot well wagon, two steel minerals also loaded with coal, a box van and a BR brake van. New into service on 7th July 1963, No. 5936 was based at Reading from early May 1959 to late March 1963, when it transferred to Horton Road. It was withdrawn at the start of February 1965. The promontory in the background is Robinswood Hill. NPC

LEFT AND BELOW: John Strange positioned himself on the bridge one Saturday in August 1964 to photograph some of the passing trains and caught No. 1444 heading to Chalford, left, with a pair of auto trailers. Some time later, he captured the same combination hurrying back to Gloucester. Despite the speed, frequency and timings of the service, the auto trains just could not compete with the buses on sheer convenience. JOHN STRANGE/NPC

ABOVE: Still looking north from Dunn's Bridge, the other Oakley, No. 6823 *Oakley Grange* of Wolverhampton Oxley shed, slogs south with a mixed goods which included a significant number of coal wagons on 1st August 1964. New on 21st January 1937, the locomotive was withdrawn in late June 1965. NPC

BELOW: Four weeks later, on Saturday 29th August, another 'Grange', No. 6872 *Crawley Grange*, was seen with a goods train that was again mainly comprised of steel mineral wagons loaded with coal. The engine had entered service on 31st March 1939 and was based at Severn Tunnel Junction when seen here but the train had clearly been sent via Gloucester. Many of the coal trains originating from South Wales seem to have been routed away from the tunnel, although the working instructions contained within the *Sectional Appendix to the Working Time Table, Bristol Traffic District, October 1960* made it clear that there was no need to do so. Perhaps it was more to do with capacity on busy Saturdays. No. 6872 moved on to Cardiff East Docks shed in early November 1964, from where it was withdrawn on 21st July 1965 but it was then reinstated at Worcester two weeks later, on 6th August, its career finally ending on 31st December, the last day of WR steam. NPC

Turning round to look south from Dunn's Bridge, ex-GWR Class '28XX' No. 2882 was seen with a short Down freight of box vans and tank wagons heading north past Haresfield on 26th June 1963. The train has just passed the station, the platforms on the Midland side only just being visible in the right background. The elderly 2-8-0 was nearing the end of its long career when seen here, having entered service in April 1919. Based at Taunton, to where it had moved from Tyseley in April 1959, it was withdrawn six months after the picture was taken, on 16th December 1963. The engine's home location suggests that the train will have come up the Midland line from one of the Bristol yards. NPC

The GWR had no interest in serving the small village of Haresfield (population 458 in 1891 and 378 in 2011), so never provided any platforms on their pair of lines, leaving the passenger traffic for the Midland. Goods traffic meanwhile never amounted to much more than parcels, so no sidings were ever provided. Space between the two pairs of lines was also limited, so the Down platform was squeezed between the the Western Down Main and the Midland Down Main (the two companies operated their Ups and Downs in opposing directions between Standish Junction and Lansdown Junction at Cheltenham). The camera lens has not quite managed to 'stop' the smokebox end of No. 1458 here, as it propelled the Chalford auto back to Gloucester. A date of June 1962 had been added to the slide mount but this cannot be correct as No. 1458 was based at Oswestry at that date. More likely is April 1964, when the photographer made an extended visit here to photograph the station (see Vol. 4A), this view being taken from the level crossing at the south end. Trains speeding by so closely must have been quite scary for anyone standing on the platform and as a result, most travellers stayed on the Up side platform until their train was due. There was similarly no space for a footbridge, so crossing the line had to be undertaken with care and under the watchful eye of the Haresfield signalman. Note the train approaching on the Up Main, hauled by a Brush Type '4' with the Distant signal 'off' for a clear route through Standish Junction to head towards Stroud and Swindon. JOHN STRANGE/NPC

RIGHT: A slightly out of focus but nevertheless interesting view of the line just south of Haresfield, which is also a tad earlier than we generally see. Taken circa 1958, an ex-GWR 4-6-0 heads towards Gloucester with a Down express that includes several coaches in the 1950s carmine and cream livery. Meanwhile, an ex-LM&SR 4-4-0 passes on the adjacent Midland Down line with a four coach 'stopper' to Temple Meads. NPC

BELOW: Showing the same stretch of line but photographed from Martin's Bridge (MR No. 93 in the *Gloucester District Midland Bridge Register*) and looking back towards Haresfield station in the left distance, No. 8491 speeds by with a single auto trailer bound for Chalford on 26th June 1963. Built for British Railways by Robert Stephenson & Hawthorn Ltd and new into service on 31st August 1952 at Bristol St. Philip's Marsh shed, the '94XX' Class pannier tank was based at Horton Road from May 1959 until withdrawal on 23rd July 1963, a month after this picture was taken. It was not auto fitted, so would have to run round the trailer at Chalford. NPC

LEFT: We saw 'Large Prairie' No. 4109 deputising for a smaller tank engine on the Chalford auto a while ago and here we have another of Horton Road's stalwarts, '45XX' Class 'Small Prairie' No. 5545 strolling southwards with a single trailer on Thursday 25th June 1964. It all goes to show that in the days of steam, even on such a simple basic service as the Gloucester to Chalford auto, the dedicated photographer/ enthusiast/spotter never quite knew what to expect next! Were the service still running today, it would be in the hands of two or three different classes of DMU, in either two or three car sets, but all of fairly uniform conformity. NPC

LEFT: Class '57XX' pannier tank No. 4629 was also not auto fitted, hence why it is seen here on Wednesday 26th June 1963 passing Martin's Bridge and dragging its single trailer back to Gloucester having run round at Chalford. New into service from Swindon Works on 6th October 1942, the locomotive spent much of its life working from Kidderminster shed, moving to Horton Road in January 1963. It was enjoying its final few weeks in service when seen here, withdrawal taking place three months later in September 1963. The bridge, which was of similar design to No's 92 and 94, the two spans immediately to the south and north, carried a farm access track across the line but was demolished circa the late 1970s. NPC

RIGHT: No. 6848 *Toddington Grange* heads north towards Martin's Bridge with a long van train, which is likely to have originated from Avonmouth Docks, on 25th June 1964. New into stock on 22nd October 1937, the engine had transferred from Pontypool Road to Worcester in January 1964, from where it was withdrawn at the end of December 1965. Toddington Grange is in the Cotswolds village of Toddington, just north of Winchcombe, whilst its nearest station has been the home base of the Gloucestershire Warwickshire Railway since the early 1980s. This line will be explored in *Volume 6 Cheltenham and the Cotswolds Lines*. NPC

LEFT: Horton Road's 'Large Prairie' No. 4100 was seen passing Tuffley Junction on page 173, with a stopping service to Swindon and this would appear to be a corresponding return service, this time with classmate No. 4109 in charge, heading bunker first back to Gloucester on 25th July 1964. The train would have called at all stations from Swindon as far as Stonehouse but not at the Stroud Valley halts which were the preserve of the auto services.
TONY BOWLES/COURTESY THE RESTORATION & ARCHIVING TRUST/REF. ARC05543

Viewed from Butt's Bridge, the adjacent bracket signal frames No. 1409 as it heads past with the 11.20am Gloucester to Chalford service on Wednesday 29th August 1962. The arm for the Up Main Line is 'off' for the passage of the train, whilst the two smaller arms were for the two Up Goods Loops, which commenced just south of the bridge. Our only previous glimpse of the engine in this series was at Sharpness, where it was also to be cut up by Coopers Metals after withdrawal, but we shall see much more of it on the Chalford autos from here on. JOHN CARTER/NPC

Just twelve years later and the view from Butt's Bridge had changed markedly. In September 1974, 'Peak' diesel electric No. 45012 powers south with train No. 1V71, 'The Cornishman', the 07.00am express from Bradford to Penzance. All semaphore signals on the route had now gone, whilst the bracket signal seen in the previous picture had in any case become redundant with the removal of the two Up Goods Loops. The four tracks had also been reduced to two but, as mentioned previously, some of this track was retained as new Up and Down Loops, which remain today. They are staggered, with the Up Loop to the north of Haresfield Crossing, whilst the Down Loop is to the south of it. Note too that the Midland had ultimately won out over the Western as regards direction of travel on this section of railway, with the two remaining lines today being Up towards Gloucester and Down towards Standish. Pictures showing either of the loops in use are scarce, so this view is particularly interesting in showing a Class '37' hauled freight waiting in the Down Loop for the express to pass. No. 45012 went new from Crewe Works to Derby as No. D108 on 28th July 1961 but was based at Leeds Holbeck when seen here. It remained allocated there until withdrawal on 27th July 1988 and was cut up by MC Metals of Springburn in November 1992. The picture also shows Martin's Bridge still in situ, indicating its demolition took place at some date after this. NPC

LEFT: An unidentified '72XX' Class 2-8-2 tank passes the Haresfield Down Distant signal as it heads north beneath Martin's Bridge in 1960. This is the first of two pictures that were sent to me as colour prints, which I marked AG but have otherwise lost the details.

RIGHT: With his Up express apparently coasting with ease, the fireman of No. 6924 *Grantley Hall* has time for a breather as he leans from the cab on the fast section of four track main line between Haresfield and Standish Junction. New into service on 5th August 1941, the engine did have a short stint at Horton Road but only from October 1952 to March 1953. The slide is undated but is likely to be summer 1963 or 1964, when No. 6924 was based at Reading, with this being a London-bound express. The engine moved to Oxford in November 1964 and was withdrawn in October 1965. Martin's Bridge features again in the background. NPC

BELOW: The fireman of No. 1472 peers from the cab at the photographer as they speed through the arch of Butt's Bridge (MR No. 92) with a Chalford-bound auto on Saturday 25th July 1964. On the left is Bridge Farm House; the farm was a later addition to the scene, not appearing on the 1924 25 inch OS, and is still there today. TONY BOWLES/COURTESY THE RESTORATION & ARCHIVING TRUST/REF. ARC00270

LEFT: As we saw in *Vol. 4A: Gloucester Midland Lines South Part 1*, there were two goods loops on the Up side of the Western Region lines, installed in 1943. Coming into use on 26th September that year, they were used to hold slow freights until there was a clear road up the Stroud Valley to Sapperton, most of which also needed to halt for the assistance of a banking engine from either Stroud or Brimscombe, or south to Charfield on the Midland line, where there were further goods refuge loops. In July 1961, No. 1472 hurries past the loops with trailer cars No's 237 (a 63ft steel-panelled open built June 1954 to diagram A43) and 189 (a 62ft 8ins steel-panelled open built January 1933 to diagram A30 and condemned in November 1961) in tow. Note that the right-hand loop had been recently relaid with concrete sleepers; however, the other loop was never done.
JOHN STRANGE/ALAN SAINTY COLLECTION

ABOVE: In July 1961, No. 5035 *Coity Castle* of Swindon shed had no need to wait as it hurried past the exit point from the loops with an Up freight, which the engine may well have been capable of taking up Sapperton Bank on its own in any case. Entering service on 21st May 1935, the 'Castle' spent its career at top main line sheds, with allocations to Cardiff Canton (from new), Wolverhampton Stafford Road (from December 1935), Old Oak Common (from April 1940) and finally to Swindon in September 1960. It was withdrawn on 17th May 1962, four days short of its twenty-seventh birthday. NPC

RIGHT: Auto-fitted 0-6-0PT No. 6412 passes the same point with a Chalford train on 31st October 1964, the final day of the service. Note that the single post signal in the view above had now been replaced with a bracket signal, provided as a result of the new junction at Standish which had only been operational for five days when seen here, from Monday 26th October. NPC

Looking north now from Gloucester Road Bridge (MR No. 91), this is a rare colour view of an Up freight exiting the Up Goods Loops behind No. 7805 *Broome Manor* in the summer of 1962, with the bracket signal arm indicating that it was going to cross over to the Midland lines in front of Standish Junction signal box to head towards Bristol. This is a member of the class that we have not encountered before, although sadly is in a very neglected state here. New into service at Shrewsbury shed on on 27th March 1938, it spent nearly two years presumably working mostly Cambrian main line services before moving to Banbury in February 1940, remaining there for just over a decade. From September 1950 to October 1953 it was based at Newton Abbot, moving next to Hereford, from where it would no doubt have worked occasionally to Gloucester on Ross line trains. A fifteen week stay at Plymouth Laira in 1958, from June to late September, preceeded its next allocation to Cardiff Canton, where it was still based when seen here. On 17th June 1963, No. 7805 made its final move, to Tyseley, being entered into London Midland Region stock and from where it was withdrawn in December 1964. It was scrapped by Cashmores at their Great Bridge yard. NPC

ABOVE: An intriguing picture on 20th June 1964, with No. 6953 *Leighton Hall* having come to a halt at the bracket signal despite the arm for the route to Bristol being 'off'. Meanwhile, the fireman has set off along the 'four foot', presumably on his way to Standish Junction box to notify the signalman. Had the 'Hall' failed or was it suffering a problem which would require it setting back into one of the Goods Loops? New on 27th February 1943, *Leighton Hall* was converted to oil burning in April 1947 as No. 3953 but reverted back to coal fired and its original number in September 1948. Most of its BR career was spent based at Oxford, from where the engine was withdrawn when WR steam ended. RODNEY LISSENDEN

RIGHT: A rather dark view of No. 1426 hurrying back to Gloucester with an auto service from Chalford on 18th March 1961. However, the picture is included here because it again shows one of the Goods Loops in use, occupied by what appears to be (under heavy enlargement) a Class '4F' hauled coal train, which would be heading south to Bristol once the line was clear. MARK B. WARBURTON

RIGHT: The chance to photograph what was to all appearances a branch line train on the main line was too good to miss for many railway photographers of the early 1960s, particularly as the realisation dawned that such services had a limited life span. Consequently, we have a plethora of views of the Chalford auto from this period from which to choose but I have tried to hone it down to a representative selection of the best ones. We shall of course see much more of these trains as we head up the Stroud Valley. Here, No. 1440 propels its single trailer back to Gloucester in the summer of 1963. This was one of the class that was turned out in plain black livery, as we saw in the view of it in Horton Road yard on page 85. NPC

LEFT: On 8th August 1964, No. 1474 makes its way towards Butt's Bridge with a typical two-coach Saturday service ... ALAN JARVIS

LEFT: ... and is then seen again making the return journey around an hour and half later. The timings varied slightly but the trip took 40-45 minutes each way, usually slightly faster in the Down direction, presumably because it was downhill from Chalford and therefore the getaway from some of the halts a little quicker. In addition, some services had a layover at Chalford of up to 40 minutes whilst others crossed over to the Down Main Line and returned 10-15 minutes after arriving. So for instance, the Up service from Central at 2.10pm would pass Standish Junction signal box at 2.21pm and then again at 3.34pm after a quick turnaround at Chalford. However, the 11.20am from Gloucester arrived at Chalford at 12.05pm but did not then depart until 12.45pm, so the wait at Standish for the return was an hour and 46 minutes. ALAN JARVIS

No. 1472 on its way back to Gloucester with train No. 2H82 (the reporting number used in the *Working Time Table* for the rail motor service) on a summer Saturday in 1961. As the timings in the previous caption show, a journey time of between 40 and 45 minutes from Chalford, potentially including up to ten intermediate stops, was creditable indeed, with passengers being deposited around ten minutes walk from the city centre. Despite this, the service was withdrawn in the face of BR's drive for efficiency and modernisation, and also the failure of railbus services to pay their way, such as those on the Cirencester and Tetbury branches. NPC

A classic panorama showing the four-track approach to Standish Junction as we would all like to remember it. On 8th September 1962, ex-GWR 4-6-0 No. 5014 *Goodrich Castle* was about to take the Swindon line with an Up express which included three coaches still in chocolate and cream livery at the rear. The locomotive, which had entered service at Plymouth Laira on 7th July 1932, was based at Bristol Bath Road when seen here and was paired with Hawksworth slab-sided 4,000 gallon tender No. 4046, which records indicate had been from this day. On 14th June 1964, No. 5014 was transferred to LM Region stock when it moved to Tyseley, from where it was withdrawn in early February 1965. The unusual looking signal in the centre foreground was the Midland line Down Home for Standish Junction which, because of the limited clearance between the tracks, had its arm raised on a small bracket so that it was centrally positioned above the post. ALAN JARVIS

Smart looking No. 1476 makes the return journey in June 1962. Technically, the service started from Chalford, as the first train of the day commenced from there at 6.27am, the corresponding train from Gloucester departing at 6.55am. These two workings passed each other on the section between Haresfield and Standish Junction, the Chalford train arriving at Central at 7.06am. The service comprised thirteen trains each day in the Down direction, although one daytime train only ran Chalford-Stroud and another started from Brimscombe. One late night train also missed out some of the halts. In the Up direction there were twelve trains, one of which only ran Stonehouse-Brimscombe. In addition, there was also a late evening 10.31pm from Gloucester to Stroud on Thursdays only and a similar departure Saturdays only that ran right through to Chalford arriving 11.16pm. The Sunday service comprised four trains each way, with the first running in the early afternoon. Note the Midland Down Home signal 'off' for a train on that line.
PAUL STRONG/NPC

A slightly soft focus picture but again worth including because it raises questions, despite none of the locomotives being identifiable. Taken in August 1965, the ex-LM&SR '8F' 2-8-0 is running 'wrong line' along the Up Main with a Down loaded coal train bound for Bristol, whilst behind a pair of engineers wagons stand on the WR Down Main Line and behind them a convoy of five 'Light Engine's cross from the Up Main to the Down Main to steam towards Gloucester. Engineering works would seem to be the most likely explanation behind all this but the major works undertaken here, the laying in of the new double junction permitting WR trains to and from the Swindon direction to run directly onto the Midland pair of lines, had been carried out in October 1964. Part of this new junction can be seen immediately to the right of the '8F'. Also, the fact that the 2-8-0 is running south on the Midland Down line suggests that any trackwork that was being carried out was either on the Midland Up line or around the double junction in front of Standish Junction signal box that allowed trains on the WR pair of lines to access the line to and from Bristol. The convoy, which has an ex-GWR 'Mogul' at the rear, also includes a 'Britannia' Class 'Pacific', so is unlikely to be withdrawn engines going for scrap (only two 'Brits' had been withdrawn by this date, both in the north-west), so had they brought engineeering trains to site? NPC

ABOVE: '61XX' Class 'Large Prairie' tank No. 6106 was caught passing through 'Light Engine' on Saturday 8th August 1964. New in May 1931, the 2-6-2T moved from Reading to Swindon in January 1964 and then up to Worcester in the July. No. 6106 then returned to Swindon four weeks later, quite possibly after being given an overhaul in the Worcester Shops as its paintwork looks pristine here and this could well be the move back south. Further moves to Didcot (November 1964) and Southall (January 1965), precced its final allocation to Oxford shed in early September 1965, from where it was withdrawn at the end of December. ALAN JARVIS

LEFT: 'Britannia' Class No. 70045 *Lord Rowellan* cruises south with a summer Saturday holiday express on 7th August 1965. Courtesy of the apparently now unavailable Gloucestershire Railway Memories website, we know that this was in fact train No. 1V53, the 8.00am from Wolverhampton Low Level to Ilfracombe, which was loaded to eleven coaches. At Cheltenham Malvern Road the train was running four minutes late but, by the time it was seen here at Standish Junction, it was a couple of minutes ahead of schedule, whilst its 11.17am arrival at Temple Meads was ten minutes early. However, this was due to a generous time table rather than any outstanding performance by No. 70045. The engine came off the train at Temple Meads, handing over to an ex-GWR 4-6-0 which would take it on south to Taunton, where the train was split. *Taunton to Barnstaple Line* author Freddie Huxtable notes that a North British Class '22' would have taken the six coaches heading to Ilfracombe, whilst the other five went to Minehead behind a 'Hymek'. The 'Brit' meanwhile returned later that day and there is a picture of it passing just north of Yate in *Vol. 4B Gloucester Midland Lines Part 3: South* (page 419). Note the engine had lost its nameplates, replaced by a chalked inscription possibly for the local (to its Wolverhampton Oxley depot) football team. Incidentally, these were the last time-tabled steam services over the Honeybourne line, ending a month after this picture was taken. DON MANN

The Avonmouth to Bromford Bridge oil tanks had just crossed over from the Up Midland to the Down Western line at Standish Junction when photographed here from Butt's Bridge on 31st October 1964. Class '9F' No. 92137 will then be able to take the Avoiding Line at Gloucester to continue its journey northwards to Birmingham. New to Saltley shed on 31st July 1957, the 2-10-0 was still based there at the date of this view, moving to Croes Newydd in early August 1966 and then on to Carlisle Kingmoor four months later. It was withdrawn in early September 1967. The locomotive is passing over the new connection allowing trains from the WR Swindon line to run directly onto Midland metals (and *vice versa*) for the first time, the work having been completed just a week earlier. Two weeks prior to this, the trailing crossover in the middle distance had been moved around 100 yards northwards to allow space for the new double junction. MARK B. WARBURTON

Gloucester Road Bridge is on a near forty-five degree skew to the line, as shown here in this view of Brush Type '4' No. D1645 thundering northwards on 7th August 1965. The photographer recorded no details as regards the train but the '3V' headcode generally referred to north to south parcels workings, whilst the locomotive was based at Swansea Landore at the date of the picture, none of which helps particularly in identification. Built at Crewe Works and going new to Cardiff Canton on 24th December 1964, the two-tone green livery, whilst attractive, clearly did not wear all that well in traffic. Renumbered under TOPS in April 1974 as Class '47' No. 47061, the locomotive has been renumbered twice more since, becoming No. 47649 on 22nd May 1986 and then No. 47830 on 29th June 1989. The locomotive is now owned by Freightliner Heavy Haul and has become something of a company celebrity, having been repainted into two-tone green livery as No. D1645 and named *Beeching's Legacy*. DON MANN

RIGHT: Seen from the fields on the west side of the line at Standish and with the highpoint of Haresfield Beacon looking down from behind, No. 1445 propels its train back to Gloucester on 13th June 1964. JOHN GRANGER

BELOW: 'Mogul' No. 6365 heads for Swindon with a mixed freight in the summer of 1960. New in October 1925, the 2-6-0 arrived at Horton Road in early July 1954 and, apart from a month at Wolverhampton Oxley in mid-1955, spent the rest of its working life there, up to withdrawal on 21st October 1963. This is another print that I marked 'AG' but have otherwise lost the provenance. If whoever sent them can make contact again I will credit them in Vol. 5B.

BELOW: No. 6864 *Dymock Grange* trundles past the new double junction on 11th August 1965, hauling a very mixed fitted freight, probably heading to Swindon and including a breakdown crane and match truck. The engine was new into service at Old Oak Common on 24th February 1939 but was much travelled subsequently, with allocations successively to Oxford, Cardiff Canton, Penzance, St. Philip's Marsh, Oxley and finally Tyseley, where it was based when seen here; it was withdrawn two months after the picture was taken. The GWR Standard 6-ton crane is one of twenty-three built at Swindon between 1898 and 1923. Ahead of it is a recently painted 44-ton strip coil wagon, converted from a 50-ton 'Warflat' to BR diagram 421, code 'COIL E'. DON MANN

ABOVE: The much simplified layout at Standish Junction on 23rd August 1976, as Class '47' No. 47262 (formerly Brush Type '4' No. D1962) takes the Swindon line with a Cardiff to Paddington train which had been diverted to run via Gloucester – presumably the Severn Tunnel was undergoing maintenance. The locomotive was to be renumbered three more times, as No. 47608 in March 1984, No. 47833 in June 1989 and No. 47788 in March 1995. From 25th January 1993 it also carried the name Captain Peter Manisty RN, along with an explanatory plate: '*Captain Peter Manisty, MBE, DSC, RN, was a founding member of the British railway preservation movement having shared in the setting up of the Association of Railway Preservation Societies of which he was Chairman for many years*'. Stored unserviceable in August 2000, the '47' was scrapped two months later. Note the two emergency crossovers by the rear of the train. Operated from a new ground frame, they were installed over the weekend of 12th-14th October 1968, after the resignalling had been completed. BILL POTTER/KRM

ABOVE: A little later, Cardiff Canton depot's Class 37 No. 37228 was captured heading south 'Light Engine'. Coincidentally, we saw this same locomotive heading north 'Light Engine' on page 171, passing Tuffley Junction two days earlier on 21st August. The new diamond crossing laid in here was a switch diamond; these had moveable frogs that were switched away from the running rails, allowing trains to pass through at a faster speed whilst significantly reducing wear on the point. BILL POTTER/KRM

RIGHT: Finally, another Class '47' was caught on film – although Bill missed getting its number – hauling an Up goods with several very scruffy looking fitted wagons at the head of the consist. BILL POTTER/KRM

ABOVE: From the east side of Gloucester Road Bridge looking north west on 13th November 1976, a train of vans is seen taking the Swindon line headed by two unidentified locomotives, with a 'Peak' leading and a Class '31' tucked inside. MIKE SPICER/COURTESY THE RESTORATION & ARCHIVING TRUST/REF. MSZZ4186

BELOW: A little later on, Class '37' No. 37143 was photographed passing through the junction with a Gloucester to Swindon parcels train. New to Cardiff Canton as No. D6843 on 29th May 1963, the Type '3' was renumbered under TOPS in May 1974 – by which time it had returned to South Wales after an eight year spell in Scotland – and then again as No. 37800 in 1985. The locomotive is in service today with Rail Operations Group and used for *ad hoc* movements of rolling stock on behalf of various of the Train Operating Companies. In the early 2000s, when owned by EWS, No. 37800 also enjoyed stints in France and Spain working on the construction of new high speed lines. MIKE SPICER/COURTESY THE RESTORATION & ARCHIVING TRUST/REF. MSZZ4190

With the driver seen at the controls in the driving end of the trailer whilst the guard stands in the doorway, a Gloucester-bound auto clatters through Standish Junction on Saturday 13th June 1964. As we shall see, there were numerous excellent viewpoints around the immediate area of the divergence of the two routes, providing excellent panoramic scenes and we shall not compromise on the size of many of the pictures over the coming pages. Whilst the photographer failed to establish exactly the identity of the '14XX' here, we know it was either No. 1445 or No. 1453, which were both working the service that day. The Great Western Railway had secured a clause in the 1846 Act of Amalgamation which led to the formation of the Midland Railway, giving them running powers over the route between Standish and Bristol, hence why the junction between the two lines to allow running between Gloucester and Bristol was established much earlier. The first junction here was in fact opened in 1844 but was closed ten years later on 19th May 1854 and it was then not until the removal of the broad gauge rails that another junction was provided, opening on 21st April 1873. However, this too was subsequently closed, on 3rd January 1887, so the junction seen in these photographs was brought into use on 1st July 1908, at a period when the GWR were pushing new opportunities to serve Bristol from Birmingham via the then newly opened Honeybourne route. JOHN GRANGER

No. 7023 *Penrice Castle* negotiates the junction between the Midland and WR lines on Saturday 8th August 1964. This is another holiday express that we can identify thanks to the Gloucestershire Railway Memories site, as train No. 1M34, the 10.05am from Kingswear to Wolverhampton. The 'Castle' was a BR-build, entering service from Swindon Works on 24th June 1949. It had moved from Worcester shed to Wolverhampton Oxley on 14th June 1964 – eight weeks before the picture was taken – and was withdrawn early the following year, on 13th February. The lever frame, incidentally, was at the rear of the signal box, hence the stove chimneys being to the front. ALAN JARVIS

A fine view from Gloucester Road Bridge into the cab of No. 6937 *Conyngham Hall*, as it takes the route to Bristol on 14th August 1965. Standish Junction was an early installation of switch diamond crossings and we get a good view here through the one that the engine is about to negotiate. Note that we have an extra man on the footplate too, either an inspector or perhaps another driver cadging a lift back to Bristol. New from Swindon Works on 11th July 1942, the 'Hall' was based at Didcot from February 1960 but had transferred to Oxford around six weeks before this picture was taken. It was withdrawn on the last day of WR steam. The 18th century Conyngham Hall is a Grade II* listed mansion at Knaresborough, in Yorkshire. DON MANN

No. 5914 *Ripon Hall* drifts down the bank and over the junction with what is probably a Swindon to Gloucester 'stopper' on Wednesday 26th June 1963. In fact the WR lines were on quite a gentle gradient here but made to look much steeper by the Midland lines climbing up from Stonehouse. No. 5914 was one of the earlier 'Halls' completed at Swindon in July 1931. It was at Horton Road by early July 1952 but moved to Worcester a few weeks later and did not return until January 1958. Then, in March 1961 it went to Southall, followed by a move to Reading in July 1962. The engine made its last move, back to Horton Road, in March 1963 for its final ten months in traffic, withdrawal taking place on 22nd January 1964, which was followed by scrapping at Cashmores Newport yard in June. Note that the first two carriages of No. 5914's train are still in the rapidly being phased out by this date WR chocolate and cream livery. NPC

An evening shot, with the sun sinking in the west just lighting up Collett 0-6-0 No. 2251 and its train of assorted goods wagons heading north in August 1963. New in March 1930, the '22XX' had had two brief allocations to Horton Road, for three months between November 1957 and February 1958 and then a further three months from March to June 1958. The next four and a half years were spent in mid and west Wales and the borders, with the engine then moving to Bristol Barrow Road for a year and where it was based when seen here. It was withdrawn off Templecombe (S&D) shed in December 1963, a month after arriving there, not surprising given its tatty condition here. NPC

ABOVE: Saltley shed's '9F' No. 92125 heads across the junction to the Western lines with an Up express on 8th August 1964. Again we are helped by the Gloucestershire Railway Memories website, with this being one of three '9F's seen with northbound trains: a relief train going north to Bradford in the morning, train No. 1N01, behind No. 92160 of Kettering shed; No. 92125 here was on 1N40, the 10.20am Newton Abbot to Bradford and it was immediately followed by No. 92000 of Bristol Barrow Road with an Up relief service to Bradford, train No. 1N14. Halcyon days! All also used the Avoiding Line to by-pass Gloucester. ALAN JARVIS

Standish Junction was a Midland Type '4C' box opened on 28th June 1908, when a junction here between the MR and GWR lines that was removed in early 1887 was re-established. The box frame was extended from 40 to 44 levers in 1943, to control the new loops and signals on the GWR side. It closed on 14th October 1968. Here, on 18th March 1961, No. 1409 scoots past on its way to Chalford as a competing double-decker bus crosses Gloucester Road Bridge behind. MARK B. WARBURTON

On 17th October 1965, 'Hymek' No. D7004 glides beneath Gloucester Road Bridge and past Standish Junction signal box with a Cheltenham St. James to Swindon passenger service, train No. 2B29. This ran six times a day, Mondays to Saturdays, and called at Gloucester Central, Stroud and Kemble; three of the services also stopped at Stonehouse, whilst prior to their closure on 2nd November 1964, one of these three had also called at Brimscombe and Chalford, and another had called Chalford but not Brimscombe. One other service called at Chalford but not Stonehouse. Like the carriages that it is hauling, the locomotive is in fairly dirty condition but keeping the new diesels clean when they were generally shedded alongside smokey, sooty steam engines in the old steam age sheds was no easy task. However, No. D7004, which had been in service since coming new from Beyer, Peacock's Gorton Works on 15th August 1961, spent its entire career based at Bristol Bath Road shed, which had closed to steam in 1960 and been rebuilt as a modern diesel depot. It was withdrawn on 16th June 1962. The train includes a parcels coach at the front and note that, in a nod to steam age practice, the 'Hymeks' were graced with cast numerals applied just beneath the cab windows. TREVOR OWEN/COLOUR-RAIL

We saw No. 6412 and its two trailers on the last day of the Chalford autos a little earlier, on page 183 passing the south end of the loop sidings just north of the junction, and here it is seen again, moments later having just cleared the junction – the signal box can be discerned through the smoke beyond the rear coach. The bracket signal on the left held the Midland Up Home arms for the junction, that on the right reading for trains that were crossing over to the Western lines to head past Gloucester on the Avoiding Line. ROY DENISON

An unusual aspect from track level on the west side of the line, again taken on 8th August 1964 and looking back across the Midland metals as No. 1474 hurried past on the way to its first stop at Stonehouse. The ex-GWR, wooden, square-posted signal inbetween the tracks carried the Down Home arm for the junction and note too the yellow speed restriction sign below the bracket signal, with an arrow below pointing to the junction denoting that the maximum speed through it was 35mph. The dark clouds glowering overhead belie the summer Saturday date but a brief burst of sunlight had fortuitously penetrated through to illuminate the scene as the '14XX' scampered by. ALAN JARVIS

As the Midland lines drop away in the foreground, Swindon-built 'Western' Class diesel-hydraulic No. D1018 *Western Buccaneer* makes its way up the gentle climb from the junction and towards Stonehouse on 17th July 1965. Train No. 3A24 was the 8.55am parcels from Fishguard Harbour to Paddington, which included a portion picked up en route, probably at Carmarthen; the 6-wheeled milk tank for instance is likely to have originated from one of the two milk depots and creameries north of Lampeter, on the Aberystwyth to Carmarthen line. Note too the 4-wheeled flat wagon at the front with its sheeted load. *Western Buccaneer* was delivered new to Old Oak Common on 2nd April 1963, having taken almost 500 days for Swindon to build. The locomotive, which was based at Swansea Landore when seen here, was to be the first of the class to be broken up, in March 1974, having been withdrawn from Plymouth Laira depot on 4th June 1973. BILL POTTER/KRM

LEFT: Looking from the Midland lines, No. 6437 is seen hurrying through the arch of Standish Black Bridge (MR No. 90) spanning the Western lines with a Chalford train circa 1962. The auto-fitted pannier tank was based at Horton Road from May 1960 to withdrawal on 2nd July 1963. NPC

BELOW: No. 1472 on the same stretch of track with a two coach auto train circa 1964. For those a little concerned about the photographer's obvious vantage point – perched on a bracket signal on the Midland side of the railway – it should be pointed out that, as a Swindon apprentice, he would have secured a permit to cover his being there. The engine was one of several members of the class put into storage at Horton Road as soon as the service ceased. DAVID POLLARD

BELOW: We venture slightly 'off line' for this view of No. 92119 heading south on the Midland main line on 5th September 1964, passing the base of the embankment carrying the Western lines as they curve away towards Stroud and Swindon. It missed being included in Vol. 4A *Midland Lines South Part 1* but merits publication as a charming period study of a very young chap watching the mighty 2-10-0 as it rumbled through with the Bromford Bridge to Avonmouth empty oil tanks, so I have taken the opportunity to slip it in here. New from Crewe Works on 28th February 1957, the '9F' was allocated to Leicester Midland shed at the time of this view. It was to be withdrawn from Carlisle Kingmoor shed almost exactly three years later. The driver leans nonchalantly from his cab and would no doubt give the youngster a wave as he passed by. MARK B. WARBURTON

Photographer David Pollard then climbed up the WR Standish Down Distant signal to get this lovely shot of No. 6986 *Rydal Hall* leaning into the curve as it made its way to Swindon with a mixed freight comprised mostly of coal and a little bit of oil in 1964. This 'Modified Hall' Class 4-6-0 emerged from Swindon Works very early in the BR era, on 3rd March 1948, its first allocation being to Bristol St. Philip's Marsh shed. It then alternated between there and Bristol Bath Road for the next twelve and a half years, until moving to Swindon in October 1960. However, when seen here it had been based at Southall shed since early December 1962, from where it moved on to Didcot in March 1965 but was then withdrawn a month later. Standish Black Bridge, which carries an access lane to a farm, has changed little since these pictures were taken, although its parapets are now more green than black! DAVID POLLARD

Another fine shot from the camera of Bill Potter, as 0-4-2T No. 1453 climbs away from Standish Junction with its single trailer, past Black Bridge and towards Stonehouse on 3rd October 1964. Note the lattice post supporting the bracket signal on the left. The LM&SR used lattice posts for signals over 30ft in height up to 1944, increasing it to 35ft thereafter. BILL POTTER/KRM

Class '50' No. 50037 comes round the curve towards Standish Junction with an express from Paddington in August 1976. New from English Electric on 20th September 1968, the 'Hoover' (a nickname bestowed on the class for a fairly obvious reason) was based at Bristol Bath Road at the time of this view. Moving to Old Oak Common on 4th October 1987, it was withdrawn from there on 9th September 1991. Mike Spicer/Courtesy the Restoration & Archiving Trust/Ref. MSZZ4233

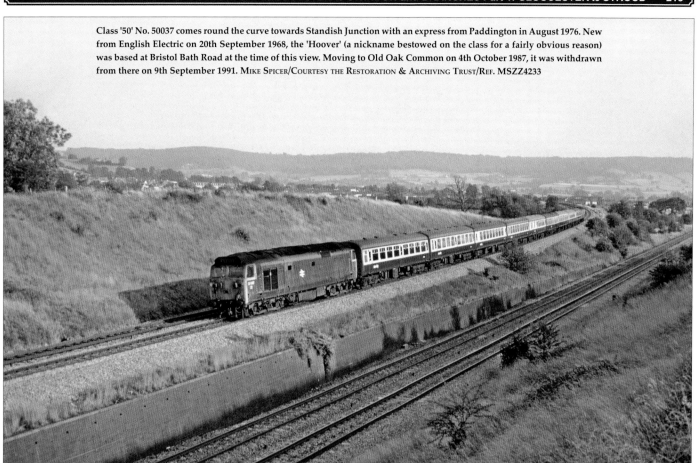

A little further round the curve towards Stroud and from just below the level of the line, 'Hymek' No. D7072 was photographed with train No. 1H57, the 11.35am from Paddington to Cheltenham express of just five BR Mk 1 coaches, on 3rd October 1964. Note the first carriage is still in chocolate and cream livery and thus matches nicely with the two tone green 'Hymek'. No. D7072 was new on 22nd March 1963 and based at Plymouth Laira at the date of the picture. It moved to Old Oak Common early the next year and was withdrawn off Cardiff Canton depot on 3rd October 1971. Bill Potter/KRM

We are now on the opposite side of the line, looking back towards Standish on Saturday 22nd August 1964, a gloriously warm sunny day of the sort that photographers and spotters loved, as the heat brought out the smell of the creosote in the sleepers which, combined with the scent of a hot steam locomotive, added greatly to the lineside 'experience'. A little further up on the right, three more enthusiasts wait to capture No. 6412 on film and in notebooks as the pannier tank propels its train back to Gloucester. ROY DENISON

No. 8403 climbs the gentle rise away from the junction with an auto working to Chalford on 17th October 1964, a fortnight before the service ended. New from W.G. Bagnall of Stafford on 30th September 1949, the engine was based at Horton Road for only a short time, from September 1964 to January 1965, when it moved to Bristol Barrow Road, from where it was withdrawn on 16th June. TONY BOWLES/COURTESY THE RESTORATION & ARCHIVING TRUST/REF. ARC00407

We cross back over the tracks again for this view of non-auto fitted Class '57XX' No. 3775 passing the Standish Down Distant in February 1962. ROY DENISON

ABOVE: As well as No. 6412, No. 1458 was also on Chalford auto duties on Saturday 22nd August 1964 and is seen here heading back to Gloucester. ROY DENISON

BELOW: No. 1458 propels the 15.10pm Chalford to Gloucester Central towards Standish Junction on 3rd October 1964. Incidentally, the glorious conditions depicted in this series of pictures that Bill took at Standish that day did not seem to equate with an October date, so I queried this with David Postle at Kidderminster Railway Museum but was assured the information was correct. I then did a web search of the weather for autumn 1964 and found the following: '*The first 5 days of October were dry, sunny and warm. The temperature on the 5th reached 20°C. The weather then became unsettled and cooler.*' An Indian Summer! BILL POTTER/KRM

Bill made the most of the fine weather that graced Saturday 3rd October 1964 and on the same curve away from the junction took this view of 'Castle' Class 4-6-0 No. 7013 *Bristol Castle*, at the head of an Up goods train. This engine was one of the first of the class built, completed at Swindon Works in April 1924 as No. 4082 *Windsor Castle*. Appropriately, it then had a long association with the British Royal family, being chosen as the Royal engine after being driven from Swindon works to the station by King George V, accompanied by Queen Mary, on 28th April 1924, with plaques to commemorate the occasion being mounted on the side of the cab. However, when King George VI died suddenly in February 1952, No. 4082 was in Swindon Works awaiting repair, so in order to maintain the tradition, the number and nameplates, and the commemorative plaques, were transferred to the much newer (July 1948 BR-built) No. 7013 *Bristol Castle* to haul the funeral train, the engine then assuming the identity permanently. Thus the engine seen here is the original 1924-built No. 4082 as driven by King George V. Allocated to Tyseley shed in June 1964, No. 7013 was withdrawn in February 1965 having travelled around two million miles in service. Sadly, the engine's illustrious past was not enough to save it from being scrapped, by Cox & Danks at Park Royal, whilst it had already lost its nameplates when photographed here. BILL POTTER/KRM

Back to February 1962 again, when this three-coach auto was photographed heading back to Gloucester, with an unidentified auto-fitted '64XX' 0-6-0PT providing the power. This strengthened service shows that, whilst it was the practice for trailers to have their driving compartment at the Gloucester end, as the maximum number allowed to be propelled was two, the third one had to go behind the locomotive. ROY DENISON

Still down the slope a little way again for this dramatic view with the sky as a backdrop, as an unknown '28XX' 2-8-0 drifted past with a mixed goods. ROY DENISON

SECTION 4

STONEHOUSE BURDETT ROAD to STROUD

The ex-GWR main line from Standish Junction to Stroud, as shown on the 1961 1 inch OS (enlarged by 200%). The freight only (by this date) branch on the opposite side of the valley, from Stonehouse Bristol Road to Dudbridge, Stroud Midland and Nailsworth, is also shown; this was followed in Vol. 4A.

As the ex-GWR line curved away westwards from Standish Junction, it passed through the small town of Stonehouse, which lies at the foot of Doverow Hill. Once having two stations serving a population of just 4,350 inhabitants at the end of the 19th century, this has now grown to around 7,300 but only the GWR station, opened with the line on 1st June 1845, is still in use. It was renamed Stonehouse Burdett Road in 1951 to distinguish it from the station on the Midland line, which was also renamed as Stonehouse Bristol Road. However, it reverted to simply Stonehouse from 1968, BR having closed Bristol Road station. Sadly, in an all too familiar act of corporate vandalism, British Railways demolished the original listed Brunellian station buildings in the mid-1970s after threatening complete closure of the station if they were not permitted to do so. The goods shed had gone in the late 1960s, the signal box survived until the 1990s but has now gone too; however, the footbridge remains. The much simplified

A Saturday service rounds the curve between Stonehouse and Standish Junction in May 1963. The train has just passed over Oldends Lane Bridge, whilst in the left background is part of the Cotswold Green Estate, then on the northern edge of the town but soon to be swallowed up by further development. NPC

station has also benefitted from a recent £300,000 upgrade, which saw the platforms lengthened from two to four coaches and a new ticket office and information centre provided.

The four miles of main line between Standish and Stroud is relatively level, the climb up the valley to Chalford not starting until after Stroud station. Although we refer here to the Stroud Valley, the town is in fact the hub for five valleys, none of which are called Stroud! Clockwise from north-west of Stonehouse they are: Ruscombe, Painswick, Slad, Chalford and Nailsworth, and it is the Chalford Valley, popularly known as 'The Golden Valley', up which the railway wends its way from Stroud. The Stonehouse Valley, which the line

traverses to Stroud, is not a part of the 'Five Valleys' group. Ribbon development along the lower south facing slopes of the Stonehouse Valley produced a number of smaller villages which the railway was able to serve from the early years of the 20th century via a series of halts, the three provided on this section of line, at Ebley, Cashes Green and Downfield, following each other in quick succession. Sadly, despite the seeming sheer convenience and frequency of the service provided, it was not to survive BR's vicious cull of secondary passenger services in the 1960s and all of the halts closed on and from 2nd November 1964. Such was their basic nature, nothing remains today to mark their existence.

LEFT: The embankment between Stonehouse and Standish, looking from what are now the playing fields on the north side of Oldends Lane, as No. 6437 propels back to Gloucester on Saturday 17th March 1962. NPC

BELOW: On 22nd August 1964, a similar two trailer combination to that already seen behind No. 6412 (page 216) and No. 1458 (page 218) was photographed heading back to Gloucester on a later service, crossing Oldends Lane Bridge, about half a mile to the east of Stonehouse station. The trailers are clearly not the same, so this will also be a different engine, which means that three locomotives were required to work the service, which was normal. Taking into account the preparation involved, it all goes to show why the labour intensive steam railway was failing to compete with road transport. No one then foresaw the horrendous expansion in road use over the subsequent decades. A housing estate now occupies the land in the foreground, with Ryelands Road running across where the photographer was standing. ROY DENISON

Also on the auto service on 17th October 1964 with No. 8403, seen just now, was one of Horton Road's complement of '14XX' 0-4-2Ts, although photographer Tony Bowles was too far away to record the number. This train was also seen crossing Oldends Lane Bridge but we are now on the opposite side of the line, so it is heading to Chalford. The land on this side of the railway is no longer green fields either, with development here beginning within a couple of years of this picture being taken. The Shrubberies – a school for children with learning disabilities – now occupies this field in which the photographer was standing.

Tony Bowles/Courtesy the Restoration & Archiving Trust/Ref. ARC00408

RIGHT AND BELOW: These two views of No. 1473 waiting in the Stonehouse Up Refuge Siding on Saturday 12th August 1961 are most unusual. Placing an auto working here would have been a rare occurrence, as reversing a passenger train in over what was now effectively a facing point meant it had to be clipped open and then closed again once the train was inside, with the process reversed to bring it out again. The clips were kept in the signal box and the process could be carried out by a trained porter. However, it all took time, so would only be carried out in exceptional circumstances, particularly as it meant that the auto service was now behind time. We can surmise that the likely course of events on this day began with the Up 'Cheltenham Spa Express' running late, perhaps delayed for some reason in leaving Cheltenham. The crew of the auto were thus probably

warned before leaving Gloucester Central that they were going to be refuged at Stonehouse to allow it to pass and not delay it any further heading up the Stroud Valley. They were obviously held here for a little while, as the driver has had time to go round with the oil can, seen on the bufferbeam as the 'Castle'-hauled CSE sped past. It is just possible that, if there had been only a few passengers on board the auto, they could have been politely asked to get off the train at Stonehouse and wait in the Up shelter, which meant that clipping the point would not then have been required. The photographer (John Strange almost certainly took both pictures) was thus very lucky to have been on hand to record this rare event. Incidentally, there was a footpath which crossed the line here to The Globe Inn, which because it bisected the siding and could therefore be deemed a hazard for folk trying to cross if there was a lengthy train parked there, required a special instruction – see the extract below from the *Sectional Appendix to the Working Time Table, Gloucester Traffic District, October 1960.* ABOVE: COURTESY RAIL ONLINE; BELOW: JOHN STRANGE/ALAN SAINTY COLLECTION

STONEHOUSE (BURDETT ROAD)

Globe Footpath Crossing
    Whenever a train is shunted into the Up Refuge Siding at Stonehouse and stands foul of the above crossing, the Guard must part the train to give free passage for pedestrians.
    Enginemen must sound the engine whistle when shunting into this Siding.

No. 1453 departs Stonehouse for Gloucester over the narrow, headroom restricted Queen's Road Bridge on Saturday 23rd May 1964. Since these pictures were taken, the bridge has been rebuilt with a new deck and the stone pillars have gone. The cast iron sign in the foreground would now be a very collectable piece of railwayana. BILL POTTER/KRM

On the same day, No. 1444 was also seen on auto duties but with a single trailer. This would have been the 4.05pm auto from Chalford, which had arrived here at 4.30pm and after a short wait, would then use the crossover in front of the engine to form the 4.40pm service from Stonehouse to Brimscombe. The crossover was equipped with a facing point lock (the point is already in position) and a disc signal (already showing 'clear'). The photographer's wife and daughter pose with the driver and guard. BILL POTTER/KRM

No. 1424 draws into Stonehouse Burdett Road with an Up service in April 1962. Note that the name addition was appended on a separate board beneath the main nameboard. M.E.J. Deane, courtesy Dr Simon Fosbury

Two months later, on Tuesday 5th June 1962, No. 1409 was photographed at the same spot with the usual single trailer that made up a mid-week service. Entering service at Exeter on 14th October 1932, the 0-4-2T moved to Gloucester in the summer of 1942, where it spent the next fourteen years, mostly sub-shedded at Lydney, before being put into store in November 1956. Subsequently reinstated at Gloucester on 16th June 1959, it was based at Barnwood from April 1963, working Sharpness Branch services for its last six months in traffic, until withdrawal on 14th October. A long rake of vans can be seen parked in the Up Refuge Siding in the left background. Alan Jarvis

No. 1409 again, starting away for Gloucester in October 1962 after dropping off several passengers, an evocative scene lit up by a burst of sunlight after a shower of rain. The picture is only spoilt by the cement post and chain link fence on the left, which jars with the ex-GWR wooden paling fence on the right, but presumably the original on this side had rotted and had to be replaced. The main approach to the station was via Great Western Road but for those who lived at the north end of the town there was a short cut off the end of the Down platform and along a little footpath descending to Queen's Road. This no longer exists, whilst the platforms in any case now end around 50 yards short of where they used to. ROY DENISON

LEFT: As we travel up the Stonehouse Valley to Stroud we shall see some more unusual auto workings and here is our first glimpse of one, with an unknown '14XX' tank and three trailers at the station in 1961. Although we do not have an exact date, this will have been a strengthened Saturday service. GERALD PEACOCK

ABOVE: An unidentified 'Hymek' drifts into the Up platform in November 1964 with train No. 2B29, the same Cheltenham to Swindon service that we saw a picture of in November 1965 on page 208. Departures from St. James station were at 7.05am, 8.55am*, 11.55am, 2.35pm*, 6.00pm and 6.55pm*, with only those asterisked stopping here at Stonehouse but it is not clear if this was one of those trains or one of the other three heading straight through. NPC

RIGHT: Passengers alighting from and boarding an Up train hauled by No. 1424 on 5th June 1962. ALAN JARVIS

A view west towards Standish Junction in October 1964, as No. 1458 pauses with a Saturday train during the final days of the auto services. One of the boards bottom left no doubt holds the BR notice detailing the cessation of the service and the closure of the halts and stations that it served. The original broad gauge station buildings, accredited to Brunel, have sadly not survived, despite being listed, being demolished in the late 1970s after British Railways threatened total closure. Even then, the local parish council had to raise £13,500 as a contribution towards the cost of 'improving' the station. We get a glimpse here inside the main building on the Down platform and of the cast iron brackets supporting the canopy of the smaller shelter on the Up side. Note that both platforms had road access, as they still do today. The crossover in the foreground was used by the once daily Down auto service that terminated here and then crossed over to run back to Brimscombe. However, it was originally provided in September 1891, in conjunction with the laying of a new loop siding on the Up side serving the Stonehouse Brick & Tile Company's new works. NPC

LEFT: A general view of the station and the main building looking from the Up platform circa 1962. Notice the drop in height at this end of the Down platform, reflecting the length and height as originally built in the 1840s. Early broad gauge trains were much shorter, so most stations built during that period had to have their platforms lengthened subsequently or be rebuilt completely. However, at Stonehouse, no effort was ever made to raise the height of this section of the Down platform, no doubt because it would have involved significant work to raise the building too, although this was done elsewhere. At Chepstow, for instance, the main building was lifted up on jacks in 1877, so that the platform could be raised by 2ft. Interestingly, as can be seen, this drop in height was not replicated on the Up side, where the platform was simply lengthened at the same height. NPC

RIGHT: No. 1453, with its distinctive homemade replacement smokebox numberplate, starts away for Gloucester in May 1963, having been seen off by the station master and a porter. The extra height of the lengthened Down platform at this end of the station meant that auto workings stopped here for the convenience and safety of passengers. However, this section was only a little over two coaches in length so those on longer trains were advised to take care and to alight from carriages nearer the engine. Note the Stonehouse Burdett Road totem bolted to the fence at the rear of the Up platform. NPC

LEFT: The view looking west from the footbridge in December 1966. Whilst the buildings look the same and platform trolleys still abound, numerous changes had taken place. The crossover had been removed in January of the previous year, as had the Up Refuge Siding in the right background. The wooden paling fence at the rear of the Up platform had also now gone, replaced by iron railings, whilst all trains passing through the station had been diesel hauled since the start of the year. NPC

On the last day of the service, Saturday 31st October 1964, No. 6437 prepares to leave at the head of the 10.20am auto working from Gloucester Central to Chalford. The official closure date was almost always on a Monday and from the start of the day, so with many lines not having a Sunday service, most 'last trains' ran on the preceding Saturday. The Chalford autos were unusual in that there was a Sunday service but it seems that this was not operated on 1st November 1964 and consequently, the official closure date is noted as being 'on and from Monday 2nd November 1964', which is in line with all of the other Gloucester area local passenger services that were withdrawn on the same day. A footbridge was not provided when the station first opened, nor is one shown on the 1st edition 25 inch OS surveyed in 1882 but it does appear on the 1901 survey. To a standard late 19th century GWR design, it may have been erected when the new brickworks siding and connections were added in 1891. It survives with some minor alterations today. BILL POTTER/KRM

ABOVE: For the benefit of modellers and historians, the next few pages present various aspects of the Brunellian station buildings in the years preceding their demolition. This first view is looking west in 1968-70. The signal box was still in operation controlling the few remaining semaphores, whilst in the foreground, the last remaining connection into the goods yard was not taken out until 7th September 1970. Comparison with the view from a similar position on the previous page will show how much of the steam age railway paraphernalia had gone. Note, however, the overloaded coal bunker, which supplied the signal box stove. The ground level angle of this view also clearly shows the low height of the Up platform, which was only raised after the buildings had been demolished. SEAN BOLAN

ABOVE: Looking east towards the derelict goods yard on a rainy day in late 1970 or 1971, with the drizzle having slightly affected the camera's ability to focus. A large scale 50 inch OS map published in 1969 does not include the goods shed, which is likely to have been demolished around the time the Stonehouse Coal Concentration Co. began using one of the sidings in the yard in 1966. Of the three original Brunellian goods sheds built for when the line opened, at Brimscombe, Stroud and here at Stonehouse, fortunately the one at Stroud has survived. The Coal Concentration siding is recorded as closing on 5th October 1970 but it is probable that their operations here had ceased much earlier, as the depot is not shown on the map mentioned above. SEAN BOLAN

ABOVE: Plain track running right through the station in this circa 1971 view looking east. SEAN BOLAN

RIGHT: A view of the station, signal box and footbridge looking north in the early 1970s. SEAN BOLAN

ABOVE: Stonehouse Signal Box in the early 1970s, after closure. The box seen here dated from 1922 and was a replacement for an earlier box that was in place by 1882 (according to the 1st edition 25 inch OS surveyed in that year), which was on the same or an immediately adjacent site. The 1922 box had a part timber upper storey on a red brick base and measured 25ft by 11ft, with the operating floor at a height of 8ft. It housed a GW Type VT3 frame with 40 levers at 4ins centres and closed on 5th October 1970. However, it was not removed, finding a new use as a permanent way storage shed and mess room, in which guise it survived for another two decades at least, being demolished eventually circa the early 1990s. SEAN BOLAN

LEFT: An unidentified 'Western' cruises through the station with a Down express. The locomotive's livery of maroon sides with full yellow ends again puts a 1969-70 date on the picture and note the BR(WR) brown & cream totem still hanging from the railings on the left, which would now sell for around £1,500 at a railwayana auction. SEAN BOLAN

ABOVE AND BELOW: Front and rear elevations of the Down side main building circa 1970. By this date the station was no longer fully manned and the entrance into the building from the approach along Burdett Road had been closed and boarded up. BOTH SEAN BOLAN

ABOVE AND BELOW: These front and rear elevations of the stylish Up side shelter were taken on the same occasion. The attractive Italianate chimney was a typically Brunellian touch. The terrace of houses in the background facing Upper Queen's Road still remains. BOTH SEAN BOLAN

With his lever cloth in his hand, the signalman gives a wave as No. 1424 sprints away with a Chalford-bound auto service on 5th June 1962. The acceleration of these small tank engines on short trains such as this was impressive and hence they were perfect for the auto workings, with their frequent stops and tight time-tabling, which they were well able to maintain. Note that the footbridge was still painted in WR cream at this date. ALAN JARVIS

A couple of months earlier, on 14th April 1962, No. 1409 was photographed propelling back into the station past the goods shed. This was also a typical Brunel design, with one side for rail access and the arches on the other side for road vehicles. The yard crane was of 5-ton capacity. MARK B. WARBURTON

Moments after the previous picture was taken, No. 1409 is seen easing past the signal box into the Down platform. This view just shows the vehicular access gateway into the goods yard, with the ground dropping away slightly behind the station, and also the end loading dock adjacent to the signal box, the area around which was all looking rather untidy at this time. MARK B. WARBURTON

2nd - SINGLE   SINGLE - 2nd
       Stroud to   Stroud
Stroud   Stonehouse
Stonehouse   Burdett Road
Burdett Road
(W) STONEHOUSE BURDETT ROAD (W)
            9d. Fare 9d.
For conditions see over For conditions see over
6467
6467

RIGHT: The 3.10pm from Gloucester Central sets off from Stonehouse behind No. 1445 on Saturday 9th May 1964. If running to time – and these services almost invariably were – the time was now 3.31pm, with the next stop at Ebley Crossing Halt a mile further along scheduled for 3.33pm. NPC

LEFT: Looking across the tarmacadamed section of the goods yard on the same day, as No. 1451 propels in with two trailers forming the 3.05pm from Chalford to Gloucester. This was due here at 3.31pm, so must have crossed with No. 1445, above, a few moments earlier. The guard/conductor stands in the open doorway of the trailer next to the engine, ready to alight first and moniter those leaving or joining the train. NPC

RIGHT: Back to October 1963 for this view of an Up trainload of coal passing through, headed by Class '28XX' 2-8-0 No. 3823. This is likely to have been South Wales coal, with the locomotive having just moved from Oxford to Neath Court Sart shed at the time of the picture. New into service on 6th May 1940, it moved on to Severn Tunnel Junction in early November 1964 and was withdrawn on 2nd July 1965. NPC

On Saturday 3rd October 1964, No. 1453 is seen starting away with the 4.40pm Stonehouse to Brimscombe auto, past the Stonehouse Brick & Tile Co. Ltd's offices. Note the lovely little Morris Commercial Series Z 5cwt van in the yard behind. Based upon the Morris Eight, it had separate headlights rather than having them incorporated into the front wings. Introduced in late 1939, they were widely used by GPO Telephones and Royal Mail. The front end of the vehicle was basically a Morris Series E (introduced in late 1938) with modifications insomuch that it used the Series E engine but was fitted with the earlier type 3-speed gearbox. They remained in production after the war until replaced by the Minor based van. The registration number, KDC 906, was Middlesbrough issued. BILL POTTER/KRM

On the last day, No. 6412 heads off to Chalford with the 10.20am from Gloucester Central. BILL POTTER/KRM

Another '28XX' 2-8-0, No. 2841 of Reading shed, rumbles through with a mixed goods carrying an express unfitted freight lamp code on Saturday 14th April 1962. The first member of this class, No. 2800, was constructed at Swindon in 1903, with a further twenty following in 1905 and ten more in 1907, and so successful was this new design, the first 2-8-0s in this country, that they were still being built, with little change, thirty-five years later. No. 2841 was one of a batch of ten completed in 1912, emerging from Swindon Works in October of that year. It moved on from Reading to Southall in March 1963 and was withdrawn from there near the end of the year on 16th December, by which time it had completed over fifty-one years in traffic, a testament to the success and durability of Churchward's original design. The yard closed to general goods traffic in the first half of 1964, with the loop siding beyond the goods shed, the main line connection at that end and a siding serving the livestock pens all being lifted on 21st June. The line running into the goods shed was retained, as was the siding branching off to the right, which was later used by the Stonehouse Coal Concentration Co., probably from the same time as they established their depot at Stonehouse Bristol Road station, on 7th October 1966. MARK B. WARBURTON

Looking towards Stroud from the footbridge in October 1964, the bright sunshine and blue sky suggesting that we are back to the fine weather of Saturday 3rd October again. We are also almost certainly looking at the same two services that we saw on page 238, at just after 3.30pm, with the outgoing 3.10pm from Gloucester crossing with the incoming 3.05pm from Chalford just by the goods shed. The Stonehouse Brick & Tile Co. Ltd was established in 1891, with a new loop siding to serve the works being provided in that year; the Private Siding Agreement (PSA) with the GWR was dated 9th September 1891. Rail transport had ceased in 1959, with the PSA being terminated on 8th November, but the siding remained in place for several more years, being lifted on 21st June 1964, although clearly only the rails were taken away initially, leaving the sleepers to be collected at a later date. As the selection of lorries in the yard shows, road transport was used after 1959. By the date of this picture, the goods yard was only in use by the engineers. NPC

ABOVE: The three trailer service we saw at the platform on page 228 is here seen arriving past the goods shed in summer 1961, with the impressive brickworks chimney dominating the background. Part of the site was levelled before construction of the works began in 1890, with brick making starting the following year. The clay was dug from Gay's Hill behind, with the pit gradually eating further into the hillside over the decades. The success of the works enabled the original No. 1 plant – kilns, brickmaking machinery, horizontal high pressure steam engine, Cornish boiler, grinding rolls and haulage gear – to be augmented by the construction of No. 2 plant in 1898 – a new steam engine, boiler, brickmaking machinery, dryers and five new kilns – more than doubling capacity. The chimney, which we shall see again shortly, was completed in 1900. Further improvements were made in the late 1930s, after a consortium of Gloucester building companies had purchased the works, with additional kilns being constructed and a ground-mounted monorail system installed to move the brickearth from the clay face to the brickmaking area, supplementing the 2ft gauge tramway in the clay pit on which tram tubs were pushed around by hand. Around 1960, an extension into a new clay pit was worked by a 4-wheeled diesel mechanical engine of unknown origin. However, after running profitably through the first half of the 20th century, competition from larger producers, such as the London Brick Company,

began to have a detrimental effect and this, coupled with production difficulties, forced the company into voluntary liquidation at the end of 1962. After purchase of the works the following year, a new company, the Stonehouse Brick & Tile Co. (1963) Ltd, was formed, which traded until early 1968, when it finally closed for good, although it took several months to remove the three million bricks still in stock. The site is now covered by the Rosedale housing estate. For anyone interested, typing Stonehouse Brick & Tile Company into a web search brings up a film on You Tube, 9 mins 34 secs of black & white and colour cine shot in 1945, showing the clay being dug and moved in tubs on the 2ft gauge tramway, bricks being fired in the kilns and other shots around the works – fascinating, although there is only the briefest of glimpses of the railway. GERALD PEACOCK

RIGHT: With the driver visible through the trailer cab window and the fireman peering out from the cab of the engine, a Gloucester-bound service arrives past the goods shed in October 1962. ROY DENISON

ABOVE AND BELOW: The track layout at Stonehouse station was rationalised in stages. First to be taken out of use, on 31st March 1963, was the east end main line connection of the brickworks loop siding. As already noted, the sidings at that end of the goods yard were removed on 21st June 1964, along with the brickworks siding. On 26th January 1965, the Up and Down Refuge sidings were taken out of use, along with the two trailing crossovers. These two views, dated Sunday 4th April 1965 and annotated '*removal of crossover*' (above) and '*2-6-2T ballast duties*' (below), now confirm the date of their actual removal. A date for when the Refuge sidings were lifted has not yet been found but there is no sign of the Down Refuge in the centre distance, so a March 1965 date would seem likely. The remaining trackwork in the goods yard was taken out of use on 7th September 1970 and removed on 5th October when the Stonehouse Coal Concentration Co's PSA was officially terminated. The brickworks is again busy with lorries being loaded. BOTH JOHN STRANGE/NPC

The most unusual sight of 'Hall' Class 4-6-0 No. 5983 *Henley Hall* shunting coal wagons in the goods yard on 5th June 1962. New into service on 12th October 1938, the pristine engine was ex-Swindon Works on a running in turn when seen here, so this was either a very fortunate 'cop' for the photographer or the result of a tip off from a railway contact. The engine had transferred from Wolverhampton Stafford Road to Tyseley shed in late September 1961, so was being eased back into traffic to check everything was in order before being sent back to Birmingham. It would have been given a light Swindon-Gloucester duty from the works or possibly even sent 'Light Engine' to Gloucester, where it was turned and worked back to Swindon on a pick-up freight turn, which is how it came to be in the yard here at Stonehouse. On reaching Swindon, if all was well it would then have been returned to Tyseley. We get another good view of the crane here and a couple of the local coal merchant's men at work in the coal pens in the left background. Note, too, the equally gleaming carmine and cream liveried parcels lorry on the right, its driver also interested in the sight of the 'Hall' shunting the yard. No. 5983 was withdrawn off Tyseley shed on 10th April 1965. ALAN JARVIS

The east end of the goods shed, with No. 5983 *Henley Hall* framed by the arch as No. 2876 of Aberdare shed heads past with a load of South Wales coal. On the right, the Down Refuge Siding can be seen joining the Down Main Line; the goods shed loop crossed both of these via diamond crossings to join the Up Main Line. ALAN JARVIS

There was no restriction on locomotives running through the goods shed, so a short while later this picture was also taken of No. 5983 framed by the arch at the east end. It was the trackwork at this end of the shed that was removed in June 1964. Note the GWR wooden posted Siding signal on the left and the catch point at the end of the Down Refuge Siding. ALAN JARVIS

A more complete view of the Stonehouse brickworks chimney as No. 1424 accelerates away towards Ebley in 1963. The chimney was a major landmark for sixty-five years, 202ft high, 17ft in diameter at the base and was reputedly the tallest chimney in the county. There is a suggestion that it was originally planned to be only 190ft in height but to beat a slightly taller chimney near Bristol, the Stonehouse chimney was increased by the addition of the decorative section at the top so it could then lay claim to the title. It has been calculated that it contained 273,000 bricks weighing 1,100 tons and was built by the firm of Orchard & Peer of Stroud, at a cost of £790. It became redundant after modernisation of the plant by the new owners in 1963 and was felled on 14th October 1965. On the left is the Down Refuge Siding, the polished rails showing that it was clearly still being regularly used, and note that a Gloucester-bound train was also due, as indicated by the Stonehouse Down Home signal being 'off'. NPC

The main line is on a curve through Stonehouse station and this carries on for about half a mile, straightening out as it crosses over Foxmoor Lane via a low bridge and then reaching Chapel Lane, which was a minor crossing. Here, immediately on the west side of it, the GWR opened Ebley Crossing Halt on 12th October 1903 for the new steam railmotor service along the Stroud Valley and to and from Gloucester. In this view, No. 1473 has paused with an Up Saturday service again strengthened to three trailers in May 1961, so a certain amount of shunting would be required at Chalford before the return journey could be made. Note that the halt as seen in this and the following pictures had been rebuilt, at an unknown date but probably in the early 1950s, the original wooden platforms having been replaced with cast concrete. Meanwhile, the corrugated iron, pagoda style shelters were replaced with rather soulless square wooden huts, which probably all goes to explain why in later years this was one of the least photographed of the halts. M.E.J. DEANE, COURTESY DR SIMON FOSBURY

Late afternoon autumn sunshine lights up a damp day in October 1962, as a Down service heads away to Stonehouse and Gloucester. ROY DENISON

No. 1444 pauses with its single trailer in August 1964. As with all of the other halts we shall encounter on our journey up the valley, it closed officially on 2nd November 1964. NPC

Shortly after the previous picture, No. 1444 heads away over Chapel Lane Crossing, watched by a young mother and group of children who had just left the train; the one little girl clearly did not like noisy hissing steam engines! The halt took its name from the village of Ebley on the south side of the line. The youngsters on the Down platform do not look like spotters, so were probably waiting for an auto to take them to Stonehouse or perhaps Gloucester. However, a glance into the left distance reveals a Down passenger service had passed through whilst No. 1444 was stopped at the Up platform, so they would have a few minutes to wait yet before the next auto followed through. The crossing is still in use today and is now tarmacadamed and gated, although vehicular use is at the responsibility of the driver and is clearly not encouraged; signs give instructions how to use it, there is a phone for anyone driving large or slow vehicles to use before crossing (although the gates are very narrow) and red and green lights giving an indication of approaching trains. NPC

Looking north east from Chapel Lane Crossing on 18th March 1961, No. 5032 *Usk Castle* speeds along the level straight stretch of track separating Ebley Crossing Halt from Cashes Green Halt, just visible in front of the overbridge in the right background. The Old Oak Common based locomotive, which had entered service on 25th May 1934, was hauling a Paddington to Gloucester and Cheltenham express. MARK B. WARBURTON

A lone schoolgirl waits to board a morning Up auto service arriving at Cashes Green Halt behind an unidentified '14XX' tank in August 1964. She is wearing the uniform of Stroud High School, so may only be travelling the short distance to the next stop at Downfield Crossing Halt, adjacent to the school, although the picture was taken in what would be the summer holiday recess, so she may simply be smartly dressed. JOHN STRANGE/ALAN SAINTY COLLECTION

No. 1440 arriving at Cashes Green Halt in the summer of 1964. Whilst the stops were listed in the time table, in practice the auto workings only stopped as required. On leaving Stonehouse, the guard would enquire of passengers where they wanted to leave the train and let the driver know. If there was no one for a particular halt and no passengers waiting on the platform as they approached, then the service would not stop. Most services therefore did not need to stop at all of the halts, thus helping to maintain the tight timings. NPC

A fine panorama of the halt at Cashes Green on 1st June 1963. This was a later opening but there is conflicting information as to the actual date. Robertson (*Great Western Railway Halts Vol. 1*) and Cooke (*Track Layout Diagrams of the GWR & BR(WR) Section 20*) both give 22nd January 1930, whereas Quick (*Railway Passenger Stations in England, Scotland & Wales, A Chronology*) notes that it first appeared in the time table in March 1931. In addition, the *Great Western Magazine* issue for November 1930 states: '*A halt is to be provided at Cashes Green, between Stroud and Stonehouse*' but a perusal of the years 1929-1931 of this publication found no other mention of it, not for a contract being let or an opening notice. Robertson further notes that construction of the halt did not appear in GWR Engineering Department minutes until November 1930, wherein it was stated that materials from the closed Chalvey Halt on the Windsor Branch were used to build it, at a cost of £185. However, Robertson then muddies the water in his entry for Chalvey Halt: '*Opened 6th May 1929. Closed on 7th July 1930, but materials re-erected at the new Cashes Green Halt in the Stroud valley*'. On balance therefore, I rather think the opening date was 22nd January 1931.

A major advantage of the site of the new halt was the adacent road bridge, carrying Cashes Green Road over the line. Gates at either end led to footpaths down to each platform, the bridge thus forming a footbridge with no need for a hazardous foot crossing of the line such as at Ebley and, as we shall shortly see, Downfield. Here, on Friday 13th September 1963, No. 1424 gets ready to propel its trailer towards Stonehouse and Gloucester, after disgorging several passengers who are now heading off via the path to and from the Down platform. When the halt was built, the footpath was also extended to run behind it (from where the mother and young family are coming in on the left), to join up with a much older path about a hundred yards further on, which ran down the west edge of what later became the cricket field, to St. Matthew's Church and Church Road. The footpath is the only reminder left to show of the halt's existence. The GWR, incidentally, had a reputation for re-using materials and existing timber or corrugated iron structures, such as signal boxes and huts. The wisdom of this is shown in the differing figures for the two halts built using the materials seen here: the estimate for Chalvey had been £840, whereas simple re-erection at Cashes Green came in at £655 less! It seems unlikely, however, that the concrete platform lamps were those provided when the halt was built. BLAKE PATTERSON/COURTESY THE RESTORATION & ARCHIVING TRUST/REF. 1N20

RIGHT: No. 1445 at Cashes Green Halt Up platform with a single trailer in August 1964. The house behind was still relatively new when the picture taken, No's 42 and 44 Cashes Green Road being the first of one of what were four pairs of these redbrick semis built sometime after 1954. JOHN STRANGE/NPC

RIGHT: The same engine and trailer combination on the same day but photographed from the gate off Cashes Green Road and probably a later service given that the stop here was only around a minute in length. All four pairs of semi-detached houses can be seen in this view, which shows their then fairly rural location. Since these views were taken, unsurprisingly the fields behind have been lost beneath further housing development which, despite the onset of the 'Age of the Motor Car', still rather makes the decision to withdraw the railmotor service and close the halts it served all look rather short-sighted. One of the two wooden nameboards from the halt was sold recently at a local auction, for what seems the reasonable sum of £300, albeit in faded and slightly distressed condition. JOHN STRANGE/NPC

LEFT: This is probably the same train heading smartly away towards Downfield Crossing Halt and Stroud a few moments later, seen from Cashes Green Road as it rises to cross the bridge. There is a fair selection of vegetables growing in the allotments alongside the line, which, as they are not fenced off from it, were almost certainly the preserve of local railwaymen. JOHN STRANGE/NPC

A fine study looking eastwards from Cashes Green Road Bridge in May 1964, as an unknown '14XX' tank propels two trailers back to Gloucester. There is an excellent view into the driving cab of the trailer, showing the driver was preparing to stop, with his right hand on the regulator and his left on the handle of the screw brake. In the middle distance, just beyond the colour light signal on the Up side, can be seen the parapets of Carpenter's Viaduct, which carried the line over an old mill pond, part of a water system that ran down the hill from Puckshole and that served several mills and a brewery on the way, before running to the Stroudwater Canal; the pond is now mostly silted up. The railway is today fenced off from the land on the right and some housebuilding has taken place in the foreground but otherwise the allotments still remain. Note the 103 milepost (from Paddington) bottom left, whilst Downfield Crossing Halt, the next stop for Up auto trains, can just be glimpsed where the line curves to the right in the far distance. JOHN STRANGE/NPC

RIGHT AND BELOW: With the driver leaning out from the cab – probably to make sure he got himself into the picture – ex-GWR '28XX' 2-8-0 No. 2807 clanks its way westwards past Downfield Crossing Halt with a Down part-fitted freight in June 1961. This was a venerable old engine when photographed here, one of the oldest we have encountered, having entered service in October 1905. It was based at Bristol in 1921 and Llanelly in 1934 but by the end of the GWR era had moved to Hereford. No. 2807 then spent much of its BR era career on or near the 'North & West' route, between Newport and Chester, moving to Worcester, back to Hereford, back to Worcester, then Chester West, Newport Ebbw Junction and lastly Pontypool Road in June 1958. It then went to Newton Abbot in December 1958 before moving back up to Severn Tunnel Junction in December 1960, its base when seen here and from where it was withdrawn, after over fifty-seven years service, on 7th March 1963. BOTH ROY DENISON

LEFT: No. 1455 arrives at the halt with a single trailer in tow in April 1964. The building behind the engine is interesting. Named Downfield Crossing Cottage, it was built in 1933 presumably to house a crossing keeper. The 1936 25 inch OS shows a signal box as having appeared at this end of the halt's Up platform, which must be an error as no box ever existed here. As the photographs which follow show, it was very close to the running line and the porch entrance also faced onto the railway, so it must have been quite entertaining inside when express trains thundered past! It survived closure of the halt and in 1982 was bought by a nurse, Conrad Mills, who worked at Standish Hospital but who also had a strong interest in railways. He lived there for twenty-six years until, very sadly, one day in October 2008, the bungalow was burned to the ground in a suspected arson attack, leaving Mr Mills homeless and destroying all his possessions, including his collection of railway books and artefacts. The building contained significant amounts of asbestos in the walls and roof, so was not insured. JOHN STRANGE/NPC

From a viewpoint just to the west of Downfield Crossing Cottage, No. 6956 *Mottram Hall* was photographed storming through with a Down freight in the summer of 1964. The 'Hall' had entered service on 28th March 1943 and alternated its home between Wolverhampton Stafford Road and Shrewsbury throughout the 1950s. In 1961 it had four month stays at first Oxford and then Stourbridge Junction, before moving in early October of that year to Gloucester Horton Road, where it remained until July 1965. It then returned to Oxford where it survived until the end of WR steam. On the opposite side of the line to the photographer, to his right and behind him, are the playing fields of Marling School, opened in 1889. The large house just glimpsed on the right, named Grafton House and to which the brick building was some form of annexe – a stables and hay loft originally perhaps – pre-dated the school but at some stage was purchased by it and has since been demolished to allow for expansion of the school facilities. NPC

RIGHT: Another unusual auto working was photographed arriving at Downfield Crossing Halt under a heavy sky on 5th June 1964. An unidentified '14XX' 0-4-2T is sandwiched between a trailer, with the driver visible in the driving compartment, and a GWR design 'Fruit D' van, which was almost certainly loaded with parcels. These 'brown' vehicles were classed as non-passenger stock but were vacuum fitted, so could be attached to passenger services. HOWARD BURCHELL

LEFT: The same train moments later, heading away towards Cashes Green and its ultimate destination at Gloucester. The 'Fruit D's were a useful design which BR continued building in small batches up until 1958. We get another glimpse of Downfield Crossing Cottage here too, showing just how close to the railway it stood. In fact it is something of a surprise that BR did not demolish it after closure of the halt but presumably it was retained initially for the crossing keeper. The crossing, which can be seen here between the end of the platform and the cottage, was finally closed in 2016, having been deemed to be too dangerous to remain in use due to the curvature of the line at this point and the 90mph linespeed. HOWARD BURCHELL

RIGHT: No. 1458 calls at the halt on Saturday 3rd October with the 2.10pm train from Gloucester Central, watched by a man tending his roses in the right background. The substantial nature of the platforms is worthy of note, as they were not originally built like this, the halt, when it first opened on 12th October 1903 being equipped with wooden platforms similar to those at Cashes Green. It would seem likely that they were rebuilt in 1933, when the cottage was also built, which had a similar brick base. BILL POTTER/KRM

A busy moment for the guard of this Down train propelling back to Gloucester on Monday 1st May 1961, as he steps down to watch a small crowd of passengers climb aboard. No. 1453's fireman can also be glimpsed through the cab spectacle plate. The platforms were widened when they were rebuilt, so that the two corrugated iron pagoda shelters, which appear to be the originals, now stood on the platforms rather than being perched on wooden stilts behind. In later years, grass was allowed to grow on the sections of each platform which were not used by passengers, with Up and Down services favouring the west ends of each. ROY DENISON

Following on from the previous picture, with a late afternoon sun on 1st May 1961 imparting a golden glow on a scene which had shortly before clearly been given a soaking, No. 1453 is seen again with a single trailer. This could well be the 4.40pm 'shuttle' from Stonehouse to Brimscombe, which called here at 4.47½pm. ROY DENISON

A panorama of the halt on 16th June 1961, minus trains but with the crossing keeper posing with a bucket and what looks to be a can – perhaps he was filling the oil lamps which hung from the lampposts; these would be extinguished and locked away after the passage of the final train each day. At the unmanned halts, it was the duty of the guard to do this. JOHN STRANGE/NPC

A few passengers wait to board the trailer which has just arrived behind No. 1453 in May 1964, as a schoolboy uses the foot crossing immediately behind. This sylvan scene, a moment in time of an age now lost, is further enhanced by the blossom decorating some of the surrounding trees, whilst from a modeller's perspective, notice the GWR pattern platform seat (there was another on the Up side hidden by the shelter), the proliferation of lampposts, cast iron signs and the '3 Car' stop notice to prevent longer trains from fouling the crossing whilst stopped. JOHN STRANGE/NPC

Looking east in April 1964 from the foot crossing, as an Up train starts away from the halt. The railway divided Downfield Lane in two, although it did not in fact exist as a throughway when the line was built. The crossing itself apparently came into existence sometime between the OS's 1885 and 1901 25 inch surveys and whilst it may have been used by the odd horse cart in its earlier years, vehicular traffic was never encouraged and was probably in fact prohibited later on. Downfield Crossing was easily the most photographed of the three halts between Stonehouse and Stroud and having such a fine selection of pictures from which to choose, I have erred on the side of staying here to enjoy this delightful location as long as possible! JOHN STRANGE/NPC

Another Up service heads away past the end of the Up platform and the '3 Car' stop sign for Up trains in 1964. These signs were a late addition and generally associated with diesel multiple units, so was there a thought at some stage that the autos might be replaced with DMUs? Beards Lane Crossing is just ahead, the crossing keeper's cottage, on the Stroud side of the lane, being provided from quite early on, possibly when the line first opened or soon after. There was also a gate box, Beards Lane Crossing Signal Box, which again seems to have been an early provision but certainly by 1885. A non-standard timber box on a brick base and with a 6 lever double twist frame, it acted as a block post too but was reduced to ground frame status on 23rd November 1958 and removed circa 1970. It was also positioned on the Up side but on the opposite side of Beards Lane to the cottage. Given it was in place when the halt first opened, it seems slightly perverse that the halt was built adjacent to Downfield Crossing and not next to Beards Lane Crossing. JOHN STRANGE/NPC

RIGHT: The driver of No. 1472 leans out of the cab checking the injector overflow of his engine whilst paused at the halt in 1964. The water draining out indicates that the mix of steam was not set correctly in the injector on this side. A steam injector delivers cold water to a boiler against its own pressure, using its own live or exhaust steam, instead of using a mechanical pump. If the injector cannot initially overcome boiler pressure, the overflow allows it to continue to draw water and steam. Injectors are simple and typically over 98 per cent energy efficient overall, most of the heat energy in the condensed steam being returned to the boiler. JOHN STRANGE/NPC

OPPOSITE PAGE TOP: An unknown guard poses in front of the Up side nameboard with a pair of Tilley lamps in April 1962. The large pair of semi detached houses behind, with their half-timbered upper storeys, still remain. Built probably just before the First World War (they are not on the 1901 OS), they are shown as being named 'Cartref', on the left, and 'The Limes', right. JOHN STRANGE/NPC

OPPOSITE PAGE TOP: The 'Cheltenham Spa Express' powers through the halt behind a 'Castle' Class 4-6-0 in June 1961. Whilst the locomotive is not positively identified, it can be seen to be carrying an 85B Horton Road shedplate, so it is likely to be No. 7003 Elmley Castle, which was allocated there at this time. ROY DENISON

ABOVE: Passengers leave a Gloucester-bound train in 1964. The large bell over the driver's window was for warning of the approach of the train. Another bell in the cab allowed the fireman to remain in communication with the driver, who operated the regulator via a system of mechanical linkages, whilst a valve in the brake pipe also gave him control of the automatic vacuum brake. Meanwhile, all alone on the footplate, the fireman's job remained, as before, to keep the firebox fed and water in the boiler but with the added complication of having to get the blower on smartly before the driver closed the regulator, not easy when he could not see him. NPC

RIGHT: The Up side pagoda shelter circa 1960, still with the iron embellishments in place along the roof line. NPC

Another more unusual working is seen here, about to start away from the halt on Friday 16th June 1961, with an unknown '14XX' propelling trailer No. W169W whilst also hauling a 'Fruit D' and two fitted box vans almost certainly again filled with parcels. The time table suggests that the wagons had most likely been attached at Stroud. The long shadows caused by the lowering sun indicate that this is an evening service and the date is close to the longest day of the year, so we are probably looking at a time around 7.00-7.30pm. Two minutes were normally allowed in the time table for the call at Stroud but the 7.00pm return from Chalford stopped there at 7.13½pm and stayed for 4½ minutes, departing at 7.19pm; the extra 2½ minutes are likely therefore to have been for the parcels vans to be attached or collected possibly from the goods loop on the Down side. No. W169W was a 59ft 6ins steel-panelled open trailer, built in January 1929 to Lot No. 1349. Its time in service was coming to a close when seen here, withdrawal taking place five months later in November 1961. Sister coach No. W167W is preserved on the Dean Forest Railway. JOHN STRANGE/NPC

Another gem from the camera of Bill Potter, as non auto fitted Class '57XX' 0-6-0PT No. 3775 heads over Beards Lane Crossing with the 2.00pm from Chalford on 3rd October 1964. The noticeboard on the right warned against crossing whilst the bell mounted up on the pole alongside was ringing, an audible indication of an approaching train. This clearly was also a foot crossing only, despite the railway apparently dividing Beards Lane in two when it was built. Like the foot crossing at Downfield, it is also now locked out of use with a footbridge having been provided instead, sited just behind where the photographer was standing. However, although the crossing keeper's cottage stands so close to the railway, it has survived and is now a private dwelling. BILL POTTER/KRM

Horton Road-based No. 5017 *The Gloucestershire Regiment 28th, 61st* passes over Beards Lane Crossing with what is likely to be a Gloucester to Swindon train – albeit carrying an express lamp code – on 14th September 1962. Note that this end of the crossing cottage was devoid of windows. Lineside tree growth, coupled with the curvature of the line at this point, has badly obscured the view from the crossings today and there is also the inherent dangers posed by two trains passing in opposite directions at the same time; as noted overleaf, Network Rail has therefore locked them out of use and erected a huge new disability compliant footbridge in their place, on the west side of Beards Lane. PAUL RILEY/COURTESY THE RESTORATION & ARCHIVING TRUST/REF. PR1429

Looking back towards the halt from Beards Lane Crossing, as No. 1455 heads away to Stroud on 13th September 1963. The vegetable plots on the Down side of the line have today been swallowed up by the expansion of Marling School. BLAKE PATTERSON/COURTESY THE RESTORATION & ARCHIVING TRUST/REF. 1N18

'Large Prairie' No. 4100 has just passed Beards Lane Crossing with the 5.45pm 'stopper' from Gloucester to Swindon in the late summer of 1964. BILL POTTER/KRM

One of the lesser photographed members of the 'Castle' Class, No. 5058 *Earl of Clancarty*, scoots past Beards Lane Crossing with a Swindon-bound express on 16th March 1962. New into service on 19th May 1937 as *Newport Castle*, the locomotive was another of the class given the names of eminent personages which had originally been destined for 'Earl' Class (or 'Dukedogs' as they came to be known) 4-4-0s. No. 5058 was renamed from 1st September 1937, whilst in a rather convoluted sequence of events, the *Newport Castle* plates were bestowed on No. 5065 *Upton Castle*, then being named *Upton Castle* when built in 1939. No. 5065 *Upton Castle*, with No. 5093 then being named *Upton Castle* when built in 1939. No. 5058 spent most of its career in the West Country, at Newton Abbot and Plymouth Laira, before moving to Gloucester on 11th September 1961. The engine was clearly well looked after by the Horton Road shed staff but was to enter Swindon Works exactly two months after this picture was taken, where it stayed for sixty-two days undergoing a heavy intermediate overhaul, emerging on 16th July. However, it was then apparently put into store at Horton Road on 12th November and was subsequently withdrawn on 6th March 1963. ROY DENISON

The first of two views of the Down 'Cheltenham Spa Express' approaching Beards Lane Crossing. Here, on 23rd June 1962, No. 7035 *Ogmore Castle* of Horton Road shed was in charge of this prestigious train, which was introduced by the GWR in 1923, as a result of the first members of the 'Castle' Class entering service. BR dropped the name after the end of WR steam but it was brought back again in 1984 and continues in use today. JOHN STRANGE/ ALAN SAINTY COLLECTION

A little further east, by the Stroud Up Outer Home signal, seen in the distance in the picture above, there was another foot crossing of the line, which carried a footpath running between Stratford Road and Gannicox Road, and where, in June 1959, a 'Castle' Class engine was photographed leaning to the curve at the head of the Down 'CSE' again. The locomotive is supposedly No. 4087 *Cardigan Castle* but this seems unlikely, as that engine was based at Plymouth Laira at the date of the picture and is recorded as being coupled with a Collett tender, not the slab-sided Hawksworth tender seen here. More likely perhaps is that the number was mistranscribed and it should be No. 4085 *Berkeley Castle*, which was on Horton Road's roster at this date. ROY DENISON

Class '8F' No. 48410 glides round the curve and down the gentle decline away from Stroud with a lengthy train of coal empties on 11th May 1961. This ex-LM&SR locomotive actually had strong Western connections, firstly having been built during the Second World War at Swindon Works, entering service on 22nd September 1943. It then later enjoyed three successive allocations to ex-GWR sheds under BR – Bristol St. Philip's Marsh from August 1955 to January 1960, Old Oak Common (where it was based when seen here) to October 1962 and then Stourbridge Junction to July 1966. Moving then to Wigan Springs Branch shed, its final allocation was to Rose Grove, from December 1967 to the beginning of August 1968, shortly before steam on BR ceased once and for all. The Stroud Up Outer Home signal is indicating that an Up train was also due, whilst the rear of No. 48410's train is passing over Stratford Viaduct. Note the allotments on the left, again in very close proximity to the line. ROY DENISON

The signal was 'off' for the 6.32pm auto working from Gloucester to Chalford, which passed by a few moments later. The uniformed railwayman looks rather an important chap, possibly an inspector and perhaps accompanying the photographer. However, Roy worked for the railway himself, in the District General Manager's office at Gloucester, so would not have had a problem getting lineside access. Note too the jacket draped on a post near the base of the signal – Roy's perhaps? A footpath passes under the line near where he was standing and a view taken from this point today would reveal little change apart from the removal of the signal in 1970. Even the allotments remain although they no longer run right up to the railway. Roy DENISON

One of the last day auto services crosses the four-arch Stratford Viaduct, spanning a valley along which runs the Painswick Stream, on 31st October 1964. The viaduct took its name from the adjacent Stratford Mill, part of which is visible through the arches. First recorded as a cloth mill in 1607, it was converted for use as a corn mill around 1735 and by 1901 it was an extensive steam and water powered flour mill, belonging to R. Townsend & Co. Ltd. Badly damaged by fire in 1908, the mill continued to trade until 1984, by which time it had changed hands twice more, Townsends having been absorbed by Rank Hovis Mcdougall in 1962. The workforce numbered ninety workers in 1972 but, in 1983, the mill was taken over again by Dalgety Spillers, who closed it the following year. After closure, the mill building was demolished and a supermarket was built on the site. The mill had a rail connection, which was installed probably soon after the railway was built. This comprised a wagon turntable at the end of a siding on the Up side of the line, which led to two more sidings that formed a loop, running down the side of the valley and through a covered loading bay. The rails were finally lifted in May 1970 but the siding agreement was not terminated until 1978. ROY DENISON

ABOVE: Also on Thursday 11th May 1961, following on from the pictures on pages 272-73, the 'Cheltenham Spa Express', the 4.55pm ex-Paddington to Cheltenham train, was photographed coasting through Stroud and over Stratford Viaduct headed by a 'Castle' Class engine that the photographer did not have time to identify. However, it is likely to be Horton Road's No. 7003 *Elmley Castle* again. Note the scaffolding on the right with repointing of the brickwork underway. ROY DENISON

BELOW: Later, Roy then captured the 7.08pm Chalford to Gloucester auto crossing the viaduct, which again included some additional wagons. The siding serving the mill ran parallel to the Up line, curving away slightly at the far end to a wagon turntable behind the temporary 20mph speed restriction board. The house in the right background, called 'The Hill', is today Stroud Masonic Hall. ROY DENISON

Class '28XX' No. 2876, which we saw passing Stonehouse a little earlier on, produces a fine head of steam as it heads away over the twelve span Stroud Viaduct leading away from the north west end of Stroud station on 17th March 1962. New in January 1919, the 2-8-0 was based at Aberdare but was on a running in turn from Swindon Works when photographed here (having been recorded by the Stephenson Locomotive Society as being in Swindon 'A' Shop on 4th March), hence its pristine black paintwork; however, as the picture on page 245 shows, it was not to stay this way for long. Moving to Newport Ebbw Junction in August 1963, it was withdrawn on 15th January 1965. The train, which was just getting underway again, had been given the road by the signal on the left, the Down Advanced Starter, positioned 'wrong side' for sighting purposes due to the curvature of the line. The arm had also been equipped with a sighting board so it could be clearly seen by the drivers of Down trains but was hidden from Up train crews. Beneath the signal is the point for the Stratford Mill siding, which was controlled from Townsend's Ground Frame in the cabin alongside, which was electrically released from Stroud Signal Box. Stroud town centre can be seen in the background. NPC

No. 7006 *Lydford Castle* steams across Stroud Viaduct with an Up Paddington-bound express on 6th April 1963. Entering service on 28th June 1946, No. 7006 was on its final allocation when seen here, to Old Oak Common shed, but had enjoyed two spells at Horton Road earlier in its career, from 25th August 1948 to 20th January 1950 and a much longer second visit, from 28th May 1951 to 26th February 1958, so would have known this route well. However, its time in service was drawing to a close at the date of the photograph, withdrawal taking place on 16th December 1963, a short working life for a 'Castle' of just seventeen and a half years. ROY DENISON

No. 1472 heads into Stroud with a three trailer Saturday service probably in autumn 1961. The date estimate is based partly on the Kodak slide mount – white card with a solid blue border; other examples I have of this type of mount date from 1960-61. As noted earlier, No. 1472 was at Cheltenham from May 1959 until August 1960, when it was put into store. On 6th April 1961 it then went into Wolverhampton Stafford Road Works for a Heavy Intermediate repair, from where it was despatched to Horton Road on 11th May. It would seem unlikely that Wolverhampton sent it back out after repair in the filthy state seen here, so I believe that a date of around October 1961 is more likely. Also, services strengthened to three trailers seem to have been much less common after 1961. Note the rake of wagons on the Stratford Mill siding in the left background, beyond which can be seen Stroud Technical College, which moved to these new buildings in 1954, and also the Rosary Roman Catholic School garden shed and allotments to the right of the engine. JOHN STRANGE/NPC

A similar view but three years later, as No. 1453 trundles across the viaduct with a service to Chalford on 3rd October 1964. Note the proximity of the Down Advanced Starter signal (in the 'off' position for a Down train) to the Up Home signal, both on the same side of the line and hence the requirement for a back board behind the arm of the former. On the right is the distinctive roof of the malthouse for Stroud Brewery, the main buildings of which, as we shall shortly see, were on the opposite side of the railway viaduct. Note that the school allotments had been abandoned since the previous picture. BILL POTTER/KRM

The twelve span bridge carrying the railway across the bottom end of the Slad Valley is variously known as Stroud, Merrywalks or Watts Viaduct, the latter either after the Watts family who owned Cuttle's Mill at Wallbridge from 1779 to 1850, or more probably Joseph Watts, who owned Stroud Brewery from 1818 to 1855; the two families may well have been related but this is not clear. Merrywalks is the name of the road being travelled by the double-decker bus in the foreground, and is part of the A46 trunk road which originally ran across country between Bath and Cleethorpes; motorway development has seen parts of the route now lost. Merrywalks runs from Beeches Green (by the big house in the distance through the first arch) and Bath Road, just behind the photographer. The malthouse buildings, which still survive, are visible through the other arches. On Saturday 7th March 1964, an unidentified '14XX' propels June 1954-built, 63ft steel-panelled open trailer No. W244W away from Stroud. BLAKE PATTERSON/COURTESY THE RESTORATION & ARCHIVING TRUST/REF. 1Y14

With the fireman leaning from the cab looking down on the scene below, No. 1453 propels away from Stroud on Saturday 6th April 1963. Roy Denison

No. 1472 leans to the curve as it arrives at Stroud on 5th June 1962. Note that there was a 50mph speed restriction for Up expresses heading non-stop through the station. The platforms at the Gloucester end run a considerable way onto the viaduct, so are cantilevered out from it on either side. Some wagons can just be made out in the background, behind the Down side water crane, on the mill siding and note the Stroud totem fixed to the lamp bracket on the right. Alan Jarvis

Mark Warburton and Roy Denison were clearly at the station together on 6th April 1963, with the former taking this shot of No. 1453 arriving at the station with trailer No. W227W. At the station end of the viaduct, Rowcroft was crossed by a steel girder span, the deck of which is seen here just in front of the locomotive. Trailer No. W227W was built by BR in June 1951, Lot No. 1736 to diagram A38. Twenty-five were built in total, fifteen between May and August 1951 and ten more in June 1954. Six of them have been preserved – five of them by the Dart Valley Railway, although one has since moved to the Severn Valley – but No. W227W was not amongst them. Condemned dates for these vehicles were not recorded but it was presumably taken out of use after the Chalford service ceased on 31st October 1964. MARK B. WARBURTON

ABOVE: The Gloucester end of the station from beneath the footbridge in June 1967, showing on the left the ornate base, in stone and two colours of brick, of the Stroud Brewery chimney. The brewery had its origins in 1760 and went through various changes of ownership over the two hundred or so years of its existence, with the Stroud Brewery Co. Ltd being formed in 1888. It closed around the time of this photograph and the brewery buildings, which occupied a triangular site bounded by the railway to the north east, Rowcroft to the south and Merrywalks to the west, were demolished in 1973. The chimney was added in 1901 and had been a prominent local landmark. As they still do today, the platforms extend onto the viaduct for around 100ft and the Georgian buildings on the right fronting onto Rowcroft still remain. Note the beech tree on the left, more on which shortly! NPC

RIGHT: No. 1409 departs for Gloucester past the chimney on 6th April 1963. MARK B. WARBURTON

No. 7035 *Ogmore Castle* again, calling at Stroud at 12.31pm at the head of the 11.45am Cheltenham to Paddington express on 16th June 1962. As detailed earlier, No. 7035 is the engine that finally ended up with the *Ogmore Castle* nameplates after No. 5056, which was given them first but subsequently became *Earl of Powis*, and then No. 5080, which was renamed *Defiant* during the Second World War. Built by BR and going new into service at Shrewsbury shed on 9th August 1950, No. 7035 moved to Horton Road in September 1953, where it stayed for three years. It then had stints at Bristol Bath Road and Swansea Landore until arriving back at Gloucester on 29th February 1960, remaining until 12th November 1962, when it moved on to Oxford. The engine's last allocation was to Old Oak Common shed from 4th March 1963 up until withdrawal on 1st June 1964, another short life – less than fourteen years – for a member of this class. On the platform, the porters wait to load parcels from a trolley, whilst the prominence of the brewery chimney is clear. NPC

No. 5986 *Arbury Hall* pauses with a Gloucester to Swindon train in June 1961, the engine being based at the latter's shed at this date. New into service on 21st November 1939, shortly after the outbreak of the Second World War, No. 5986 was converted to oil burning in May 1947, in which condition it ran as No. 3954, reverting to its old number when converted back to coal fired in February 1950. Three months after this picture was taken it moved on to Reading shed and then to Westbury a year later in September 1962. Twelve months after this it was withdrawn. Whilst Brimscombe shed was where the banking engines for the climb up to Sapperton were generally based, they sometimes waited here at Stroud, hence the 'Large Prairie' tank standing in the bay, although No. 5986 would not require its services. M.E.J. Deane, courtesy Dr Simon Fosbury

A most unusual view, for which we must be grateful as few photographers bothered with peripheral railway scenes such as this, particularly as all these structures have sadly – but unsurprisingly – now gone. The round tank on its circular stone base housing the pumping equipment certainly dated from broad gauge days, featuring in an early painting of the station executed by the Gloucestershire artist Edward Smith (1821-1893), who painted many local scenes including of the docks at Gloucester. Sadly, it has not been possible to decipher the lettering for the maker's name on the tank side but the centre line may be a date with a forward slash in the centre, possibly '18/55'. The rectangular tank was a later addition but is shown on a large scale 1 in 500 OS map of 1884. The tanks held the water supply for the station and also supplied the cranes at the end of each platform. The picture was taken on 4th June 1962, with our unknown photographer looking up from the approach road to the rear of the Down side platform. NPC

RIGHT: A typical scene beneath the Down side platform canopy on 5th August 1963, as a group of passengers board one of the trailers of the 11.40am from Chalford to Gloucester, whilst the fireman of No. 1424 and the guard take a short break sitting on a platform trolley. The driver will have stayed in the end driving compartment of the far trailer, waiting for the guard's green flag.
SEAN BOLAN COLLECTION

ABOVE: We saw No. 1453 with its single trailer departing across the viaduct on 6th April 1963 a few pages ago and here it is again prior to that, waiting whilst a group of passengers, including a couple of young mums with babies in prams, get aboard. In the far distance it can just be seen that the Down Starter signal has already been pulled 'off' by the signalman. On the right, the low sun has nicely lit up the detail beneath the Up platform canopy, showing the supporting ironwork and the gated passenger entrance with the ticket collector's booth alongside. The array of posters appears to include one extolling the electrification of the London Midland Region's West Coast Main Line. ROY DENISON

LEFT: We also saw No. 1409 departing on 6th April 1963 a few pages ago, so this is the corresponding view to that, showing the train arriving at the station. These services were well used and there is another small crowd of passengers waiting to board.
MARK B. WARBURTON

Looking north through the station on Saturday 24th March 1962, with a handful of passengers on the Up platform awaiting the arrival of the next auto to Gloucester. NPC

No. 1458 has just taken a drink of water here, with the fireman preparing to pull the hose back out of the tank and over the drain – the steel pipe with conical top partially hidden behind the lamppost. Stops here were generally brief, often only a couple of minutes but a few were longer, up to five minutes, which gave just enough time for a quick top up. This is a well composed view too, in that the conical tank which supplied the water can also be seen in the left background. However, the rectangular cast iron tank that accompanied it (see page 285) had been removed. The 'Large Prairie' tank in the bay on the right was on banking duties, Stroud often being where they were attached to Up freights instead of Brimscombe. We shall see much more of the Sapperton bankers and banking operations in the next volume. No. 1458 was transferred from Hereford to Horton Road in July 1964, which gives us a four month window in which this picture was taken. NPC

As we did at Stonehouse, we now present a short series of views of the station buildings all taken circa 1969-70. Designed by Brunel and dating from the opening of the line, the main station building remains today with the additions seen here, having been Grade II listed since 1989, albeit with minor detail differences some fifty years later. The Down side building, despite appearances, is not original, as noted in the listing, reproduced here: '*Railway station and footbridge c.1845 with additions of 1890 and 1914. Probably by I.K. Brunel, for the Cheltenham & Great Western Union Railway, with additions by Great Western Railway. Limestone rubble and ashlar with Welsh slate roofs. The up platform is a Brunel 'cottage' with extensions of 1890 and 1914. Bridge to down platform probably 1914. Earliest building (up side): Coursed ashlar limestone on chisel dressed limestone plinth, projecting chisel dressed limestone quoins and raised ashlar dressings to windows. Ashlar chimneys, (one partly rebuilt in reconstructed stone) with high level drip course mouldings. Parapets to gables*

and blue Welsh slate roof. Platform canopy with dogs tooth or chevron timber fascia, supported partly on cast iron cantilever brackets with circular motif. Down platform building c1914: coursed ashlar limestone with projecting details, plinth and ashlar surrounds to flat arched doorways, all generally detailed to match earlier building on up platform. Platform canopy and low mono pitched roof with modern felt covering. Various chamfered timber mullion and transom windows with some opening casements to both buildings. Original up platform building is rectangular in plan with projecting wing on north east side, with extensions to re-entrant angle, and at both ends. Down platform building is rectangular plan with bay window at south east end. Interior of both buildings divided into various station offices, waiting rooms etc, with no features of particular interest. Steel and timber covered footbridge links up and down platforms at north west end. Platforms at north west end carried over valley and roadway on bridge and blue engineering brick viaduct. Group value with viaduct, railway goods shed (q.v.) and Hill-Paul Mill building to south west. Building originally for C&GWUR with Brunel as consultant engineer. Taken over by GWR in 1844.' The earliest part of the building is the 'cottage' – the centre gable here and the single storey to the left, although the frontage to the car park that side is also a later extension. Everything to the right of the gable is later, whilst the so called '*Hill-Paul Mill building*' – actually the ex-Williamson, Tratt & Co. Ltd clothing factory – can be seen in the right background. There is also here an interesting selection of 1950s and '60s motor cars parked in the forecourt. From left to right we have: a Morris Minor or Minor 1000 – if post-1956 it would be a Minor 1000; a Mini Countryman/ Traveller – the estate version of the Mini; a Singer Gazelle – similar to its Hillman Minx sibling but with styling modifications and the duo-tone swage line – possibly a Gazelle VI of 1965-67; a Hillman Imp; a Jaguar MKII, 1959-67, similar to the 'Morse' type; a Triumph 2000 – Triumph's rival to the Rover 2000, E registration (1967) so the 1963-69 model; and finally a Vauxhall Victor FB, 1961-64 – the sporty version, the VX4/90 had a duo-tone swage line.

The rear of the later Down side building. Unusually, the GWR had made some considerable effort to provide something that matched closely to the original broad gauge building it replaced, in stone and with very similar chimneys. The area behind is now the main car park for the station. SEAN BOLAN

A Seat in the Shade

HOW A GREAT WESTERN STATION ADOPTED A STATELY TREE

STROUD station, Gloucestershire, rejoices in a fine American beech tree growing on the platform. When the station was opened in April, 1845, there was a plantation of trees and shrubs at the back of the down platform. It remained unmolested for many years, forming an oasis between the down side approach road and the main Bath Road. As traffic requirements grew, however, some of the trees had to be cut down to make room for new buildings, and the extent of the plantation was gradually reduced.

Alterations to the station in 1890 included extensions to the platform, but an American beech was left standing just behind the down platform railings. For over three decades it continued to flourish there, casting a welcome shade on to the platform when the sun was high. In those days a seat was placed where full advantage could be taken of the tree's shelter, and many thousands of passengers have rested in its grateful shadow while waiting for their trains.

Further extensions to the station and down platform in 1913 and 1914, including the shifting of the fence, brought the beech tree on to the platform itself. At this time its fate hung in the balance. There was much talk of felling the tree, for the sake of the space this would clear. Thanks, however, to the appeals of many who had rested beneath its shadow, the beech was spared the axe ; instead of its being removed, a seat was built right around the truck, increasing the accommodation beneath the leafy canopy.

Americans Take Seeds Home

During the war, many hundreds of our friends of the United States Army sat beneath those wide spreading branches, admired the tree's shapeliness and stature, and came to feel toward it a sort of affectionate possessiveness. Often they collected the fallen seeds, to take " back home " and plant as a permanent memento of their wartime sojourn in " this England ".

Our beech tree is of the American " fern-leaf " species (*Polypodum Phegopteris*), believed to be rather uncommon in this country, although several are to be seen in Lypiatt Park ; its age is estimated to be approaching a hundred years. Many attempts have been made in this country to grow similar trees from seed, but there is no record of any such efforts having proved successful.

The tree does not fruit regularly each year, the beechmast being thrown at intervals of sometimes one year, sometimes two years. Beech foliage is graceful and pleasing to the eye, and the great tree makes a splendid picture, especially

THE GREAT AMERICAN BEECH ON STROUD STATION PLATFORM.

when it is decked in all the glory of springtime green. Unfortunately, owing to traffic requirements, some pruning of the lower branches has been necessary, slightly impairing the tree's full natural beauty of symmetry ; but as *Polypodum Phegopteris* has afforded rest and pleasure to generations past, so we trust it may long flourish to dispense charm and shade to future generations.—E. M. BERRY.

ABOVE: The story of the beech tree at the Gloucester end of the Down platform, from the *Great Western Railway Magazine*, August 1946. The locomotive in the picture is No. 5988 *Bostock Hall*, which had entered service on 28th November 1939 and was based at Horton Road when seen here. It was to be withdrawn off Tyseley shed in early October 1965. Note the early clerestory coach body behind the tree, presumably in use as a store – does anyone remember it or know when it was removed? Happily, the tree still stands.

RIGHT: The footbridge, Up platform and building from the Gloucester end of the Down platform, with the beech tree just getting into the picture on the right. The footbridge, which was provided as part of the circa 1914 improvements to the station, was a replacement for an earlier bridge erected some years after the station first opened. SEAN BOLAN

The Down side building from the Up platform. Note the platform trolleys loaded with magazines or brochures awaiting collection. However, the doors and windows had all been boarded up so the rooms within the building were clearly no longer in use by the date of these pictures. However, it has since been brought back into use, with the doors and windows being opened back up and the building now looks much smarter again. In the right distance, the siding serving Stratford Mill can still be made out, so the views pre-date the removal of that on 31st May 1970. SEAN BOLAN

RIGHT: Looking towards Swindon, with the goods shed and signal box visible beyond the end of the Up platform. The box, which will be looked at in more detail in Volume 5B, was closed from 5th October 1970, with the semaphore signals all being removed at the same time. The shutters are down on the bookstall – was it Wymans? Can anyone confirm – but the array of advertising posters in front suggests that it was still trading rather than closed completely, meaning that these pictures were most likely taken on a Sunday.

BELOW: Looking back towards Gloucester from the Down platform ramp, with a single box van in BR blue livery parked in the siding behind the Up platform. Note that the GWR nameboard on the left had been removed, leaving the posts standing on their own. BOTH SEAN BOLAN

LEFT: The Down side building again, with the magnificent old Hill Paul clothing factory behind. Williamson Tratt & Co. established a wholesale clothing business in Stroud in 1879 but this building, apparently to a design provided by Henry A. Cheers of Teddington in Middlesex in 1886, was not built until 1898. It was executed mostly in red and yellow brick but with stone details in place of the latter at the front. After Williamson Tratt & Co. went into liquidation in 1902, another firm of clothing manufacturers, Hill, Paul & Co., took over the factory, continuing successfully for much of the rest of the 20th century with a workforce of 110 still employed in 1971. Production finished in 1989 and the building was purchased by a developer, whose intention was to turn it into flats but no progress was made and it was in imminent danger of demolition. A determined campaign by local people, including barricading the building to stop contractors starting work, coupled with the formation of the Hill Paul Regeneration group, happily saw it saved at the eleventh hour and restored as luxury housing apartments, with an additional two storeys built on top. SEAN BOLAN

We finish the first part of our journey here at Stroud, as No. 1453 waits to depart for Brimscombe and Chalford with the 11.20am from Gloucester Central on Saturday 3rd October 1964. Note the 'Siphon G' in the siding bay. A total of 130 of these were built by the GWR between 1913 and 1927, specifically for carrying milk churns, with all surviving into BR ownership. However, with transport in milk largely going over to road after the Second World War, these vehicles were converted for parcels traffic instead. The GWR-built 'Siphon G' vehicles were withdrawn between 1954 and 1962 but in the meantime, BR had built further small batches of them at Swindon between 1950 and 1955, many of which were used specifically for newspaper traffic. The vehicle seen here is one of the later BR-built examples. And for anyone feeling a little disappointed that our visit to the station has been rather brief, don't worry, there is much more still to be covered, including the signal box and goods yard, in the next volume. BILL POTTER/KRM

APPENDIX

The PAINSWICK RAILWAY

Readers of this series of colour books of Gloucestershire railways will be aware of how I stretch the self-imposed boundaries on a regular basis, for all sorts of what I believe to be valid reasons. Datelines do come forward from the roughly 1975 cut-off point, whilst county boundaries are ignored for the purposes of completing a journey. We will now stretch things even further to bring you the story of how the businessfolk and worthies of Painswick fought for three decades to bring a railway to their small town (population 4,019 in 1871), a campaign which was ultimately to prove unsuccessful, although they did instead get a railway operated bus service for twenty-four years.

This otherwise forgotten footnote of railway history, involving a noted Gloucestershire railway engineer, is based on a rare colour map purchased many years ago and is illustrated with period views of the area to be served, colour views of similar stations which were built in the Forest of Dean and pictures of the GWR buses that eventually ran between Stroud and Painswick. Part of the reason for telling it here is because the map is in colour and I have been able to reproduce it in full, as it was originally drawn up in 1873-74 by George William Keeling (1839-1913), engineer of the Severn & Wye Railway and of the Severn Bridge, and later engineer of the Gloucester & Hereford Division of the GWR. Keeling's proposed track layouts at the two projected stations were understandably similar to some on the Severn & Wye system, hence the use of pictures of Upper Lydbrook (a valley side location similar to Pitchcombe) and Coleford (which had a similar triple track arrangement to that proposed at Painswick). However, given the less industrial nature of the Painswick Valley, in comparison to the coal and iron industries in the Forest of Dean, coupled with the greater wealth in the area, might perhaps the station buildings have been constructed from local stone, rather than the William Eassie timber 'sheds' that were supplied to the S&WR.

The first suggestion for a railway branch line between Stroud and Painswick, a small but prosperous Cotswold mill town, came in November 1866 from Mr E. Little of Pitchcombe House. Some 200 people are reported to have attended the public meeting he called, at which a Chairman was appointed, being Mr Croome, Lord of the Manor of Painswick, and a railway engineer, a Mr Edwards, was introduced. There were several mills in the Painswick Valley and it was noted how they were suffering as manufacturing moved to the areas around Stroud that were now railway served. Edwards' estimate for the construction of the line, a detailed proposal for which he presented to the meeting, came in at £12,500. However, Mr Matthews, owner of Matthews Mill, thought the estimate much too low, suggesting it should be doubled, whilst crucially the plan did not garner the support of another important personage, Mr W. Hyatt of Painswick House, who also doubted the costings. As a result, the scheme failed soon after without, it appears, the GWR having even been consulted as regards joining their line at Stroud.

No. 1453 arriving at Stroud on 6th April 1963, with the siding serving Stratford Mill at the far end of the viaduct. As the plan overleaf shows, the intended branch would have also come off at this point, carving through the side of the cutting where the Up Home signal here stands, to then curve round and run across the far side of the playing field in the right background. If history had been different, might this have been an auto train arriving from Painswick? MARK B. WARBURTON

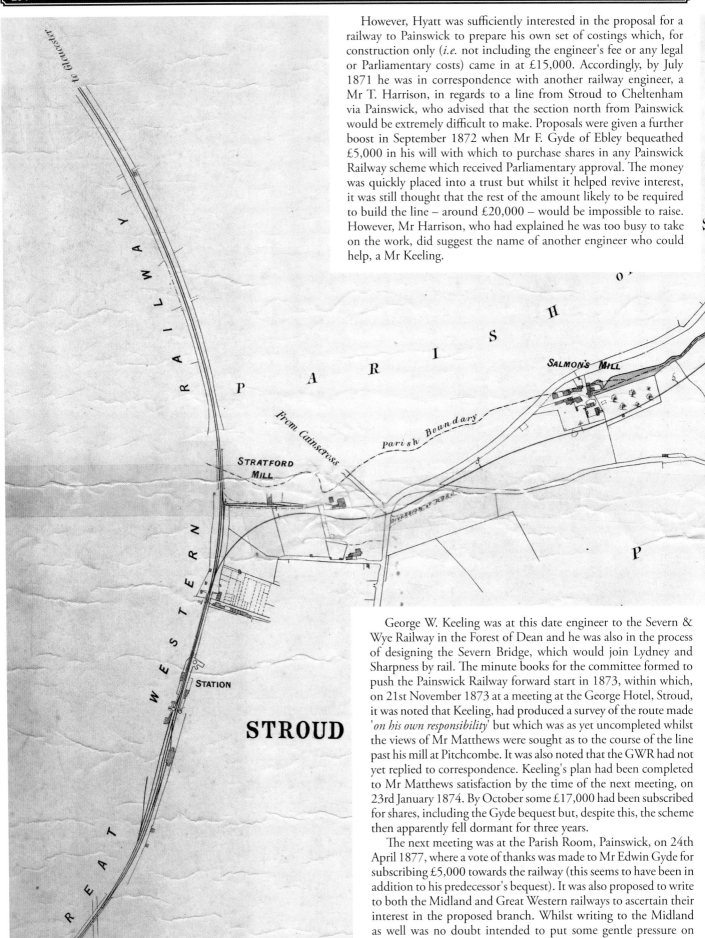

However, Hyatt was sufficiently interested in the proposal for a railway to Painswick to prepare his own set of costings which, for construction only (*i.e.* not including the engineer's fee or any legal or Parliamentary costs) came in at £15,000. Accordingly, by July 1871 he was in correspondence with another railway engineer, a Mr T. Harrison, in regards to a line from Stroud to Cheltenham via Painswick, who advised that the section north from Painswick would be extremely difficult to make. Proposals were given a further boost in September 1872 when Mr F. Gyde of Ebley bequeathed £5,000 in his will with which to purchase shares in any Painswick Railway scheme which received Parliamentary approval. The money was quickly placed into a trust but whilst it helped revive interest, it was still thought that the rest of the amount likely to be required to build the line – around £20,000 – would be impossible to raise. However, Mr Harrison, who had explained he was too busy to take on the work, did suggest the name of another engineer who could help, a Mr Keeling.

George W. Keeling was at this date engineer to the Severn & Wye Railway in the Forest of Dean and he was also in the process of designing the Severn Bridge, which would join Lydney and Sharpness by rail. The minute books for the committee formed to push the Painswick Railway forward start in 1873, within which, on 21st November 1873 at a meeting at the George Hotel, Stroud, it was noted that Keeling, had produced a survey of the route made '*on his own responsibility*' but which was as yet uncompleted whilst the views of Mr Matthews were sought as to the course of the line past his mill at Pitchcombe. It was also noted that the GWR had not yet replied to correspondence. Keeling's plan had been completed to Mr Matthews satisfaction by the time of the next meeting, on 23rd January 1874. By October some £17,000 had been subscribed for shares, including the Gyde bequest but, despite this, the scheme then apparently fell dormant for three years.

The next meeting was at the Parish Room, Painswick, on 24th April 1877, where a vote of thanks was made to Mr Edwin Gyde for subscribing £5,000 towards the railway (this seems to have been in addition to his predecessor's bequest). It was also proposed to write to both the Midland and Great Western railways to ascertain their interest in the proposed branch. Whilst writing to the Midland as well was no doubt intended to put some gentle pressure on the GWR, it would undoubtedly have been optimistic in the extreme – at this date the branch to Nailsworth came no closer

In sweltering heat on 6th June 1962, No. 1473 heads past the Stratford Mill Siding towards Stroud station with an auto service to Chalford. If the Painswick Branch had been built, it would have curved away right where the signal stands and climbed up through the side of the cutting to run along the valley side towards its destination. Note the tank wagon in the background, parked near the wagon turntable which provided access to the two mill sidings. JOHN STRANGE/NPC

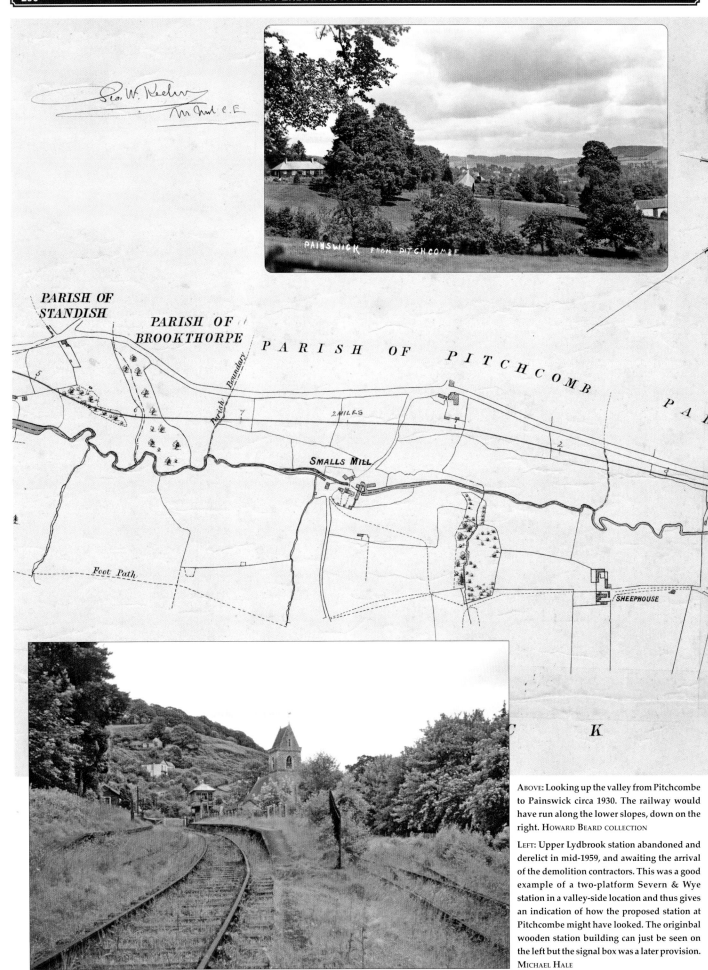

PAINSWICK FROM PITCHCOMBE

PARISH OF
STANDISH

PARISH OF
BROOKTHORPE

PARISH   OF   PITCHCOMB

PAR

2 MILES

SMALLS MILL

Foot Path

SHEEPHOUSE

C   K

ABOVE: Looking up the valley from Pitchcombe to Painswick circa 1930. The railway would have run along the lower slopes, down on the right. HOWARD BEARD COLLECTION

LEFT: Upper Lydbrook station abandoned and derelict in mid-1959, and awaiting the arrival of the demolition contractors. This was a good example of a two-platform Severn & Wye station in a valley-side location and thus gives an indication of how the proposed station at Pitchcombe might have looked. The originbal wooden station building can just be seen on the left but the signal box was a later provision. MICHAEL HALE

ABOVE: Keeling's plan for the proposed terminus at Painswick envisioned twin platforms with three tracks between – a run round line flanked by loops either side. It was a track layout which he clearly favoured, as indicated by this view of the Severn & Wye Railway's station at Coleford, terminus of the branch from Coleford Junction, near Parkend. The loading wharf here on the right would have been about where Keeling planned for a goods shed at Painswick, with platforms then each side of the three tracks. The S&W passenger service north of Lydney Town was withdrawn in 1929, so this view, showing a Stephenson Locomotive Society tour departing the station on 13th May 1961 is only representative of how things had been over thirty years before. Had the Painswick Railway been built, it seems likely that it too would have lost its passenger trains well before Dr Beeching came along. Services on the nearby Midland branches to Nailsworth and Stroud ceased in 1947. ALAN JARVIS

BELOW: Stroud Road, Painswick, with Whitehall on the right, circa 1905. The station approach would have turned off to the right just behind the photographer. NPC

than Dudbridge and the Midland had just been forced to absorb the bankrupt owning company rather than let the line close. It also could only serve to increase costs, as the GWR main line would have to be crossed to reach the Midland. However, it did open the enticing prospect of a direct connection with the line over the Severn Bridge and therefore Forest of Dean coal.

In July 1877, following a walk along the proposed route with the committee, Keeling was instructed to take another survey for Parliamentary purposes and to peg out the line for the benefit of landowners affected. At a meeting at the Volunteer Armoury, Stroud in December, it was resolved to contact shareholders to advance 10 per cent of the value of their intended holding in order to raise the amount required for the Parliamentary Deposit, a circular letter duly being sent out on 21st of that month. The plans for the Painswick Railway – incorporation of the company, construction of the railway, working and other arrangements (the GWR had consented to work the line) and running powers over part of the GWR into Stroud station – were duly deposited in time for the 1878 Parliamentary Sessions but did not gain assent. By this time, the mill industry in the Painswick Valley was in serious decline, unable to consider converting to steam power due to the cost of transporting coal.

In 1887 the scheme was revived once again, following an offer by the Reverend & Mrs Seddon to purchase £2,500 worth of shares. A meeting in November 1888 was informed that £13,000 out of £15,000 required had been raised, with the result that a further £1,450 was subscribed by the end of the evening. The proposal now was for a light railway, promoted under the heading of 'The Painswick

(Light) Railway', which was put forward in the Parliamentary Session for 1889, where it received the Royal Assent. The contractor was reported to be a Mr Firbank (Joseph T. Firbank, son of the well known railway contractor who died in 1886?) and Keeling was now consulting engineer to the railway.

Despite gaining assent, no progress was made with construction and in the meantime, over the next few years, the scheme continued to grow to what now seems fantastical proportions – the line was going to extend past Painswick with branches up the hill to Paradise and along the valley to Cranham, whilst at the Stroud end it would connect to the GWR and also run across their line to join the Midland at Wallbridge. Now entitled 'The Stroud & Painswick (Light) Railway', yet again a bill was put before Parliament in the 1895 sessions and again received Royal Assent.

And there, essentially, the story ends. Money had been spent on plans, newspaper notices, legal costs, Parliamentary fees, etc, but no

LEFT: The S&W terminus at Coleford looking the opposite way in 1965. As can be seen, the platform here was on a curve whilst Keeling's plan for Painswick was for a station with two straight platforms. However, it seems unlikely that it would have been built like that had the project come to fruition – almost certainly the cost of a second platform would have been dispensed with. It is also the case, however, that the site allowed for the possible future expansion of siding accommodation, should traffic to and from the numerous local mills justify it. The brick buildings seen here were a replacement for the timber originals which burnt down. BILL POTTER/NPC

BELOW: Keeling's gradient profile for the branch, as drawn up and deposited in the Office of the Clerk of the Peace at Gloucester in November 1877. Despite the hilly nature of the area, the branch was able to run along the north west side of the valley mostly at a relatively gentle climb. GLOUCESTERSHIRE ARCHIVES

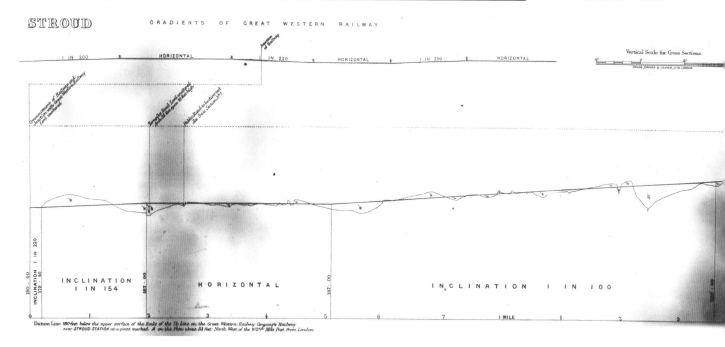

contracts were ever let and no spade was ever placed in the ground. The mills had closed, so ending the prospects for goods traffic, whilst the lines now proposed were aimed at day trippers as much as residents. From here the story goes very quiet but the probability is that there was little prospect of raising the finance required and that calls for shares to be paid up met with little success. The plan was finally abandoned in 1906 and the money held was used for other essential services, such as lighting the town, whilst in early January 1905 the GWR commenced a motor bus service to Painswick which, in various forms, operated until 1929.

THE MOTOR BUS AT STROUD.

RIGHT: Whilst Painswick was destined never to get its railway, it was railway served for a number of years courtesy of a GWR motor bus service which, eventually, after some trials, settled down to run between Stroud and Cheltenham. The first service, from Stroud to Painswick, operated from 9th January to 28th February 1905, then being extended to start from Cainscross from 1st March. This service was evidently not a great success, ending on 10th June and reverting to simply Stroud-Painswick from 12th June. However, from 4th October 1906, it was extended to Cheltenham, along what is now the A46, and this service then operated until 9th July 1921, when it was cut back to Painswick again. The Stroud to Painswick buses continued until 30th August 1929, when this became another of the routes taken over by Western National buses, whilst briefly, from 26th July to 19th September 1926, a Sundays only extension of the service to Cranham was also trialled. The vehicle shown here is a 20hp Milnes-Daimler open charabanc with roof, registration No. AF-84, which entered service on 18th May 1904. The picture was taken after the service was extended to Cheltenham, probably in 1907. Note the Hill, Paul & Co. Ltd mill building in the background and the fine collection of railway posters on the wall, right. HOWARD BEARD COLLECTION

RIGHT: If the railway had been built, Stroud Road might have been renamed Station Road. AEC 45hp bus registration No. T-8464, which entered GWR service on 30th April 1920, heads down the hill away from Painswick in the mid-1920s, after the service had been cut back from running to Cheltenham. This is today the A46 trunk road. H.G.W. HOUSEHOLD

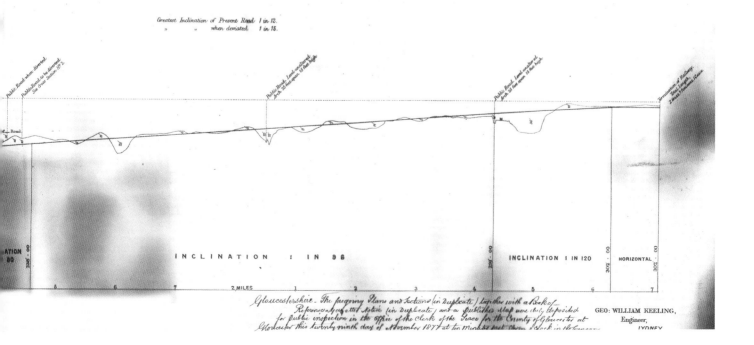

Greatest Inclination of Present Road 1 in 12.
" " when deviated 1 in 15.

INCLINATION 1 IN 88   INCLINATION 1 IN 120   HORIZONTAL

2 MILES

Gloucestershire - The foregoing Plans and Sections (in duplicate) together with a Book of Reference and required notice (in duplicate) and a published map were duly deposited for public inspection in the office of the Clerk of the Peace for the County of Gloucester at Gloucester this twenty ninth day of November 1877 at ten minutes past eleven o'clock in the forenoon

GEO: WILLIAM KEELING, Engineer, SYDNEY

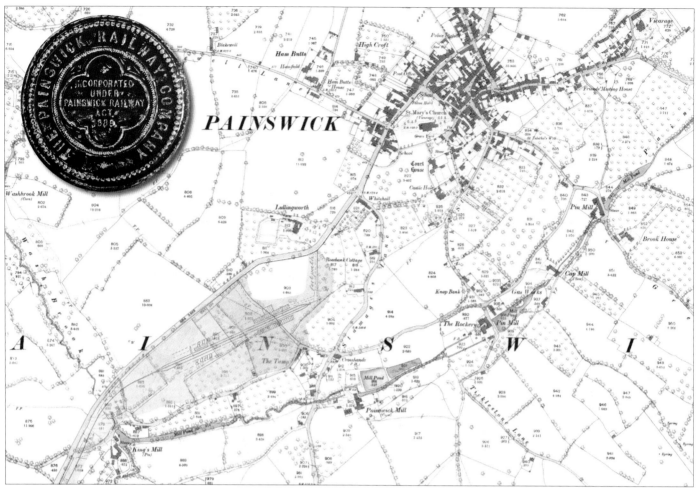

ABOVE: Keeling's plan for the terminus superimposed on the 1881 25 inch first edition OS for Painswick. Note that road access was planned from both sides and there was also a footpath leading to the end of the main platform. INSET: The company seal of the 1889 Painswick Railway.

BELOW: A general view of Painswick circa 1930, with the site of the proposed terminus outlined in red. Painswick Mill can be seen at the bottom of the valley. Housing now occupies most of the intended station site. NPC

FOLLOW UP 1

OVER JUNCTION and the LLANTHONY DOCKS BRANCH

As alluded to at the start of this book, photographer Don Mann's loan of his Gloucestershire slides not only provided a welcome boost to the amount of material from which to choose, they were also largely taken around sections of the county's railway system that I had yet to cover. Whilst there are quite a number along the Stroud Valley – his home territory – most were of the railway in and around Gloucester, where he worked. The collection was loaned in time for me to be able to include those relevant to the Midland line in Volume 4A but Don's interest leant far more to the Western side, so it is within the pages of this and the following book that will form Volume 5 that his work really comes to the fore. The pictorial surveys of Central station and Horton Road shed would both be much the poorer without having had recourse to his extensive selection of what were then everyday scenes on the railway.

However, the one part of Gloucester's railway system that had

been previously covered, in Volume 1, but of which there was a good selection of new views, was Over Junction and the Llanthony Docks Branch, on the west side of the city. Having decided to devote more pages to the west end of the station here, again courtesy of Don's slides and following on from the coverage of it also in Volume 1, it seemed sensible therefore to complete our colour study of the railway at Gloucester within this volume by also including this revisiting of Over Junction and the Llanthony Docks Branch. The latter was also a repository in the 1960s for locomotives awaiting towing to various of the South Wales scrapyards, so there are several new pictures of these.

Apart from the fireless locomotive which worked there, Castle Meads power station itself seems not to have been of much interest to photographers. I have included another colour slide of this engine but the glimpses which appear in the background of views in Volume 1 remain all that we have of the power station itself.

Crosti-boilered Class '9F' No. 92028 would have been an unusual sight on this section of line just to the west of Gloucester Central station; the locomotive appears to be on the nearer, Down line and may be reversing 'Light Engine' to Over Sidings to collect a train of wagons. The slide is undated but from others in the collection in the same mounts, was probably taken circa August 1965. At this date, the 2-10-0 was based at Saltley shed, having just been transferred back there after a four month allocation to Banbury. New from Crewe Works to Wellingborough shed on 9th July 1955, No. 92028 was withdrawn from Saltley in October 1966. Whilst the location of the picture was clearly on the west of the city, the exact position took a little pinning down due to changes in the foreground. The photographer was standing in Priory Road gardens, which have now gone, whilst Gouda Way, built in 1994 across a playing field and connecting Priory Road and Worcester Street, now parallels the railway to the right. The spire in the centre distance is that of St. Marks Church in Worcester Street and the block of flats just visible on the right is Clapham Court, a retirement housing complex built in 1963 at the end of Alvin Street. DON MANN

Alney Island is an area of land to the west of the city which is so named because it is bounded on both sides by the River Severn, which divides into the Eastern and Western Channels at Upper Parting. It is low lying and prone to flooding and thus the railway had to be built across it on an embankment punctuated by multi-arch flood viaducts. On 2nd March 1965, 2-8-0 No. 3840 was photographed from the old Over Causeway overbridge heading to South Wales with a lengthy mixed freight. Entering service on 31st January 1942, the engine was less than five months away from withdrawal, off Newport Ebbw Junction shed on 21st July 1965. The rear of the train is just clearing Ham Viaduct, whilst the locomotive is passing over a set of un-named arches spanning winter flood water – the part of Alney Island to the south (right) of the line was named Town Ham. Today, the route of the 1970s-built dual carriageway that now forms the A40 Over Causeway runs across it and is carried over the railway on the far side of these arches. The bridge from which this picture was demolished when the new road opened. Note the bracket signal had lost its leftmost arm, which had been for the by then closed Ledbury Branch. NPC

With the driver leaning out from the cab window, '9F' No. 92216 makes a fine sight as it rumbles past the junction for the docks branch with a mixed fitted goods on 6th August 1965. We saw the 2-10-0 on Horton Road shed on, page 132, when it was still officially allocated to Southall, but by the date of this view it had just been transferred to Severn Tunnel Junction, from where it was to be withdrawn on 26th October 1965. In the background, behind Over Junction Signal Box, a contractor's crane can be seen, with track lifting of the branch to Ledbury via Newent and Dymock nearing completion. DON MANN

A fascinating panorama taken from Telford's road bridge on 7th March 1964, showing the bridge carrying the A40 Over Causeway over the South Wales main line and the Llanthony Docks Branch curving off to the right, with lines of coal wagons in Llanthony Sidings. Over Junction was remodelled in September 1958, when the main lines were realigned to cross the river on a new span seen here behind the truss girder carrying a pipe line. The Over Causeway bridge was rebuilt to accommodate this new alignment. Note that there was little sign of the existence of the earlier bridge and I have also been unable to find any mention of the works in the contemporary railway press, which must have involved a temporary line closure. An unidentified ex-GWR 'Mogul' heads through the A40 arch on its way to Ross and Hereford. As mentioned, the A40 was also realigned in the 1970s to bypass Telford's bridge, so the new overbridge seen here has gone, and more recently the pipeline bridge has also been removed. DON MANN

RIGHT: On a damp and dismal Saturday 10th August 1963, an unidentified 'Large Prairie' tank makes its way past Docks Branch Junction with a three-coach train from Hereford. On the Down Main line, what looks to be a BR 'Standard' Class '78XXX' has just come off the branch and is making its way slowly over the bridge spanning the River Severn. In the foreground is part of the embankment carrying the old A40 Over Causeway across the railway and on to Thomas Telford's 1831 bridge spanning the river. As recounted in a previous volume, due to an error in the bridge's construction, freely admitted by Telford, it had sagged in the centre from the day it was completed but it was not until 1975, when it was bypassed by the new dual carriageway, that it was finally taken out of use. It is now a Scheduled Ancient Monument and can be walked over. NPC

LEFT: In similarly gloomy conditions on 2nd March 1965, '57XX' Class pannier tank No. 8745 steams towards Over Causeway bridge with a short mixed freight from the Forest of Dean. We saw this engine earlier in these pages, on Horton Road shed. Heading the other way is another mixed goods train, hauled by a tender engine and most likely heading to South Wales. From this angle it is possible to see the remains of the old alignment, to the right of No. 8745. The original bridge had curved its way across the river. DON MANN

RIGHT: Having transferred from Old Oak Common to Horton Road shed on 5th October 1964, No. 7029 *Clun Castle* was made regular use of like any other engine on the allocation. It was only right at the end of it's working life that No. 7029 started to become something of a celebrity after being used on various rail tours. It is therefore not too much of a surprise to see the 'Castle' here at Over Junction 'Light Engine' on 27th July 1965. The September edition of *The Railway Observer* had noted the locomotive's use on the 5.45am Gloucester to Cardiff 'stopper' on several occasions in July 1965, from which it returned 'Light Engine', which probably explains No. 7029's presence here. The engine is standing on the Up Main line, with its front pony truck on the flood arch at the south end of the River Severn viaduct. We shall see *Clun* again shortly, at the head of the Llanthony Docks Branch a couple of weeks later. DON MANN

No. 6961 *Stedham Hall* trundles past Over Junction Signal Box with a freight on 27th July 1965. Entering service on 13th March 1944, the 'Hall' had moved from Didcot to Oxford shortly before the picture was taken, from where it was withdrawn six weeks later on 10th September. Note the signalman's light blue Mk I Ford Cortina parked next to the box. DON MANN

On the same day, Horton Road shed's BR 'Standard' Class '2' No. 78004 waits 'Light Engine' by the box. New from Darlington Works on 21st January 1953, the 2-6-0 had moved to Gloucester in July 1964 and was to be withdrawn on 18th November 1965. It is the first time we have seen the engine in these pages but it has appeared several times in previous volumes. DON MANN

Later on, No. 5992 *Horton Hall* was photographed heading to South Wales. Taken from the footpath leading down to the arch shown in the picture of *Clun Castle* on the previous page and with the remains of the Ledbury Branch in the foreground, we get a glimpse here of the rear of the box, which was very much a non-standard BR design, all in red brick and with a steeply pitched roof. Correcting information given in Volume 1, the box was in fact built in 1952 and brought into use in January 1953, with the old box, which had been sited a little way to the right here, then being closed. Note the signalman had now moved his car and parked it behind the box. Entering traffic on 18th December 1939, No. 5992 had transferred from Horton Road to Newport Ebbw Junction a month before this picture was taken, for what was to be a very short stay, withdrawal taking place just over a week after being photographed here, on 6th August. DON MANN

An unidentified '9F' 2-10-0 heads past Over Sidings with a block train of oil tank wagons mostly wearing Shell/BP logos on 2nd March 1965. There was a Down Refuge Loop and an Up Refuge Siding here by 1881 but these were lengthened in 1904, the Up Refuge Siding also by then having become a loop. A new Over Sidings Signal Box was opened at the same time. Both loops were then further lengthened during the Second World War, in February 1942, when a bank of new sidings was also added on the Up side. In preparation for this, Over Sidings Signal Box was replaced with a larger box in November 1941. The '9F' is here passing the north end of the loops, exit from which was controlled by the right-hand bracket signal. The additional sidings were in the far distance, to the right of the passenger train just visible heading to South Wales. In the foreground, what appear to be redundant wagons had been stored on the remaining stub of the Ledbury Branch and note too the caravan park, still here in expanded form today. DON MANN

We now venture onto the Llanthony Docks Branch, where we first of all encounter No. 7029 *Clun Castle* once again, on Friday 6th August 1965. As noted a few pages ago, far from being the celebrity it is today, Horton Road used the engine as a 'Maid of all Work' during the last few months of its BR career. The October 1965 edition of *The Railway Observer* noted that it was rarely being used on passenger workings apart from specials but had been seen dragging No. 92220 *Evening Star* from Cardiff East Dock to Gloucester on 13th August (bound ultimately for Swindon for renovation) and then was seen passing through Cheltenham with the Down morning pick-up freight on 3rd September. Sadly there is no mention of a visit to the Docks Branch, so we can only speculate as to why it was here but perhaps it had brought in a freight from South Wales or tripped some wagons in from Over Sidings? Any thoughts welcome. Don Mann

Rebuilt Bulleid 'West Country' Class 'Pacific' No. 34045 *Ottery St. Mary* was parked for a time in Llanthony Sidings whilst on its way to South Wales for scrapping. Pictured here on 2nd March 1965, the 4-6-2 had entered traffic from Brighton Works in October 1946 as No. 21C145 and was renumbered by BR in January 1949. It had been withdrawn off Bournemouth shed in June 1964. Note that much of the valve gear had been removed for ease of dragging the engine. This view is looking back towards Over Junction, with empty wagons that had delivered coal for Castlemeads power station on the right. Don Mann

LEFT: No. 68012 was still languishing in Llanthony Sidings on 27th January 1968, although the other engines seen below had apparently moved on to meet their fate. Built by the Hunslet Engineering Co. (Works No. 3174) as WD No. 75124 in June 1944, the engine became L&NER No. 8012 in July 1946 and then gained its BR number in May 1951. With classmate No. 68006, it had worked the last train, an SLS brake-van special, over the Hopton Incline of the Cromford & High Peak line on 30th April 1967, in tandem with No. 68006. The last of the 'J94' Class to be withdrawn, off Westhouses shed in early October 1967, after several months working at Williamsthorpe Colliery, it was scrapped by Buttigiegs of Newport in 1968. NPC

BELOW: Photographed in Llanthony Sidings in late 1967, whilst also on their way to South Wales for scrapping, were ex-London & North Eastern Railway Class 'J94' 0-6-0ST No. 68012 and ex-Southern Railway USA 0-6-0 dock tanks No's 30067 and 30069. Ahead is an unidentified SR 'Pacific'; the November 1967 edition of *The Railway Observer* noted that rebuilt 'West Country' Class 4-6-2 No. 34002 *Salisbury* had been stored at Horton Road from 20th-22nd September 1967 before moving on, which may provide a clue as to this engine's identity. No's 30067 and 30069 were built by Vulcan Ironworks in the USA in 1942 and 1943 respectively, and worked at Southampton Docks until 1963, when both were transferred to Eastleigh, from where they were withdrawn in early July 1967. They were scrapped by Cashmores of Newport in March 1968. MIKE SPICER/COURTESY THE RESTORATION & ARCHIVING TRUST/REF. MSZZ3888

Above: No. 1424, which we have seen several times on Chalford auto duties, and 'Castle' Class No. 5049 *Earl of Plymouth* await their final journey whilst stored in Llanthony Sidings on 7th March 1964. No. 5049 entered service on 30th April 1936 as *Denbigh Castle* and was renamed on 27th August 1937. It was withdrawn off Bristol St. Philip's Marsh shed on 22nd March 1963 and broken up in April 1964 by Cashmores at their Newport yard. However, whilst No. 1424 had been sold to the same company for scrapping, it is recorded as being broken up at their Great Bridge yard, in West Bromwich, in June 1964. Don Mann

OPPOSITE PAGE FAR LEFT: Also taken on 7th March 1964, a fireman's eye view from the footplate of withdrawn No. 6943 *Farnley Hall*, looking towards Llanthony Yard, in the left distance, with the twin lines curving off round to Castlemeads power station on the left. New into service on 26th August 1942, the 'Hall' had been withdrawn off Horton Road shed on 28th December 1963.

OPPOSITE PAGE LEFT: A close-up study of the 'business' end of No. 5049 *Earl of Plymouth*. BOTH DON MANN

RIGHT: Ex-GWR 'Mogul' No. 6381 languishes on the stored line with other engines on 7th March 1964. New in July 1921 and based at Horton Road by 1956 (one source gives its arrival there as during the four weeks ending 16th July 1955), it is listed as being withdrawn in November 1963. However, the shedbashuk.blogspot website notes it as being stored withdrawn at Horton Road on Sunday 10th March 1963, along with classmate No. 6330. DON MANN

LEFT: Silhouetted against a clear sky on 1st December 1965, this is No. 5932 *Haydon Hall*, which had been withdrawn off Bristol Barrow Road shed five weeks earlier, on 26th October. Once out of use, the rust set in very quickly. New into service on 23rd June 1933, No. 5932 was scrapped by Cashmores at their Newport yard in January 1966. Flood waters can be glimpsed through the access arch beneath the engine. DON MANN

RIGHT: As we have already seen, Southern engines on their way to be scrapped in South Wales provided a diversion from the usual fare of mostly ex-GWR, ex-LM&SR and BR types to be seen at Gloucester. On 2nd March 1965, 'Q' Class 0-6-0 No. 30541 was on view at the sidings coupled behind the tender of No. 34045 *Ottery St. Mary*. New from Eastleigh Works on 23rd January 1939, the engine had been withdrawn off Guildford shed in late November 1964. DON MANN

Looking back along the Llanthony Docks Branch on 3rd February 1961, from the footbridge that spanned the entrance to the yard by the docks. This view clearly shows the Port Ham electricity sub-station in the centre right distance, which was built in the early 1950s – the city's penchant for building sub-stations on the flood plain has caused problems over the years! This site is still in operation, although was completely modernised circa 2006, with all the equipment now being housed inside a building that occupies just one fifth of the original site. The light grey steel lattice masts carrying wires over the sidings were replaced with wooden poles a couple of years after this picture was taken. Beneath them, the branch to Castlemeads power station peels off to the right. Llanthony swing bridge carrying the railway over the River Severn's Eastern Channel had not operated for many years by the date of this view. The ageing wooden structure partially seen in the centre foreground was a small cabin provided for the operator. On the left, the lock-keeper's cottage faces onto the infilled Llanthony Lock, which was abandoned in 1924 when the walls collapsed and therefore the bridge is unlikely to have been opened since then (there is a weir in the river just to the left). The lock site, surrounding land and cottage are now owned by the Herefordshire & Gloucestershire Canal Trust, who are slowly restoring the lock, which will then provide access from the docks to the restored canal at Over via the river. ROY DENISON

We saw the CEGB-owned 21-ton fireless locomotive used for shunting at Castlemeads in Volume 1 but here is another aspect of this delightful little engine posed in the power station yard circa 1962. The power station was opened by Gloucester Corporation Electricity Department in 1941 and the engine was built for them by Andrew Barclay (Works No. 2126) in 1942, delivered in wartime battleship grey livery with yellow lining and designated Gloucester Corporation No. 1. It was the only locomotive ever to work here, ceasing operation with the power station in 1969 but was then donated to the Dowty Railway Preservation Society and moved to their base at Ashchurch in 1973. In 1988, it was obtained by the National Waterways Museum, since when it has been cosmetically restored and has been back on display close to its old home, although at the time of writing it is currently stored with the Vale of Berkeley Railway at their Sharpness workshops, presumably awaiting restoration again. The power station was demolished in 1978. NPC

ABOVE: We finish this section back in the city, with two more views of Southern engines on their way to the scrap man. 'N' Class 'Mogul' No. 31870, minus its connecting rods, was photographed surrounded by steel mineral wagons on 23rd June 1964. Completed at Ashford Works in July 1925, the engine had been withdrawn off Redhill shed in early April 1964. The exact location is uncertain but is thought to be Barnwood shed or Barnwood Sidings. DON MANN

BELOW: The brutalist design of Bulleid's 'Q1' Class 0-6-0s was a response to war time austerity conditions but also incorporated numerous innovative and weight saving concepts which dramatically improved their functionality. No. 33014 was built at Brighton Works, entering service as SR No. C14 in October 1942. It was withdrawn in early January 1964 from Guildford shed and is seen here at Gloucester on 3rd July 1964 – the photographer's note on the mount states '*Glos Goods Yard*', so we are probably back in the yard next to Central station. All dead engines heading for scrap had to be routed via Gloucester and the August 1964 edition of *The Railway Observer* noted that on 17th June, '*a Southern Q1 was seen towing three of its classmates*' but does not identify any of them. However, it would seem likely that No. 33014, minus its connecting rods, was one of those being towed. DON MANN

FOLLOW UP 2

The EASTGATE LOOP and the MIDLAND DOCKS BRANCHES

ABOVE: A twilight view from the elevated Barton Street Junction cabin in late 1975, shortly before Eastgate station closed for good. The site is now a supermarket. NPC

TOP: All that was left of the once extensive 48 lever frame inside Barton Street Junction cabin. NPC

RIGHT: A Met-Camm 3-car unit (with a railcar or another set attached behind) departs Eastgate station beneath Barton Street cabin and over the level crossing sometime in 1975. Set B804, comprising driving Motor Brake Second No. 51452, Trailer Composite Lavatory No. 59551 and Driving Motor Composite Lavatory No. 51523, had transferred from Plymouth Laira to Bristol Bath Road in early June 1976, so with the line closing on 1st December 1975, this gives a five month window in which the picture was taken. As 2-car unit No. S804 and coupled with another 2-car unit, the set was involved in a non-fatal accident with a tractor on a level crossing near Llandrindod Wells on 8th August 1987 and was subsequently stored. Note the hearse parked in front of All Saints (CoE) church, with a funeral service underway inside. NPC

THIS AND NEXT PAGE: The answer to the question posed on the rear cover – the very last steam locomotive to call at Eastgate station was in fact rebuilt 'Merchant Navy' Class 'Pacific' No. 35028 *Clan Line*, which made an unscheduled stop here to take on board water via a hose run from a fire hydrant (RIGHT AND BELOW), whilst on its way home from the Stockton & Darlington 150th anniversary celebrations on 1st-2nd September 1975. No. 35028 was officially a BR build, emerging from Eastleigh Works in December 1948 in streamlined form. It was named by Lord Rotherwick, Chairman of Clan Line, at Southampton Docks on 15th January 1951 and was rebuilt to the form seen in these pictures in October 1959. Withdrawn from Nine Elms depot in early July 1967, it was bought for preservation by the Merchant Navy Locomotive Preservation Society, who are still the engine's owners today. At the date of these pictures, *Clan Line* had just moved from Ashford in

Kent to its new base at Bulmers Cider in Hereford, then recently established as a railway centre. It is now based at Stewarts Lane depot, where it had been allocated for most of the 1950s, and is operational at the time of writing. The full page view, RIGHT, from the Down Home colour light signal No. G31, shows the locomotive preparing to depart, whilst the second view, BELOW, shows it heading off round the Tuffley Loop, which suggests that it was then going to travel via the Severn Tunnel, the Maindee curve at Newport and then up the 'North & West Line' to Hereford. Its appearance on the loop line must have been quite a surprise to anyone living alongside it or caught waiting at one of the level crossings! In the left foreground of both these views is the remaining stub of the High Orchard Docks Branch. The only landmarks which remain from these scenes today are the church and, in the distance, the Gloucestershire Royal Hospital tower block, whilst the leisure centre seen in the picture right has been completely rebuilt. TOP: PETER BERRY; ALL OTHERS NPC

The Midland Railway boxes on the Tuffley Loop were well illustrated in Volume 4A but here are some further views all taken in their final months of operation:

PAGE LEFT TOP: California Crossing cabin, which was rescued after closure and now resides on the narrow gauge line at Toddington station on the Gloucestershire Warwickshire Railway. It was a replacement box, opened on 26th September 1920.

PAGE LEFT BOTTOM: Farm Street Crossing had long been pedestrian only but still retained a manned gate box as the line was on a curve.

THIS PAGE TOP: Painswick Road Crossing box, minus nameboards but showing the steps up to the operating floor. The box had opened on 15th October 1893.

THIS PAGE BOTTOM: Looking towards Eastgate from inside Painswick Road Crossing box, with the rear of colour light signal No. G60 on the right. The gates were in fact across Tredworth Road, which led to Painswick Road half a mile away. Stroud Road garage is still in operation today. ALL NPC

ABOVE: On 22nd March 1969, the Branch Line Society ran a Gloucestershire rail tour that started out from Bristol Temple Meads and visited numerous branches: Sudbrook, Caerwent, Tintern Quarry, Parkend, Llanthony Docks, High Orchard Docks, Hempsted Docks, Dursley and Sharpness Docks – what a day! The tour was operated by a Gloucester Railway Carriage & Wagon Co. Cross-Country 3-car set (Class '119'), which is seen here in the much rationalised High Orchard yard alongside a rake of box vans.

ABOVE RIGHT: Eighteen months later, the last trip to traverse the High Orchard Branch was the RCTS 'Cotswold Edge Rail Tour', on 21st November 1970. The tour had started from Birmingham New Street with the Metropolitan-Cammell Class '101' 3-car set travelling via Stoke Works Junction and Droitwich to Worcester, before then heading back to the Midland main line and south to Gloucester, where the ex-GWR Llanthony Yard was visited first, followed by the High Orchard Branch. MALCOLM BRAIN

ABOVE: The view towards Barton Street Junction signal box and crossing from the rear cab of the Met-Camm DMU after arriving back at Eastgate From High Orchard. The next stop would be at Gloucester New Yard before the return trip to Birmingham along the Honeybourne line, with a detour to Honeybourne station on the Oxford to Worcester main line on the way. MALCOLM BRAIN

Above: As a result of mentioning in Volume 4A (page 113) that no pictures of Podsmead or New Road Bridge – Bridge No. 2 on the Hempsted or New Docks Branch – had been found, reader Geoff Preece sent me some very rare scans from colour prints of it being dismantled in 1977, which were taken by his late mother. Built originally in 1900 across a short road to nowhere, it was not until after the Second World War that housing developments were started and the road was completed. The first view shows the bridge with the crane just setting up and the second shows one of the girder spans being lifted out. JOYCE PREECE